SNEAKIN' DEACON

FROM SECRET SERVICE
TO SACRED SERVICE

SNEAKIN' DEACON

FROM SECRET SERVICE TO SACRED SERVICE

GREG GITSCHIER

WITH BRYANT A. STAMFORD

BUTLER BOOKS

Front cover photo by Madison Gitschier

ISBN: 978-1-941953-68-6

Printed in the United States of America

Book design by Scott Stortz

Published by:
Butler Books
P.O. Box 7311
Louisville, KY 40257
(502) 897–9393
Fax (502) 897–9797

www.butlerbooks.com

DEDICATION

Kids Cancer Alliance is unique. It offers a variety of camp and recreational activities year-round for children with cancer and their families. There are no fees; everything is free. We are dedicated to providing once-in-a-lifetime experiences where children with cancer and their families can grow, learn, build friendships, and most importantly, have fun being kids.

Twenty years ago, God guided me to get involved with Kids Cancer Alliance, and it has been a transformational experience for me in many ways. I was the first executive director, and since then, I have been on the board, eagerly engaged with our kids and our wonderful volunteers who give so much of themselves. I believe in this organization and support it in every way I can, including dedicating a portion of the proceeds from this book to keep our camps up and going so that we can continue this important work.

To learn more, please see www.kidscanceralliance.org.

Contents

PART THREE: SECRET SERVICE AGENT: INVESTIGATIONS UNIT

PART FOUR: SACRED SERVICE: DEACON AND CHAPLAIN

FOREWORD

I have known Greg Gitschier my entire life. First as one of my mom's friends, then as a police officer and a Secret Service agent. In 2008, one of my first films premiered in Louisville and Greg became my first bodyguard. But underneath the surface, I had no idea the kind of life he really led. I knew nothing of his harrowing adventures, run-ins with thugs and fellow officers, personal encounters with US presidents and world leaders, or his life-changing experience protecting the Pope, which inspired him to become a deacon.

This book shows the personal side of Greg; one that I have come to know over the years while Greg has escorted me to family weddings, fundraisers, and yearly trips to the Children's Hospital around Christmas. These visits with brave kids who are in intensive care or fighting life-threatening illnesses have been some of the most memorable times we have shared, and Greg has truly helped give these kids a special place in my and my family's hearts. I am so grateful for his service to our country, children in need, and to my family.

— Jennifer Lawrence

This book is a memoir and depicts actual events and experiences. In some instances, dialogue has been recreated and is consistent with the character speaking and the circumstances. Some language may be offensive but is authentic to the situations depicted. All persons are real, and there are no composite characters. Some names have been changed to protect privacy. Most photos belong to the author and were taken by him or friends and family. Some were taken so long ago that it's impossible to credit the individual photographer. Where possible, photo credits have been added.

PREFACE

The year was 1983. I was a Secret Service agent assigned to the protection detail for Reverend Jesse Jackson, one of several Democratic candidates competing for the nomination in the upcoming presidential election. Jackson was a well-known celebrity, outspoken and highly controversial, and he provoked strong feelings, pro and con. Because he was an African American, there was fear that some bigoted, hate-filled goofball might try something stupid. This resulted in an early bodyguard detail, several months earlier than usual.

As part of his campaign, Reverend Jackson was scheduled to meet with George Wallace, governor of Alabama. I did the advance work, taking care of the logistics required for the meeting at the governor's mansion in Montgomery. Wallace, a Democrat, served four terms as governor, on and off from 1963 through 1987. A staunch segregationist before 1980, Wallace abandoned his position and won his last term as governor with support from black voters. Despite past animosities, Jackson was reaching out, wanting Wallace to help him win voters in the South, black and white.

Wallace was no stranger to presidential politics. He had been a candidate for president 11 years earlier in 1972, and at the time, he was polling very well and gaining momentum. Unfortunately, his candidacy was halted when he was shot five times by Arthur Bremer, a 21-year-old busboy, in the parking lot of a shopping center in Laurel, Maryland. The shots paralyzed Wallace from the waist down and he never walked again.

When I escorted Reverend Jackson into the governor's office, Wallace was sitting behind his desk in a wheelchair. Another agent followed us, and we immediately assumed our expected fly-on-the-wall stance, blending in with the furniture. At first, their conversation was the light, cordial chitchat typical of two highly skilled politicians and similar to the strategy employed by boxers in the first round as they feel each other out before the action shifts into high gear.

Governor Wallace appeared to be in good spirits as he related an amusing story. Afterward, he paused, his face changing, more serious now as he glanced over at me. I'll never forget how he studied me for what seemed like an eternity, and the discomfort I felt from his penetrating stare. Did I blunder in some way? Was there something I should be doing or not doing? A moment later, his face relaxed, and he gave me a slight nod before returning his gaze to Jackson.

"Reverend," he said, "let me give you some free advice. The reason I'm in this wheelchair is because I didn't listen to these guys." He gestured toward me, then added, "These guys, the Secret Service, they know what they're doing; they know what they're talking about. They told me not to go into that parking lot, but I wouldn't listen, and I went anyway." He paused again and frowned, no doubt reflecting on the moment that changed his life. Then he shrugged and said, "Well, I guess all I can say is, the rest is history."

Because of intense training and constant vigilance, the agents assigned to Wallace at the time had known the parking lot was wide open, and anyone could have a weapon. Worse, they had emphasized that if Governor Wallace insisted on going to the parking lot, under no circumstances should he leave the small makeshift stage that had been erected for him to make his speech. But he had ignored their advice and waded into the crowd, right into Arthur Bremer who pulled a gun, held it out between two people, and fired from point-blank range.

It was a tragic event that spilled over to the Secret Service agent who was standing beside Wallace in the parking lot. Someone had a camera and was taking a picture of the governor at the exact instant the gun was fired. The picture revealed the explosion of gunpowder and a close-up of the face of the Secret Service agent. It was a bad deal for the agent, because the photo captured him looking surprised and flinching as the governor was shot. Regrettably, this suggested that he hadn't done his job, that he panicked in the moment of crisis. Not true. Anyone, regardless of their training or experience, would flinch. How could you not, your face so close to a loud, unexpected gunshot?

I felt bad for the guy, and I'm mentioning it here because it illustrates how little the margin of error is in our line of work. One wrong move, one moment of distraction, or in the case of that agent, simply being in the wrong place at the wrong time and showing a human response, could haunt us the rest of our lives. The good news was, the agent disarmed the shooter immediately, so there was clear evidence that he did what he was trained to do. Unfortunately, the flinch got a lot more attention.

The agents did their job trying to convince Governor Wallace they knew what they were doing and knew what was best for him, but he wasn't buying it. It can be challenging at times to protect someone and save them from themselves. This is especially true for dignitaries who take themselves too seriously. Thankfully, most folks I protected do not fit this description, and quite the contrary. President Ronald Reagan, for example, was a gentleman, always cooperative and a pleasure to be around.

When I retired from the Secret Service, I continued to do private security work, but that was secondary to the demands and challenges of my next career. The seeds for my next career were planted while I was part of the security detail for Pope John Paul II during his visit to the United States. I was so inspired that I decided to get more involved with the practice of my Catholic faith. How, I wasn't sure, and I took small steps at first. But they weren't enough, so I took the leap and enrolled in studies to become a deacon. One day while we were taking a break, a fellow student, who had learned of my past as a Secret Service agent, teasingly referred to me as the "Sneakin' Deacon." The nickname stuck and has followed me ever since.

I am thankful for my career in the Secret Service, but I didn't start there. Before moving on to the federal level, I did a six-year stint as a police officer, paying my dues in local law enforcement, learning the ropes, and preparing for what was to come. Being a cop helped me develop instincts, street smarts, and the confidence that I could be trusted with the all-encompassing responsibility required to protect presidents and their families, the Pope, movie stars, titans of industry, and prime ministers and kings.

Those years as a cop, some of the best years of my life, are precious to me and are still a big part of who I am. Before sharing my experiences as a Secret Service agent and a deacon, I want to provide a glimpse of my life as a cop and you will see why, regardless of the circumstances, where I am or what I am doing, I will always bleed blue.

PART ONE

BEAT COP

CHAPTER 1

LAW ENFORCEMENT IN MY DNA

People choose to be cops for all sorts of reasons. There is the idealistic selfless desire to serve justice, to safeguard the innocent and help folks in need, to be a hero and act bravely in an emergency or in the face of extreme danger. The higher calling, in other words. And there are other more commonplace reasons, like not being bound to a desk, variety, early retirement, the uniform, prestige—the list goes on. Regardless of why people choose to be cops, after a while, the idealism and perceived perks tend to conflict with actually being a cop. Challenges include modest pay, odd hours and moonlighting that takes police away from their families, the balancing act of long stretches of mind-numbing boredom interspersed with sudden high-velocity encounters that can end in trauma or worse.

I loved being a cop, everything about it, the good and the not so good. I think most of all, I savored being someone who stood for something, someone who, regardless of the odds, would stand up and be counted when the good folks needed an ally, a protector. One of my favorite sayings is by Albert Einstein and it sums up my feelings: "The world will not be destroyed by those who do evil, but by those who watch them without doing anything." I wanted to be the guy who stood up to evildoers and put them away.

My interest and dedication started at a young age. My father, Frank, was an FBI agent for over 20 years and he spent 15 years of that time in New York City, paying his dues, as he would say. He was good at his job, probably because he loved it, ate and slept it, and eventually he was promoted to supervisor of the bank robbery squad for all five boroughs of New York City. It was heady times for me, a young kid, enthralled by seeing him come home late at night, wearing a fedora back in the 1960s, a Smith & Wesson handgun and a pair of handcuffs on his belt, and an FBI badge on his credential case. I recall the thousands of times I looked at all this, especially the gun, but never daring to get close, or heaven forbid, reaching out and touching it, despite wanting to more than anything else in the world.

In the third grade, my parents were called in more than once for parent-teacher conferences. Since my dad was always working, usually my mother would show up. and I'd get a good report, something along the lines of he's a nice kid, polite, respectful, and all that sort of thing. But, that wasn't why they were called in for one conference. The teacher said I was too easily distracted, always drawing pictures of policemen, and if I had a chance to talk about it, I'd talk about my dad arresting bad guys, handcuffing them, and putting them in jail. This annoyed my mother to no end, and she'd lean on my dad who would tell me that Sister Barbara Ann was going to tune me up if I didn't get on board with her program. In no uncertain terms, I'd better start doing better, and I did.

I was head over heels about law enforcement, and because my dad knew of my interest, he went out of his way to help prepare me for the future. He told me if I really wanted to go into law enforcement, I needed to go federal, because that's where I would make the most money and I would be able to take care of my family. In his opinion, there were two choices, either the FBI or the Secret Service. As I considered these restricted options, it bugged me that if I were fortunate enough to get on with the FBI, everybody would think I had an inside track, that I made it because of my old man.

Also, the Secret Service intrigued me in ways the FBI didn't. The way I saw it from watching my dad for so many years, the FBI was like the army, very big, and because of its size, it moved slowly and was highly bureaucratic. The Secret Service was much smaller, more like the marines, agile and faster moving, which to me meant more action, more adventure. So, getting on with the Secret Service became the brass ring.

You might ask, if going federal was the goal, and the Secret Service was the best way to go, why did I become a cop? My dad not only advised going the federal route, he also laid out the gantlet I would face in getting there. Specifically, federal agencies like to target applicants who are more mature and have meaningful experience, and therefore, it would be rare for anyone coming right out of college to get on with the feds. There are exceptions, of course, and the FBI might hire applicants who are CPAs or have law degrees, their higher education and academic skill set taking the place of on-the-job experience. But for me, the first step on the path to success meant being a cop.

I served six years. Six memorable years, every minute reinforcing the fact that I was in the right place at the right time.

CHAPTER 2

County Cop

I was a full-time student at the University of Louisville and on the football team. I majored in police administration, and I loved all the cop classes, much more than philosophy, history, economics, geography, the kinds of classes that were supposed to make me a well-rounded citizen. During that time, I was hungry for any experience I could get that would help move me toward my goal, and one fell into my lap.

I became a detective for Stewart's department store the summer between my freshman and sophomore years. I don't recall getting any training and certainly nothing formal, but I knew how to shoot, and I guess they trusted that fact without questioning it. A police friend of mine drove me over to the chief's office one day, and I vaguely remember raising my hand and swearing in. They gave me a badge and told me to cut out a picture of myself and tape it on there for my ID.

The badge said, "City of Louisville, Special Police." Admittedly, it was not an impressive badge—more like something from a cereal box or gumball machine—especially with my makeshift picture serving as my ID, but it empowered me to make probable-cause arrests. This meant, if I witnessed a possible crime, I could arrest on Stewart's property, and this might include shoplifting, employee theft, or guys stealing from the loading docks.

My goal at that time was to get on with the Louisville Police Department. I had a lot of friends there, and in many ways, I felt like I was already one of them. There were other choices available to me, including the Kentucky State Police and Jefferson County PD. I have the greatest respect for the KSP but patrolling in rural areas didn't appeal to me. The same was true for being out in the suburbs of Jefferson County. I wanted inner-city action, but unfortunately, there was a big lawsuit against the LPD and a hiring freeze.

So, I applied to the Jefferson County PD when I turned 21 in August. On the plus side, the county paid more than the LPD, and officers had the luxury of a take-home police car. The car was a big deal, because it meant that at the end of the day, instead of driving to the station and picking up my own car, I could drive straight home. In addition, driving a marked police car with the blue lights and all was good for attracting off-duty moonlighting work to supplement my modest paycheck. That might mean getting through with my shift, then going somewhere to work a security detail for four hours or working on my off days.

There was good-natured ribbing always going on between the LPD and county guys. The county was pushing professionalism, looking always sharp in uniform, shined shoes, and all that. This prompted potshots from the city guys, teasing us that we weren't real cops because we patrolled in the plush suburbs, and that we needed to carry hair dryers instead of firearms, always priming and preening to impress the good-looking upscale housewives we passed on our beat.

As it turned out, when I graduated from the academy, I was assigned to one of the busiest and roughest districts in either the city or the county. It was right on the city–county line, and I was in a one-man car, whereas the LPD doubled up. One young cop alone in a car and making as many or more dangerous runs as the LPD officers counteracted any notion that I was just going through the motions and playing at being a cop.

How did I do that first year? Okay, I guess. One thing that helped me was the confidence I had gained from my work as a store detective, but beyond that, my climb up the learning curve sure wasn't effortless. As the old saying goes, "Good judgment comes from experience, and experience comes from bad judgement." The main advice I got from experienced cops was not about courage, bravery, rushing in where angels fear to tread, and being a hero. All that sort of stuff is taken for granted. It's what cops do. The best advice was more pragmatic, emphasizing that with all kinds of challenges constantly coming my way, first and foremost, I needed to always be alert, be cautious and careful, consider every angle and detail, no matter how insignificant it might appear, and never take anything for granted. Then, with a smile, I was told that above all else, know there are a thousand ways you can screw up. Don't!

I always tried to be helpful to other cops, and especially the seasoned vets, because I never knew when I might need a favor returned. Here is an example. I was a rookie and I was riding a relief car, which means they put me wherever they needed me. It so happens that in the sector where I was assigned, this cantankerous older cop, who hated rookies and let us know it, called on the radio and told me to meet him at a specific location. A little odd, but okay, sure, I'll be there. We met, and he asked me to cover for him because he needed to do something, but he was vague about it.

I said, "No problem. Anything I can help with?"

He said, "No, nothing you can do." He looked down, then sheepishly glanced sideways at me and said, "Actually, I sharted."

I squinched my face at him and said, "Huh? What's that mean, you sharted?"

"I thought I had a fart coming, and as I squeezed it out, well, you can imagine . . ."

I laughed, assuming he was putting me on.

"No, I'm serious," he said. "Remember when all the guys went out to that party last night?"

I nodded.

"Someone showed up with a bottle of tequila, the kind with a worm in it. Not sure why, but I ate that worm, and, man . . ." He paused and frowned, then he said, "Right now I have a crime scene in my pants, and it feels like there's more on the way."

I tried to hold back, but I had to laugh. He didn't.

"You cover me, rookie, and never say a word to anyone and I'll owe you."

"Sure, I'll take your runs." After saying that, I realized it sounded like I was poking fun at his having diarrhea, and I was about to apologize when he gave me a hard look and said, "You'll take my runs, huh?" He stared darts at me a moment, then burst out laughing.

Relieved that I hadn't offended him, I said, "Yeah, but only the official ones."

I took his runs, and I'm glad I did. As I say, you never can tell when you might need a favor returned, and about a month later, I ran out of gas. That is embarrassing, especially being a rookie and seeming not to know my ass from a hole in the ground as evidenced by letting my gas tank run dry. In my defense, the reason I did was legitimate, but when guys get hold of something like that, they don't care if it's legit or not, and they'd milk it bad and get me good.

The reason I ran out of gas was because I was in an extra car that was low on gas when I got it, and I intended to fill it up after roll call. However, before I could fill up, I got an emergency call that took me all the way down to the end of Dixie Highway, almost to West Point, Kentucky. Fortunately, I made it to the call, but then ran out of gas before I could get to a gas station. True to form, my buddy, the older cop who had the runs, showed up with a can of gas, got me on my way and never said a word.

Those are two well-guarded county cop secrets that are no longer secrets.

CHAPTER 3

VALENTINE'S DAY

Police work deals with extremes. Nothing happens for prolonged periods, then suddenly we might get a hot call, a 10-32, police jargon for a trouble run with the likelihood of action. A 10-32 is automatically two cars, and we know to get there as soon as we can. If there is a greater sense of urgency, it's a Code-2, which means go with lights flashing, and a Code-3 is lights and siren. One of the most dangerous and unpredictable hot calls is intervening when there is domestic violence. We never know how a domestic violence scene started, and circumstances can turn on a dime and be completely different from one moment to the next.

One Valentine's Day, we were experiencing a whopper of a Louisville ice storm, with bitter cold temperatures and screaming winds that reduced traffic to a crawl. I was on the 6:45 a.m. to 2:45 p.m. shift, and as I drove to the station for roll call, our sergeant radioed us and told us not to come in, and instead to go directly to our beats and set up at centrally located intersections and respond only to police emergencies.

I did as instructed, then sat there observing, my windshield wipers slapping back and forth. At times like this, I had mixed feelings. On the one hand, the day was shaping up as possibly an easy gig with everything slowed to a snail's pace. As I sat there watching, I hoped the worst thing to happen would be that some fool would drive too fast for conditions and find himself in a ditch, and I'd be calling a tow. He would get what he deserved, in other words, and no one else would be involved or hurt. Routine stuff. Then, as always, my mind jumped to the potential of something more serious, with folks injured or killed in a pile-up. That tensed me up as I settled in.

Now, if you were a little bird perched nearby watching me, even though I appeared to be staring off in space, I was ready for action, somewhat like a pet dog who seems to be lazing around, but in a flash, he is in the kitchen when he hears the crinkle of a food package being opened. Once on the job, we learn and trust that we can keep ourselves alert and in tune while entertaining whatever thoughts happen by for a visit. That day, for whatever reason, I was back on the gridiron at the University of Louisville playing tight end. Go figure. Then my mind skipped quickly to it being Valentine's Day, which suggested a nice dinner date and a reminder to pick up a dozen red roses. Then I wondered about the day's namesake, Saint Valentine, and being a serious Catholic, I wondered what he had done to deserve sainthood and have a holiday named after him. I made a mental note to check it out later.

As I sat there lost in my thoughts, a call came over the radio. It was a 10-32, a trouble run, and it had to do with domestic violence. Talk about extremes: I was sitting there at peace and doing nothing but twiddling my thumbs, and a moment later, I'm on my way to a potentially highly charged and dangerous situation. What's more, it should have been a two-car response, but with the icy conditions, the likelihood of another car getting there in a timely fashion to back me up was bleak at best. Regardless, I moved ahead slowly, like 10 miles per hour, without lights and siren.

I proceeded to an apartment complex I knew was nearby. It was called the Alpine Lodge apartments. Sounds nice. It wasn't. The name came from the architect's lame attempt to mimic a ski lodge, plus there was a pretty good hill leading up to it. As I approached the hill in my rear-wheel drive Ford Crown Victoria, I knew it would be a challenge. The car was not built for traction, and the rear tended to slide sideways on slippery slopes, so I had to go uphill at an angle, keeping the tires spinning because if I stopped, I would be done. To improve traction in bad weather, we would go over to the Southwest Government Center where they had piles of sand from which we filled bags and put them in each side of our trunk in the wheel wells to add more weight on the back tires.

Eventually, and it took a while, I worked my way up the hill. The apartment building I was looking for was on the right side of the complex, and it was a good size—four stories. It was daylight, and although it wasn't bright because of the storm, I could see where I needed to go. This, unfortunately, caused me to proceed without my flashlight.

I'd been to this complex before with several trouble runs over the past year. It wasn't the worst area of town, but people had to keep their doors locked and be vigilant about what was going on around them. I exited my vehicle, locked the door, and ceased all radio contact. We had not received portable radios yet, and unlike today, we didn't have the luxury of instant communication no matter where we were or what we were doing.

I started into the staircase and up three flights to the apartment. As I climbed, it got darker and I could barely see. I wished I had brought my flashlight with me, but every second counts in situations like this and I didn't want to go back to my car. I'd have to make the best of it. Rounding a corner on the third floor, I saw a little light twinkling, and as I eased down the hallway to the apartment, I noticed that the doorjamb was splintered where someone had kicked the locked dead bolt all the way through it. Something major was going down, and instantly all my training at the academy shifted into high gear, and my hand was on my gun.

I moved closer to the door. Police officers are trained to never stand in front of a door, because it's impossible to know what's on the other side. If it's someone with a gun, they can shoot through the door. I stood to the side and knocked, aware that the door had been damaged from the outside. There was no answer. I knocked again, then cautiously pushed on the door.

I peeked inside, then leaned forward. I remember the stale, musty smell, but no distinct odors, nothing from the kitchen. I started through the opened door feeling like I was entering that part of the Mammoth Cave tour where they extinguish the lights and let you see what true darkness is. It was pitch black. No shadows. Nothing. I took a nervous breath, then announced in what I hoped sounded like a commanding voice, "Police!" I stood there waiting for a response. None came. At that moment, it occurred to me that I was completely on my own and couldn't relay any information to anyone; my only means of contact was my car radio three stories down in the parking lot. Worse, in the darkness, someone could be pointing a gun at my head and I wouldn't know it.

Was I afraid? Sure, but I wasn't aware of it. My cop self was in charge and it wouldn't allow me to be afraid. That would come later when I reviewed all the bad things that could have happened. But, right then, at that exact moment, I was following the instincts drummed into me during my training and thank God for that.

I took a few steps, stopped, and allowed my eyes to adjust to the darkness, then I put my hand on my sidearm, and again called out, "Police! Anybody here?" I cautiously moved farther into the apartment, checking for any kind of movement. As I moved forward, I heard a woman's muffled voice. I stopped and listened. She sounded like she was pleading, begging. As I moved forward, I checked the doorway to my right. It was the living room; on my left was the kitchen.

I inched along, and I could hear the woman's voice more clearly. She was saying, "Jesus, please help me." Then, "Please don't hurt him. God, please don't hurt him."

I stopped and unholstered my gun. Who was "him" and what could that mean? Did she hear me, hear my voice and my movements, and think that as a cop I might storm into the middle of a husband-and-wife quarrel and shoot her husband? It wouldn't be unusual for a wife who was being savagely beaten to defend her husband when the cops arrived. Or was "him" someone else? Maybe her child?

Confused, but knowing I was in a highly tense situation, I raised my gun. Instantly my mouth went bone dry and it felt as if my tongue were glued to the roof of my mouth. I could feel my heart pounding, the muscles in my arm suddenly aware of the heaviness of the gun. The voice was coming from the far end of the hallway, the last door on the right, which I assumed was a bedroom. That meant I still had to clear rooms on my right and left before getting there, and who knows what might be waiting for me in the dark.

I inched along past the doorways and to the last door on the right. It was partially opened and the windows in the room were not covered with thick curtains as seemed to be the case in the other rooms. I could see a bit more, and as I came around the corner, I saw a man on top of a woman in bed. She was struggling and trying to scream, but the man had his hand over her mouth. Beside her was a young boy, and the man had his other hand around his throat; a gurgling sound came from the child's mouth. The young boy was the "him" she was pleading for.

I yelled, "Police, freeze!"

The man turned his head toward me. A light outside illuminated his silhouette against a window shade.

"Get your hands up!" Immediately he raised both hands. But as I moved toward him, his right hand dropped to his waist. At that point, I cocked my .357 Magnum and yelled, "You're a corpse!" His hand went back up. Seeing this helpless woman and her young child being abused, my adrenalin took over. I grabbed the back of his shirt around his neck with my left hand and with the unusual strength that accompanies an adrenalin rush, I yanked him from the bed.

I told the man to place his hands on the wall, but once again, he lowered his right hand to his waist.

"You idiot," I screamed in his ear. He reluctantly raised both hands and gave up. I laid him down, pulled his hands behind his back, and cuffed him. I dragged him down the hallway to the living room and turned on the lights. By then I could hear multiple sirens coming my way. I put him back on his knees and searched him. To my great surprise, he had no weapon. Why would he dare to lower his hand menacingly to his waist, risking his life?

I told him, "Do you know how close you came to getting shot? When a police officer has you covered, and you reach down, you are telling me to shoot you. I need to either shoot you or risk getting shot myself."

The man, still on his knees, raised his eyes to me and, with a pathetic look, explained that he was trying to zip his pants. Can you imagine? With all that was going on, the heaviness of the implications, and all he could think to do was to zip his pants. Amazing, but not unusual; cops see crazy things every day that defy explanation.

Finally, after what seemed like two lifetimes, officers came charging into the room. They told me that earlier, as I had proceeded up the stairs to the scene and was out of radio contact (no cell phones at the time, of course), the woman was able to get to her phone, which had a long cord. She took it into her bedroom, locked the door, called, and said a man had broken into her apartment and threatened to kill her. Then he kicked the door in and that brought the cavalry with full force. They knew I was walking into the situation blind, not knowing how serious it was, but they had no way to relay that information to me.

The woman's call was interrupted when the door was kicked in, which left the phone off the hook, allowing a recording of the call to be made. Because it is so unusual to be able to interrupt a rape in progress, the call was played all over the country in police academies. Those listening heard a man kicking in the door, the woman pleading with the police to please hurry up and get there. I, of course, knew nothing about any of this as I was climbing the stairs and making my approach.

When things began to wind down, I witnessed a bit of sweet street justice, and it made me feel good. The little boy, who appeared to be about four years old, came running into the room where the perpetrator was being held, still on his knees. The little boy yelled in his face, "You're a bad, bad man." Then he launched a vicious kick as hard as a four-year-old could muster to the man's groin.

I was glad to see him express his anger and not cower in fear. Of all that had happened, I think this action by a little boy may have been the one thing that embarrassed this jerk. I don't know how much it might have hurt, but I'd like to think that kick found its mark.

The homicide detectives then appeared and congratulated me, saying I was one of the first guys around to ever catch a rapist in the act. I hadn't thought about it before they said it, but the odds are slim of ever catching one of these guys in the act, and because I did and was able to stop it, it made the boy's kick to the rapist's groin a little sweeter.

When cops are involved in something like this, time takes on a life of its own. On the one hand, time flashes by in an instant, but then it also seems to stand still at certain points, completely frozen. As I adjusted to the fact that the worst was over, the next order of business was getting the woman to the hospital. She asked me to take her, and I did. Normally, I would remain at the scene to answer questions, but accompanying her was far more important right then. It made me feel good that she wanted me and trusted me to be the one to take her; that in a brief time frame, we had established a bond that was important to both of us. The detectives understood and encouraged me to go with her, then they took the rapist to jail.

On the way to the hospital, I made sure to tell the little boy how brave he was and what a good job he did trying to protect his mother. I wanted him to have some sort of positive memories of the ordeal that he could conjure up and remember as the years go by—my words and his actions to kick the rapist where it counts.

While all this was going on, my greatest fear as a cop—shooting someone—came within a hair's breadth of being realized. And worse, shooting someone who is unarmed, because if I did, I know I would never forgive myself, even though the facts justified my actions. What's more, the public would vilify me and accuse me of being a brute who enjoyed abusing my power.

Is this fair? Is it fair to set aside the facts that this guy was raping a woman and threatening to harm her small son to gain her cooperation? Is it fair to discount the fact that it was dark, decisions had to be made in a fraction of a second, and the wrong decision could result in innocent people being harmed or killed, and that included me? Of course not. Life isn't always fair, and when you deal with life-and-death situations as part of your job, odds are good that it's less than fair too often. Be that as it may, it's what I signed on for when I joined the police force, and every cop must accept that it comes with the territory.

CHAPTER 4

PLEASE TAKE ME TO JAIL

Daylight was breaking as I was getting off shift at 6:45 on a quiet Sunday morning, ready to go home and get some sleep. Then a heartbeat later, I see this guy, an older gentleman, and he's right in front of me, zipping through a red light like it wasn't there. I do what I have to and get my lights going. I'm on his tail instantly, pulling him over as he enters a subdivision.

As I approach the stopped car from the rear, I touch the trunk of the car. One reason is to make sure the trunk is latched, because in one instance, some guys hiding in the trunk came out shooting. Another reason is, by touching the trunk, we leave fingerprints on the car, and if the car escapes the scene of a crime and they pull it over later, it can be identified because of the fingerprints.

I walk up to his window and I can see the man is alone, and immediately it is obvious that he has had way too much to drink.

I say, "Have you been drinking, sir?"

"Yup," he says with a smile.

"How many drinks have you had?"

"How old are you, young man?"

"What difference does that make?"

"How old are you?" he repeats.

"Twenty-three. Why?"

"Twenty-three, huh? Well, I've had more than that." He starts laughing.

Normally, a response might be something like, "I've had only a couple drinks, officer, I swear, and that was over a four-hour period." Never have I had anyone admit to grossly over-imbibing, and certainly not admitting to having more than 23 drinks.

As it turns out, he is very close to his house, so I have him lock up his car, and I take his keys and tell him he can get his car much later in the day and he should not try to move it in the next several hours. I told him I'll be checking back, and if he moves the car too soon, he'll be in big trouble. So, I get him into my car and drive him down the street and pull into his driveway. Safe and sound, or so it seems until his wife comes storming out the front door looking like a creature from a Hollywood horror movie. She is a large woman in a loud pink housecoat; she has rows of oversized rollers in her hair, a cigarette hanging from her mouth, and an angry, don't-mess-with-me expression on her face. The expression on the guy's face is priceless, and he starts screaming, "Oh, my God, take me to jail. Please take me to jail."

I get between the wife and her husband and calm her down as best I can, then I hand her the keys and point down the road to the car and tell her it is intact, unharmed, and can be moved later. I tell her I could have taken her husband to jail, but I wasn't going to do that. Instead, I'll write him up pretty good, making it an expensive lesson and he might lose his license.

With his wife on the scene, the guy looks up at me like a whipped puppy dog as I give him a stern cop lecture about driving drunk and tell him that he'd better never do it again. His eyes keep moving back and forth between his wife and me, like he is expecting something bad to happen, and I suspect it might when I go. But, for the moment, he responds appropriately, acknowledging that I was giving him a big break and from then on, he'd be walking the straight and narrow. Satisfied, as I depart, I give him a tap on the shoulder and tell him good luck. No doubt he'll need it.

Now, don't get me wrong, I always take drunk driving very seriously, and this case was no exception. But, I didn't take him in for several reasons.

One, he was home and wouldn't be a risk to himself or others. Two, he seemed like a harmless, hapless type, and when I checked on him, he came back completely clean, no priors for drunk driving, no outstanding warrants, the car was his, he had insurance, and all was on the up and up. Three, looking at his wife, I concluded that he likely would receive far worse punishment than he'd get spending a day in the drunk tank, sleeping it off with a bunch of other drunks, then appearing in court. Four, as I say, I was anxious to get home, and if I took him to jail, I'd be tied up a long time. I could call in and have someone coming on duty swing by and take over, but that also could take quite a while as they would be at the station a considerable distance away. And a final reason, the guy made me laugh, and on this job, a laugh can go a long way.

Let me add that later that day, I checked, and I didn't see any calls for that address, which told me he survived.

CHAPTER 5

Always Try to be Nice

I'm often asked if the way people responded to me influenced what I did and how I handled a situation. The answer is, yes, and the previous story about the funny drunk guy and his wife makes my point. I liked the guy and he made me laugh, so my natural, human inclination was to give him a break. On the other hand, since I am human and like everyone else, bad mouthing me didn't work. With that said, I wasn't real big on handing out a lot of tickets unless I witnessed something I perceived as dangerous, like someone driving far too fast who couldn't stop in time if necessary. Even so, when I pulled people over, I always started the interaction with the utmost respect and courtesy, and where it went from there was up to them. I often gave verbal or written warnings. For verbal warnings, I simply straightened them out and sent them on their way. If someone had a headlight out, I might issue a warning ticket, which meant they had to get it fixed in 30 days and show up at the courthouse to verify it was fixed, then the ticket went away.

My courtesy and respect were not always reciprocated. If someone was nasty to me, mouthing off about why I was not out chasing real criminals instead of harassing the public, or they refused to put down their window when I walked up, then instead of issuing a warning, I was likely to take the opposite path. I would write them up, and on rare occasions, send them to jail because just about anything cops can write a ticket for, they can jail someone for. What's more, a stop for something as innocuous as a burned-out taillight can open the door for any number of charges. You see this with proactive police on TV police shows. First, all someone may have is an equipment malfunction, a safety issue and no big deal; this could result in a warning ticket. But if there is a nasty attitude, perhaps the car is searched and something unlawful is uncovered, which escalates the matter, and all of it was unnecessary and brought on by being disrespectful.

One time I wrote a ticket on a guy who tossed a whole bag of White Castle hamburgers out his window, the napkins and wrappers spewing about in the wind and making a mess. It was daytime on Dixie Highway, and he was stopped at a red light. For some reason, he rolled down his window and tossed the bag, obviously unaware that I was right there on his bumper in a marked police car. I pulled him over and found that he was a nasty man with an attitude, mouthing off at me nonstop. I told him how disrespectful it was to throw garbage out his window, and I pointed to the mess. He calmed down and told me he would go pick up the mess, and he did. When he came back to his car, I handed him the ticket, which was sizeable, over $100, big bucks back in those days. Boy, that got him going, and he said, "You wrote me a ticket after I picked it all up?"

I said, "Well, yeah, of course, you threw a bunch of garbage out of your window, and you did it right in front of me."

He said, "Screw you," and he tossed the bag out again.

So, I wrote him another ticket for littering a second time, which really set him off, and he got all up in my face, which resulted in me putting him on the ground and cuffing him. The jerk went to jail for two charges of littering, disorderly conduct, and resisting arrest, all tied to his being nasty and uncooperative.

As I say, my approach was to give folks a break when I could, but I had my exceptions, and a big one was violations of handicapped parking spots. Back then, handicapped spots were not nearly as plentiful as today, which made each one that much more important and valuable. So, when people parked there illegally, it set me off and I wrote them up eagerly. You see, cops have soft hearts for kids, defenseless women, and the elderly. When I saw someone parked in a handicapped spot and a couple of 80-year-olds came along and had to park a long distance away, that bugged me. And let me tell you, it was a stiff ticket, like a hundred fifty bucks, plus court costs on top of that.

It wasn't that I went out of my way to hunt handicapped violators, but anytime I drove through a shopping center lot, I would drive past the handicapped spots to check them out. Sometimes a young guy would be sitting in his car and I'd pull up behind him.

"Where is your handicap permit?"

He'd respond, "Oh, I'm just sitting in my car, and you can't write me a ticket because I can move anytime I want to."

"Yeah, well, that's the problem, because when grandma and grandpa come around the corner, they don't see a spot and they have to park way over yonder." So, I'd write them up, which made them mad, but I figured they wouldn't do it again and that was the point.

When folks received a ticket, most simply paid it because they knew they were guilty and they got caught. But sometimes, they'd fight it just to see if I was going to show up in court. In court, a lot of discretion comes into play. For example, if I wrote someone up for going 18 over the speed limit, I might be inclined to reduce it to 14, which would count as only three points off their license instead of six. I used a coding system on each ticket, my own little mark, reminding me if someone was particularly nasty to me, and if so, I didn't budge on the charges.

Let me add here what it's like being a witness in court when you are a cop. If the defense doesn't have a good case, they resort to ruthless tactics to try to get their client off. I might be asked if I have ever been disciplined during my career. The prosecutor may object that the question is irrelevant, but the defense responds by saying they want to know what kind of police officer they are dealing with. The judge may or may not allow it, depending upon how liberal or conservative they are. Then I may be asked if I have ever consumed alcohol and driven a car? The defense attorney is trying to see how far he can go before the judge stops him. He knows he has no case, but he has to make it appear to his client that he is working hard for his fee and trying his best. From there, the defense attorney likely would take a microscope and go over my police report written some time ago, desperate to find a loophole, any sort of inconsistency. I may have done six things perfectly right and one thing almost right, and the goal would be to get me to admit I made a mistake, no matter how small or insignificant, something he can hang onto to create doubt about my competency. Perhaps on the sobriety test, I imposed walking nine steps instead of ten, and that one step difference would be blown up as a big deal.

Another game is flip-flopping. That means initially pleading not guilty, which necessitates preparing a case, including the subpoena of witnesses and all that. Then the defendant and his attorney show up for the court date and see that the prosecution is well prepared and taking the case seriously, so they flip their plea to guilty. This pisses everyone off, because it's nothing but a huge waste of time and effort.

CHAPTER 6

EASTER SUNDAY

One Easter Sunday, I was working the 2:45 to 10:45 p.m. shift. It was a slow shift, because police calls typically are limited on holidays. But on this day, a call came in about a guy named Danny (not his real name), who was all screwed up on drugs and booze, and he had just gotten into his car. Danny was a guy we all knew; he who never gave a second thought to hurting someone, and possibly hurting them badly. He also was known to be a police fighter, which meant if we arrested him, he wouldn't come easily.

The caller, Danny's girlfriend, tried to convince him not to drive, and she told him the police would get him, to which he responded, "Screw the police." Not a good sign. Then he showed her that he had taken her father's Colt .45 semi-automatic handgun and said, "I'll kill the first cop that pulls me over." He then backed out of the driveway and was on his way.

As I said, we all were quite familiar with Danny, and it was one thing to face the prospect of scuffling with him, and quite another to face him all hopped up and carrying a big old gun. Regardless, it was time to go. Fortunately, because of our intimate familiarity with this degenerate lowlife, we knew the kind of car he drove, which meant odds were good we could track him down and "interact" with him, especially since his last known whereabouts weren't far from the station.

Each of us took a different route, hoping to run into him before he got too far. Sure enough, one of our officers intercepted him and called in on the radio, then he attempted to pull him over. No luck. Danny took off as he usually does, and the chase was on. When I got the word, I realized he was heading northbound on Dixie Highway toward me, so I turned and headed southbound and saw the blue lights closing in behind him. I pulled across into the northbound lanes and put my emergency lights on. As Danny tried to get around me, another police officer pulled in front of him and blocked him off, then two more officers arrived. The four of us had him trapped, boxed in right in the middle of the intersection. Whatever happened next was up to Danny.

Mike, the officer who was in hot pursuit of Danny, drove his car up close to the driver's side of Danny's car so that he couldn't open his door. The strategy was to force him, if he were going to run, to exit from the passenger side. We were ready, and all four of us had our guns drawn. In those days, we all carried Smith & Wessons, typically a .357 Magnum with a four-inch barrel, which is what I carried. Mike was the exception with a .44 Magnum and a six-inch barrel, a big old hog-leg revolver. Gun in hand, Mike was looking straight at Danny over the trunk of his police car, yelling at him to put his hands up and exit the car. Danny couldn't go anywhere, and Mike was giving him a chance to surrender. Mike repeated the warning numerous times.

I was looking at Danny through the front windshield, my revolver pointed at him. I thank God that as I was looking at Danny, I wasn't guilty of tunnel vision, a problem that can affect those with less experience. When cops have been around the block a few times, they know they must be aware of everything around them, and not only the guy in front of them. In other words, while we focus, we also need to be tuned in to our peripheral vision to broaden our scope. So, there I was, poised and ready to shoot when a rookie officer dashed right in front of my line of fire. At the last possible instant, I caught a glimpse of him and held up, otherwise, I would have experienced a cop's worst nightmare, shooting an innocent person, and worst of the worst, shooting a fellow officer.

In situations like this, other hazards are constantly present as well. Two other officers flanked Danny, meaning there were four guns on him at that moment, creating a highly charged and dangerous scenario for us cops. We had a situation with high tension, noise, flashing lights, cops yelling, spectators gawking. There's a term, "circular firing squad," which means a scenario in which the shooters fire at each other. It's a stupid example of what can happen when chaos reigns and friendly fire brings down a comrade. Well, there we were, surrounding Danny on all four sides, guns pointed, the scene ripe for disaster.

At the moment when four guns were ready to unload on Danny, he stayed put, which allowed us to quickly assess the situation and make certain none of us were in each other's kill zone. There was no movement for what seemed like a long moment, but under those circumstances, it was probably only a few seconds. We watched Danny closely, Mike yelling at him to raise his hands and surrender. Then, without warning, Danny fired the Colt .45 inside his car. This caught us by surprise. Why would he do that? It's hard to know what he was thinking, if he was thinking, but hearing the gun go off caused an instant reaction from all of us and within seconds, he was shot four times by the police.

Mike had the kill shot, shooting him through his front teeth to the back of his skull, killing him instantly. We later learned the bullet Danny fired went through the roof of his car, indicating that firing it likely was a stupid accident.

The detectives arrived to process the crime scene, take pictures, and gather evidence. This was happening about the time we would normally get off work, and each of us had to tell what we knew. A common approach is to split up the witnesses and have each tell their story separately and in private. Then when all the stories have been told, comparisons are made to see what matches up and what doesn't. Everything is recorded in detail, and then perhaps the issues are revisited at a future date to see if the stories remain consistent. Or, witnesses could be asked to take a polygraph to see if their answers matched up to their stories told at the scene. When interviewing witnesses who are not cops, they must be made aware that it's against the law to lie, and that's why they are asked to sign their statement to make sure there was no room for misinterpretation.

As a side note, one of the things I learned later was that a brand-new White Castle burger joint had been built at this intersection, and it was stacked with customers enjoying their Easter dinner. They were immediately drawn to the drama taking place on the other side of the plate-glass window, not far from where they sat. It didn't register with me at the time, but with four squad cars blaring sirens and flashing lights and cops screaming at Danny who sat in the middle of things, it must have struck them as a spectacular show.

Through it all, time appeared to stand still, but the gunfight was over in a matter of seconds. I was told afterward that all the people in the White Castle who were standing at the front window watching the chase, the standoff, and the shootout, all dove under the tables. The witness who told me, an earthy gal from that part of town, said that all she could see were assholes and elbows disappearing under the tables. Pretty graphic description, I told her.

When the action subsides, and we've had a chance to catch our breath, there is always the sense of what could have happened if things had unfolded differently. We know that in police work, there are hidden dangers everywhere, not only when guns are being pointed. Missing one of the dangers and allowing or causing something bad to happen can be catastrophic and haunt an officer the rest of his or her life. I mentioned when the rookie ran into my line of vision how important my experience, awareness, and peripheral vision were to avoid a disaster. Beyond that, at such times, we must also consider divine interventions as playing a part, and I certainly do.

Another thing that ranks right up there with shooting an innocent person or a fellow officer is the fear of causing a traffic accident. Think about how much time police officers spend in their cars compared to normal people, and then think about all the times the officer is required to drive fast for one reason or another, lights flashing, siren blasting, and with an adrenalin rush off the charts. Under these circumstance, the public is supposed to yield, and cops have the right of way. Sounds good, but in reality, quite often someone doesn't see the flashing lights or hear the siren. Maybe they're drunk, or have earphones in, or they are arguing with someone else in the car and not paying attention. It's a perfect storm that invites tragedy.

When I approached a red light or stop sign, I had to slow down and be ultra-cautious before passing through. The person I was chasing didn't give that a thought, and all they wanted to do was to get away, whatever the cost. It was a scene we had played out with Danny on more than one occasion. The dilemma was amplified when speeding down narrow streets where a child could be playing nearby and dash out between parked cars, or an elderly person could be halfway across the street and unable to move quickly to get out of harm's way. The best advice for police is to do everything they can when in pursuit but do it with care and concern for public safety. And if we avoid an accident, avoid harming innocent bystanders and someone gets away, so be it. If we can't get it done, perhaps someone else can. That's why when you see a police chase, you may be thinking, gee, why do they need six police cars chasing one bad guy? It's because the deck is stacked against us and we must follow rules the bad guy doesn't.

CHAPTER 7

CHOIR PRACTICE

I was always looking for a reason to get together with the crew, and especially after a day like we had with Danny, so I said, "Hey, guys, how about some choir practice?" I coined the term right then, and it meant grabbing a few beers and decompressing. The term comes from the movie, *Choir Boys,* a cop movie. It's about the kind of cop nobody wants on the job, a guy who gets drunk at every opportunity off the job, and when on the job, he insults the citizens he supposedly serves. His cop buddies are cut from the same cloth, and when one of them mistakenly shoots a guy in the park while they are out letting off steam, they close ranks to try to cover up the crime.

This was to be our first choir practice, and after a while, the tradition took hold. We didn't have them often, but we knew we would be headed to choir practice after any major event that required letting off some steam. The format was the same. We would go to a small park on a dead-end street away from all the neighborhoods. It would be late and dark, and we'd park our cars, then throw some wood in a metal garbage can, and make a campfire. After a while, it would not be unusual for whoever was working the beat to stop by, which was good because he would park his car across the road at the back of our cars and basically keep everyone else out, ensuring our privacy.

At this first choir practice, we shared a few six-packs of beer as we "talked story" (a Hawaiian expression for friends socializing and catching up with each other). This helped ease the accumulated pressure. Conversation started light, like what was going on around town, when our next long four-day weekend was, and when might we hold a platoon party and where it would be, and our next poker game. Funny stories were always welcomed, particularly when somebody did something embarrassing, like lose a prisoner or come up empty on a chase or said something on the radio they came to regret. Then things would go deeper, but the topics were always in bounds. We'd never broach a sensitive topic, like when a colleague's wife left him. We'd never hammer someone about something like that, because it would be considered over the line. Plus, we always had to remember our colleague had a gun and probably had been drinking, a potentially volatile combination.

Gathered as we were around the fire and coming off a harrowing experience we all shared, eventually we'd get around to talking about it. In our way, we supported each other, but it sure wasn't sugarcoated. Usually, there was cutting sarcasm, ball breaking as we called it, in which we'd recount each step that went down, embellishing it and adding color commentary about who did what, who was wide-eyed, who saved the day and all the rest of it. But if there was a serious element, as there always is when lethal force is used, things then morphed into a more somber tone and there was time for reflection.

Such get-togethers for decompression bonded us strongly in ways we couldn't duplicate elsewhere and were important because camaraderie is critical to police work. We had to know the other guys had our backs and vice versa. I don't want to get sappy here, but we had to know they really cared. Is love too big a word? I don't know, but I do know the feeling is like the locker-room camaraderie that has to exist if a sports team is going to be successful. As the Three Musketeers used to say, "All for one and one for all."

Any time there is a gathering of cops, guys will be guys, and with a few beers in our gut and feeling our oats, stuff can happen. Once, when the weather had turned colder and we all were gathered close around the fire in the garbage can, someone said, "It's cold, we need to crank up the fire." This inspired one of the guys to abandon all common sense and take action. He quickly pulled out his gun and emptied six rounds into the metal can, ventilating it and stoking the flames. This, of course, scared everyone. Luckily, nobody was hit, and it was a blessing that he had only a six-shot revolver and it was now empty. I hate to think of him with a semi-automatic and 15 rounds.

On one occasion, we were invited by another agency to attend one of their platoon parties. They didn't call it choir practice, but for all intents and purposes, it was, or so I thought. As we sat there on tables in a picnic area, enjoying a few adult beverages, the night was moving on, and after a while, it occurred to those of us who had to be up early for a morning shift that it was time to leave. So, we got ready to take off, thanked this group for inviting us and we headed on out, no big deal.

Next morning, I got a call and the guy on the other end said in an excited voice, "Man, what happened last night?"

"What are you talking about?"

"Dude, I was in court this morning. Didn't you go down to the big police platoon party?"

"Yeah, I did, for an hour or two. Why?"

"Well, they found a dead body right there behind the picnic tables."

My heart leaped to my throat, and I said, "You've got to be kidding me."

"Not one bit. I'm serious as a heart attack."

I hung up right away and called a guy I know in the other agency and asked him what was going on. He said, "Yeah, they found a dead body right behind where we were all drinking last night. Worse, I'm afraid that when homicide takes over the investigation, they're gonna pull all those empty beer cans and bottles out of the trash cans and run them for fingerprints."

I mumbled, "Man, is this really happening?"

"Believe it. I'm trying to call the homicide detective and let him know it was us down there."

"You guys didn't kill anybody, did you?"

"No," he said and then laughed. "If it was us, they wouldn't have found the body, that's for sure."

Talk about being in the wrong place at the wrong time! The next few hours were an agonizing eternity, but thank our lucky stars, they quickly found the guy who committed the murder. This got us off the hook, and as far as we were concerned, the case went away. That was a little too close for comfort, but we learned from it, and from that point on, we created a new tradition. On choir practice nights, we made it a point to check out the area thoroughly, with emphasis on making sure there were no dead bodies nearby.

CHAPTER 8

MEMORIAL DAY

I've shared stories that occurred on Valentine's Day and Easter Sunday. It's not my intention to have a holiday theme, but here is another holiday story. This one occurred on Memorial Day. I was on day work, the 6:45 a.m. to 2:45 p.m. shift, and I was heading to roll call.

On my way across Jefferson County on the Watterson Expressway, I heard the midnight sergeant call out. He asked for any incoming cars that could divert over to I-65 near National Turnpike and help with a fatal accident so that the officers who had been working the accident could get off on time.

I advised radio to let my shift sergeant know that if it was okay with him, I'd go over there and help until one of the day-work sector cars could come by and relieve me to go back to my inner-city beat. I got the okay, and as I drove up close to the police car with my emergency equipment lights on, I realized that the officer I would be relieving was an infamous guy name Bumper. Hollywood couldn't showcase on the wide screen a better old salty, cantankerous beat cop than him. He was former military, and he looked it, spoke it, acted it, and had lots of tattoos running up and down his arms to prove it. All in all, he was the kind of guy you knew it was best to avoid. But, if you couldn't, you gave him a wide berth, especially if you saw him around the station. And if you were out and about, and especially if there was any trouble, you were glad he was on your side.

I rolled up on Bumper and said, "Hey, I'm here to relieve you."

He looked at me for a long moment, his eyes burning holes through my chest, and finally replied, "Thanks, college kid. I appreciate that."

"What do we got? What are we doing here?"

"Well, we have a fatal motorcycle accident, and the victim is underneath that sheet there." He paused a moment, then added, "Decapitated. As a college kid, I'm sure you know what that means."

"Beheaded." I looked toward the sheet. "Seriously?"

"Yeah, seriously."

Bumper stepped over and pulled the sheet back. Sure enough, there was a head lying next to a body, a helmet still on the head, eyes open. I glanced beyond the body and saw a badly crumpled motorcycle on the side of the road.

I said, "Okay, so what are we doing here?"

"We gotta stay with the body until the coroner gets here." He smirked. "Need to get official word the guy's dead."

I nodded, knowing he didn't need me to add my sarcastic comment that it wouldn't take a brain surgeon to determine that a man without a head was deceased.

Bumper looked up, scanned the area, and frowned. "The worst part of all this is the people rubbernecking as they drive by, slowing down and trying to get a good look at the mangled bike or bloody sheet." He waved his arm. "About put my flashlight through the windshield of a dozen cars, trying to get 'em to keep moving, cause they're backing traffic up all the way down the interstate."

Just a few seconds later, I saw a lady hanging out of her car so far that she was about to fall out. She reminded me of Edith Bunker, and she called out to us in a high-pitched, whiny voice. "Officers, officers, this looks terrible. Did anybody get hurt in this accident?"

I knew immediately by the look in Bumper's eyes that this woman had made a big mistake. He stared at her, then bent over and slowly pulled back the sheet. He let that sink in a moment and then moved to position himself to block the view of the car behind the woman. As he picked up the helmet containing the decapitated head, he said, "Good thing he was wearing a helmet, or it could have been a lot worse."

The woman screamed like nothing I had ever heard before, so loud, I swear if the decibel range were measured, it would rival most sirens. Then, poor thing, she was so startled at the sight of the handheld head, she banged her own head hard as she retreated like a panicked turtle back into the confines of her vehicle, continuing to scream the whole time.

It was clear that Bumper was tickled with himself.

As he placed the head back under the sheet, I said, "Oh, man, we're gonna get written up big time for this one."

Bumper started laughing and said, "Aw, relax, frat boy. You gotta have a little fun, or this job will drive you crazy."

"Yeah, well, we'll see."

"Like I said, relax. It's an out-of-state license plate, and they'll never file a complaint on us."

I took a deep breath, blew it out, and watched the out-of-state vehicle move down the line. Then, I shifted my eyes to Bumper and tried to look calm as I mumbled to myself, "Hope he's right." As he took a step toward his car, I said, "You're relieved."

He smiled real big, slapped me on the shoulder and said, "Great, got me a date with a big old bottle of Jim Beam."

As I watched him go, I thought to myself, each of us has to find ways to cope with doing what we do. For Bumper, it was dark jokes and cozying up to a bottle of Kentucky straight bourbon whiskey.

The fatal accident crew showed up and went about their business, taking their measurements and dozens of photos, the head posed like an exhibit in a gallery, the way Bumper would have liked it.

CHAPTER 9

RIDE OF A LIFETIME

After the tumultuous events of the morning with Bumper, that Memorial Day turned into a slow day, the kind we would expect on a holiday. The radio was dead, and I was back to riding my beat in the inner city. Then I got a call after lunch from the sergeant telling me to come to the station. Uh-oh, I thought, swallowing hard: that lady, the one Bumper scared to death with the severed head, probably complained, and I'm in some deep do-do.

I got to the station, and the sergeant approached me and said, "The captain's on me about getting some warrants served. There's one in there that's pretty old, and it looks bad when we have an active warrant for that long. Go and get this guy so we can take it off the books."

Any time I attempted to serve a warrant I always approached it in the same way. If the warrant says it's for John Smith, I wait for the guy to come to the door and I say, "Are you Bill Brown?" That's not his name, and he'll say, "No."

"Well, I'm trying to serve this warrant on Bill Brown. If you don't mind my asking, who are you?"

"I'm John Smith."

"Oh, good. I've got one for you, too."

Experience taught me that if I had gone up to John Smith and asked him if he was John Smith, he would likely have said no, pushing us into a bunch of foolish and possibly dangerous games.

I found the place, used my Bill Brown versus John Smith ruse, then explained to him that I was sorry to have to serve him with this, especially on Memorial Day. It was a bench warrant signed by a judge. That meant in his case I had to take him in, process him in the jail, and they would assign him a court date. I paused a moment for effect, then emphasized that he'd better make that court date.

John Smith seemed unfazed by what I had told him, and he said, "Oh, man, I was gonna have some friends over for a cookout in a little bit."

"Yeah, well, sorry about that, but it's one of those things that's out of my hands."

He understood and got ready to go.

I said, "The good news is, the radio is quiet, nothing's going on anywhere, which means chances are, you'll get down there to the jail and with a little luck, be out in a couple hours. Should be a nice, easy day for you."

I called in to the sergeant and told him I had a 10-15, meaning I had a prisoner and asked if he wanted me to transport him to jail.

To my surprise, the sergeant said, "No, Charlie 50 just came in, and they'll take him." Charlie-50 is our paddy wagon, a police van with a cage in the back with benches for prisoners.

I cuffed John Smith, hands in front because he was being a nice guy, took him to the station, put him in the holdover, filled out my arrest report, then went out to the van. There were two guys, both senior cops, more senior than me, and I asked, "What are you guys doing here working on a holiday?"

"We're on time out."

That meant they were being punished.

"For what?" I asked.

"Things got a little crazy the other night and we're both under investigation for excessive force."

"Really? So, let me understand this. You're under investigation for excessive force, and they make you both drive the paddy wagon, which is transporting a bunch of angry prisoners?"

"Gotta love the logic, the philosophy that drives decision making."

"Yeah, to be sure. So, anyway, boys, do me a favor. This guy was arrested for having a squabble with his ex-wife, a divorce thing. She got the judge to sign a bench warrant on him because he didn't appear in court. He's never been arrested before, and when I talked with him about it, he told me he had a commitment out of town and she just did it for spite to mess with him. I think he's a decent guy."

Both nodded like they understood and sympathized.

I said, "Bottom line is, could you take him down to the jail, drop him off so that he can get a court date and be out in a few hours."

"Yeah, no problem. We'll get going and run him down real quick."

"Thanks."

I left the station, checked my watch, and saw that I'd be getting off in about 10 minutes. I started down to the perimeter of my beat so when it was time for me to go, I could call in, give my location, tell them I'm okay, and the sergeant could clear me to be officially off. But about that time, I heard a call about a reckless driver near the station.

I jumped on the radio and said, "I'm leaving the station. What have you got?"

"A blue Chevy, driving crazy, a bunch of people in the car, cutting in and out of traffic, driving at excessive speeds, and they ran a couple red lights."

"Okay, I'll pull out here and wait for them."

As I pulled out, I saw the blue Chevy bearing down on me, coming fast right at me. I turned on my emergency equipment, lights and all, and tried to signal him to pull over. He proceeded to wave at me with one of his fingers, then sped northbound on Dixie Highway.

I barked into the radio the words every aggressive police officer relishes: "I'm in pursuit." That immediately got the adrenalin flowing for everyone on duty in the area.

I told them, "I'm in pursuit of a blue Chevy, northbound on Dixie Highway at Dixie Manor heading toward Shively." I gave them the license and said, "Please advise Shively police we are heading their way."

I heard a cascade of calls from cops in all directions joining the pursuit. Truth be told, in those days, it meant it was time to have some fun, and nobody wanted to miss out on it.

Suddenly, the Chevy hung a big bat turn in the middle of Dixie Highway. How he avoided hitting a bunch of cars, I'll never know. Anyway, he did this huge skid and flung his car around. In response, I did a J turn and got right back on him.

"Radio, disregard; we are now headed southbound on Dixie." My lights were flashing, siren blaring, and I was screaming out locations as other cars were trying to intercept us.

It was a slow day, which meant everyone in the area was free to get in on the chase, and we had half a dozen cars in hot pursuit. I could see four people in the Chevy as they headed back toward the station, literally cutting through the station grounds, giving us a yard job across the grass in front, which sort of annoyed me. As they spun to the back part of the parking lot, they started throwing beer cans at parked police cars. I chased them around the back of the parking lot and out again onto the street. Fortunately, traffic was light, late afternoon on a holiday, and most people were already at their destination for the day.

Again, I proceeded northbound on Dixie, picked up a couple more cars, then jumped onto the Watterson Expressway, heading east. I advised radio of my location, and by then, the police helicopter was flying overhead, and from his vantage point, he started directing about a dozen cars in pursuit. Finally, they turned down a dead-end street, heading toward a construction site. Realizing they had made a mistake, the Chevy started spinning in circles, kicking up a huge dust storm. I couldn't see in front of me and lost track of them. I slammed on my brakes to let the dust settle and get my bearings.

A moment later, I heard shots fired, which hypes the adrenalin surge. Did the shots come from the car? I couldn't tell with all the dust. Then, as the dust cleared, I could see the four people in the car jump out and take off on foot, all in different directions. I got out quickly and went after the driver, seeing him as my special project. I chased him through yards, past people grilling hot dogs and others in lawn chairs. I can't imagine what they must have thought, seeing this dirtball fly over the fence, speed past them, and seeing a cop in uniform on his tail, yelling, "Stop, police," while trying to avoid knocking over grills or plowing into innocent folks trying to enjoy their holiday.

Eventually, I was able to tackle the driver with the good form of an ex-football player. I must admit to taking more than a bit of pleasure in aggressively handcuffing this guy. The cuffs went on tight, which can happen when there is a struggle going on. On the other hand, when someone is being cooperative, we can double-lock cuffs in a comfortable position. That means they won't get any tighter once they are set, which is how I handcuffed John Smith earlier, and as I said, I cuffed his hands in front.

Once the driver was cuffed, I checked him to see if he had a gun. No gun. The others didn't have guns either and we were never able to figure out who fired the shots from the car. Anyway, I dragged him back to his vehicle and began spouting off the charges I intended to put on him.

I got back to my car and radioed in that all the perpetrators had been caught and requested Charlie-50, the paddy wagon, to fetch them. I heard Charlie-50 say, "Radio, advise that we're here already, in the back of the motorcade of police cars."

I responded, "Really? Okay, I'm coming back to you. Be there in a minute." I walked up to them and said, "Hey, guys, how the heck did you get here so fast after dropping off my prisoner?"

Then I saw the embarrassment on both of their faces as they looked at each other, their expressions saying *We forgot he was in the back of the van.*

Right in the middle of this insane pursuit going over 100 miles an hour on the Watterson Expressway, this poor guy that I had arrested on a bench warrant 45 minutes earlier was bouncing around, back and forth, up and down, in the cage in the back of the paddy wagon. The Charlie-50 drivers and I held our breath as we opened the back door of the van, hoping this guy was still alive and relatively sound.

He was, but he was also white as a ghost and he had wet his pants, perfectly understandable under the circumstances.

I said, "Sir, are you okay?"

He looked up at me, his eyes big as saucers, and said, "I don't know what happened, but I was praying for my life as I was being slung all over the place in this cage, slamming against the walls. Then I heard gunshots being fired. I just wanted to get out of this alive and never be arrested again."

I took the Charlie-50 drivers aside, and although they had seniority on me, I did my best to give them a stern look and said, "This could have turned out bad." They knew, and they nodded eagerly. Then I added with a smile, "You better be nice to this guy."

Thank goodness the guy was polite to me and I cuffed him in front and not with his hands behind his back. This allowed him to protect himself during the 26-minute chase while being tossed around like a softball in a clothes dryer.

CHAPTER 10

EXCESSIVE FORCE

In the previous chapter, I mentioned that the paddy wagon drivers told me they were being investigated for use of excessive force. What does that mean? Frankly, it could mean almost anything. Back then, there were no body cameras, and everyone nearby wasn't holding a camera, so video evidence was rare, which reduced things to eyewitness accounts and to "he said/she said" testimony. Certainly, some cops go out of their way to be brutes when it comes to effecting an arrest, doing much more than is called for to subdue someone who is resisting. The urge is natural, of course, to want to slam someone who spit in your face, cursed you out, took a punch at you, tried a kick to the groin or whatever, but you always must control such emotions and act professionally.

If you stop to think about it, using force is the last thing a cop wants. I never wanted to tangle with someone and take them to the ground, because when you do, you tear up your uniform and risk an injury to yourself or your suspect. But we do what we must if they are being so unruly that we have no choice, or they have a weapon and are threatening the officer or others. In other words, there are times when force, and possibly excessive force, is the only alternative.

Another problem with using force, excessive or otherwise, is that cops have to do paperwork and fill out a use-of-force form. And there is always the risk when any level of force is involved that the officers can face claims against them for excessive force by the person arrested. It doesn't matter whether the cops did everything right, followed protocol, used only as much force as they had to, a claim could be made simply for spite and to get police in trouble. The good news is, cops were off the hook if there were reputable witnesses around. On the other hand, if there were no witnesses, or worse, the only witnesses were hostile and were friends of the person being arrested, it could get ugly in a hurry. The consequences could range from reassignment, like working the paddy wagon, to suspension, or even charges against the officers.

In my experience, if a cop was a brutal guy who treated everybody harshly and used excessive force, especially if it was completely unnecessary, eventually he would get his just reward because other cops don't like being around guys like that. For one thing, they don't want to get complaints filed on them by association. I can think of one guy who didn't last long in the police department. For starters, he wasn't a likeable guy, and that was the universal opinion. Basically, he was a bully, but he restricted his bullying to teenagers and wouldn't torment or intimidate a man his own size or anyone who might kick his ass. Once in a while, he'd come across a kid who would fight him, and he would put out an alarm, "Officer in trouble, needs help," and we would come running to his rescue with lights and siren.

Finally, we got to the point, after making so many runs for this guy, that we concluded he was a jerk. I suspect he was one of those guys who never had many friends growing up, maybe was the object of ridicule or was bullied, and this was his way of getting even, using his badge and gun. We met as a unit and had a talk with him and told him that the next time he started a fight with some teenagers and put out a call for help, we might have a hard time finding his location.

It seemed to work and calmed down and he discontinued doing that stupid stuff. Not sure if this was the deciding factor in his quitting the force, but I suspect it helped. I might add, when people get into a pattern of doing stupid stuff, eventually it catches up with them. In this case, it showed that police can police themselves.

I remember a guy I had to hit one time, a very strong guy, a construction worker with huge thick hands, a tough guy. I had to break up a fight he was in at a bar. I was trying to get him out and convince him to go home, but he was so drunk that he turned his attention to me and tried to tackle me. That, of course, opened the gates, and I ended up hitting him over the head with my metal flashlight, which happened to be in my hand. It was night and I needed it to see, and in a situation like that, a flashlight makes a good weapon. I had no choice but to whack him good as this guy meant business. In addition, he had done some time in the penitentiary, and he knew how to take care of himself.

Head and face wounds bleed a lot, so his face was covered in blood and he looked a lot worse than he was. Finally, he went down, and we cuffed him, using two sets linked together because he was so broad and had large arms. Could he have charged me with using excessive force because I nailed him with a weapon instead of trying to subdue him? Sure, and there was no way to stop him. I've seen filled-out forms that were totally bogus, where someone who was drunk—like this guy—didn't like the fact that the officer had no choice but to subdue them by whatever means available. Unfortunately, once a form is filed, it must be dealt with, bogus or not, and it requires an investigation.

In this case, plenty of witnesses were willing to step forward and support my side, so I was in the clear. Eventually, the drunken construction worker sobered up, and I assumed the issue was over and gone. Then, some months later, he walked up to me and said, "Hey, man, you remember me?"

I was off duty at the time, no uniform, and I looked at this guy and thought, uh-oh.

He said, "Let me buy you a beer. I was an asshole that night acting the way I did, and I'm sorry about what happened." He pointed to his head and said, "Here's the scar you gave me, and I use it as a lesson to teach me not to drink up my paycheck anymore."

There we were, his arm around me and him buying me a beer at a nearby bar. I thanked him for the beer and bid him well. Then, a month or so later, he got whipped again by some other policeman, and it was the same scene: drunk as a skunk and wanting to fight everybody in the place. That's how some guys roll. They work hard and play hard and after getting paid on Friday, they head straight to the bar at four in the afternoon, drink for hours, get drunk, and by eight or nine, they're in a brawl. After that, the cops arrive, they end up in jail, and use their paycheck for fines and court costs. Or they get drunk and go home and start a domestic brawl with their wives.

CHAPTER 11

Sea Hunt

One aspect of police work that is critically important is understanding the need for rest and relaxation. In a sense, it's like what we have learned about physical training. If you keep pushing your body relentlessly hard, trying to become more fit by running more miles faster and faster, your body will break down from the unending stress of "overtraining." Similarly, for cops, the stress and pressures of rotation can build, pushing us to a point where there has to be a release, a decompression phase that allows us to recharge and come back for more.

During my first couple of years in the police department, we'd all start off in our platoon (the same set of guys) working in three-week rotations. We'd start with the three-to-eleven shift for seven days. Then we'd get one day off and be back the next day at seven in the morning, working the seven-to-three in the afternoon shift for seven days. Then one day off and we'd be on seven days of the midnight shift, eleven at night to seven the next morning.

Let me tell you, constantly changing shifts can screw you up. It's like flying back and forth from LA to New York City and never adjusting to the time change. It's all about circadian rhythms (the body's natural biologic clock) that regulate body functions. The body can adjust to day-versus-night demands, but it takes time, and a lot longer than one week. Without adequate time to adjust, sleep is disrupted, and the resulting relentless sense of fatigue makes it difficult to focus and concentrate. This causes irritability, nervousness, and the potential for a short fuse and bad temper, leading to bad decisions. It also promotes dependence on stimulation from caffeine and nicotine to stay alert and keep going, and the use of alcohol to unwind. All told, too much shift work over too long a period wreaks havoc on the body, especially in the stomach and GI tract. There's also a toll on the cardiovascular system that increases the risk of heart disease.

Okay, you get the point. Shift work is bad news. The only good thing about it was that after three grueling weeks of shift work, we'd get a five-day weekend break. Moving into our break, we'd get off at seven in the morning. From there, some of us would change clothes and head on down to Rough River Dam State Park, less than two hours away. There was always someone down there who had or could get a cabin or a houseboat, and we would head straight down there without sleeping or rest of any kind, very much looking forward to enjoying the peace and tranquility of the lake. Right off, most of us would fall into a nap, which we undertook at our own peril, because while we slept, it was likely that someone else would mess with us in all kinds of creative ways that would get a laugh.

But eventually, we'd hit our stride and swim, water ski, fish, play cards, cook out, all the ingredients required for a couple days of decompression. And even though it seems perfectly contradictory to the concept of decompression and recovery, and even if we were exhausted from being up all night drinking and with barely an hour or two of sleep, there was something magical about getting out on the lake early. I usually had my 19-foot speedboat in tow, and one thing I especially enjoyed was awakening before sunrise and taking the boat out onto the lake. The water would be calm and look like glass, and I would be going 40 or 50 miles per hour, the wind in my face, light breaking on the horizon, unspeakable beauty all around me. It was exhilarating, and the release of stress from my body was incredible.

Another option was driving to the ocean and chartering a boat for deep-sea fishing, leaving cop-life far behind. There would be a dozen of us and we'd go out not far off the coast. On one occasion, the fish were not cooperating. No bites at all, no matter what the captain tried to do. Jasper (not his real name), one of the older guys, was a hard-core drinker who was known to whine a lot when he got loaded. He was complaining about how he always came on these trips, and how he'd go all day long without so much as a single bite, never catch a thing. After hearing it for about the 10th time, one of the guys decided he'd heard enough and he came up from behind and bit Jasper's shoulder—hard. Jasper screamed like a banshee, and we all, of course, given the compromised state we were in, thought it was funny and started laughing.

Then things really heated up, with Jasper getting physical and lashing out with his fishing pole, screaming that he was bleeding. The whole while, we were laughing our asses off, watching him chase around the boat, knocking over everyone's beer and getting fishing lines tangled. Suddenly, Jasper stopped dead in his tracks, grabbed his chest, and said, "I think I'm having a heart attack!" He fell over and slammed his head against the deck of the boat. We were all watching this and thinking it was a joke. Nice try, Jasper, to gain sympathy, but it wasn't going to work.

I was an EMT (emergency medical technician) and rode with the medical unit on occasion. I looked hard at Jasper and thought this could be real, so I said, "Boys, he's not looking too good." I went over and started checking him, and sure enough, he wasn't faking. He was having a heart attack right there in front of us. Obviously, the laughter turned immediately into concern as I and another EMT started treating Jasper as best we could to save his life. We started CPR and I told the captain to call the Coast Guard and get a helicopter out there right away or this man might die.

Jasper moved in and out of consciousness, and he would ask, "What's going on?" Then, he'd go out, and we'd pick up the CPR again. Of course, an ambulance, or a helicopter in this case, always seems to take forever, but actually, the Coast Guard did a great job of getting out to us quickly. The next thing we knew, a helicopter was hovering overhead, and they started lowering a rescue basket down to us. The guys unhooked it and put it on the deck, and we put Jasper in there carefully and cinched him in with the series of seat belts to make sure he wouldn't fall out. We got him all fixed up and gave the helicopter a thumbs-up sign that Jasper was ready to go.

Up he went, and when he was up about 75 feet or so, the basket started spinning, and it looked like one of the cables that should be attached to the basket had let go. That meant he was hanging by only one cable and spinning like a top. Down below, we could hear him yelling and screaming, "What'd you do to me?"

We were all looking up, aghast at the sight, and before they got him into the helicopter, the other line detached and dropped him like a big rock into the ocean. My God! We were all watching in horror as this unfolded before our eyes, Jasper screaming all the way down, then he disappeared like a platform diver. Instantly, we were all taking off our life jackets, ready to jump in after him when the floatation devices on the basket kicked in, and he came up like a missile out of a submarine. He shot out of the water about 10 feet, cussing a blue streak the whole time, calling us every name in the book, laying it on us that he's so tired of us screwing with him all the time, and saying we did all this on purpose and he's going to get all of us.

By now, the helicopter had come in low and a team of divers jumped in to save Jasper. They hooked him up again, the correct way this time, not letting any of us touch the basket, and off they went with him to the hospital. He survived, which when you think of someone having a heart attack and being treated that way, it was truly a miracle. But it wasn't a miracle that would last long, as Jasper had another heart attack a few years later and died. A real shame, doubly so, because it was another cop who never got to enjoy his well-earned retirement.

That deep-sea fishing expedition took its place in the annals of police lore as one of the premier decompression adventures of all time.

CHAPTER 12

PREACHER PURSUIT

Many of our officers who had served in Vietnam brought home horrific memories and experiences. Worse, when they got home, not only were they burdened mentally and emotionally, and some had physical injuries, the public shunned them, spit on them, and called them warmongers and worse.

Nowadays, they call what these men had PTSD, post-traumatic stress disorder, and we have learned a lot more about it. A challenging aspect of dealing with these vets at the time was the lack of predictability and consistency. Some days they ran hot, to the point of boiling over, and other days they were cold, morose, like walking zombies. With that said, for the most part they were fine, good officers, and we got along very well as a platoon.

One thing in the police culture that cops learn quickly is if you get yourself into trouble—and it doesn't matter if it's trouble with drinking too much too often, or trouble with your spouse, or gambling or drugs—there's only one way you ever have a chance of saving your career, and that's getting yourself some help. A good first step is meeting with a police chaplain. From there, more serious issues might require turning yourself in to Our Lady of Peace psychiatric hospital. I cannot overemphasize the importance of asking for help.

We had chaplains for different faiths, and one of the guys who ministered to the officers was called Preacher Pete. Pete traveled to the beat of a different drum, and he was proud of it. I guess you could say he was somewhat of an ego maniac, which, of course, is the antithesis of what we expect from men of the cloth. Flamboyant is a word many would use to describe him. He was obsessed with having every hair in place and he was always impeccably dressed, looking the part of one of those discredited TV evangelists always asking for money, then taking it and living a lavish lifestyle. If an officer reached out to Pete for help, it probably was because he was the only choice for their faith or religion, and it was clear that most did not feel comfortable confiding in him. There was a lack of trust, a perception—legitimate or not—that Pete was a direct pipeline back to the chief's office, and you'd better be careful if you shared something confidential and revealing with him, because what you exposed and the details surrounding it might come back to haunt you.

Preacher Pete always seemed to have ideas, creative ways of doing things, and he decided that he would like to start marriage counseling for officers and their spouses. This, of course, was at face value a good thing, something desperately needed because marriages were failing right and left, especially among Vietnam vets, so the news was well received by the male officers, despite the fact that it was Preacher Pete who was behind it. Wives were eager to save their marriages as well, and when they were informed, they signed on immediately. Things seem to go along okay, and one might say the idea was productive. Certainly, the counseling of the male officers was viewed as a good thing. However, when it came to the wives, Preacher Pete seemed to want to take his up-close-and-personal counseling to a deeper level.

After a while, rumors started to circulate that Pete was able to convince some of these wives to submit to probing interviews, intimate explorations, particularly of their sex life, and from there, he was able to convince some to participate more actively. Things progressed and reached a point when these were no longer rumors; one day he got caught by a police officer in a highly compromising position with one of the wives. This started a cascade of events that led to some chaotic moments at the station and ultimately brought the matter to a head.

Preacher Pete had an unmarked police car. This was typical at the time, but it is no longer the case as speeding through traffic while hurrying to a scene proved to be too dangerous without proper training. But, one day, there he was, Preacher Pete, flying in his unmarked police car while screaming into the radio in extreme agitation, saying: "Radio, hold me 10-7 to Our Lady of Peace." Hearing this, we thought, he must have an emergency where an officer was on the verge of disaster, and hopefully, the officer was heading to the hospital to turn himself in. After a few moments, Pete got back on the radio and said, "I'm going lights and siren," which is highly unusual for a chaplain, even one as flamboyant as Preacher Pete.

It turned out to be more than a bit unusual, and as we listened, we heard an officer on the radio with his lights and siren on, saying that he was in pursuit of a subject wanted for sexual misconduct. It took a few moments for us to figure out that both events might be related, and it was our lieutenant who got on top of it first. The officer was chasing Preacher Pete, one police car chasing another to the psychiatric hospital.

I need to add two relevant facts here. One, the officer who was in hot pursuit of Pete was someone we all knew very well, a member of our platoon who had committed himself to Our Lady of Peace on more than one occasion, seeking help in his battle with the demons he brought back from Vietnam. And, two, it came to light that while this officer was convalescing in the psychiatric hospital, Preacher Pete was attending to his wife.

So, there we were, hearing this conversation on the radio, knowing that Preacher Pete was in trouble and for good reason. Once the lieutenant put two and two together, he instructed officers from another district near the hospital to get there ahead of Preacher Pete and told them to get the preacher through the doors and to safety before the pursuing officer arrived. Thankfully, *for Pete's sake* (I'm not sure where the saying comes from, but it's highly applicable here), he was ushered inside and just in time.

It was a chaotic situation to be sure, particularly as the lieutenant pleaded with the officer to stop the pursuit. The officer's response on the radio was a classic line I'll never forget. He got on there and, in a sing-song voice, said, "LT (short for lieutenant), sometimes I feel like a nut, and sometimes I don't." (This was a reference to a famous Almond Joy versus Mounds candy bars TV commercial back in the 1980s.) The implications of this officer's well-known psychiatric history of voluntary admissions to Our Lady of Peace combined with that statement sure stoked the fires of anticipation about how this episode might end.

If civilians had been aware of what was happening, they wouldn't have believed it. A cop was flying in pursuit of Preacher Pete, a police chaplain, hot on his tail and nearly catching him, and while he was at it, he sang a jingle into the radio that had an ominous interpretation tied to it. On the one hand, we couldn't help ourselves and it was hilariously funny as all get out, like some cop spoof movie. After the fact, of course, reality hit and we all realized it could have ended badly for everyone involved. Luckily, the good Lord intervened, and the pursuing officer came up short. After that, he was admitted to a different psychiatric hospital (not Our Lady of Peace for fear of running into Pete) where he did more work on exorcising his demons. As it turned out, he wouldn't have run into Pete at the hospital because Pete was gone, vanished into thin air. We never saw him or heard from him again.

One thing about all of this, it provided additional fodder for slapstick conversations at choir practice while we all gathered around the barrel fire, beer in hand.

CHAPTER 13

THE IMMACULATE INFARCTION

Coming out of the academy, I was one of the two young officers who did not get assigned as a full-time member of the EMS (emergency medical services) for the first year of duty on the job. I felt fortunate, I was. But, when certain officers were off, and they needed somebody to fill in, I would get pulled in to ride in the ambulance since I was a trained EMT. We called it the meat wagon, and I would have to ride for that shift, or for a couple days if somebody was on vacation or whatever.

When we got calls, the meat wagon would scream down the road, running like crazy with lights and sirens. I was a youngster and they usually put us with older officers, because they found that when they put us with younger officers, we would get bored. And when we did, we would run our radar gun out of the back of the EMS unit, pull over cars and write them up a ticket. That didn't sit well with the community and members of the chief's office, because even though we were fully sworn police officers performing what in our view was a necessary service, giving out tickets from the back of the meat wagon was bad publicity for EMS units, so we had to stop.

One of the older officers I always enjoyed riding with was a very large and powerful African American guy with a pleasant and friendly disposition, and he was like that all the time. We called him Med Ted, and when he wasn't getting a medical call he liked hanging out at a particular convenience store because it had coffee, Cokes, and what not. The clerks loved having us around, because in our area, where robberies were a commonplace occurrence, having that police vehicle in their parking lot and two uniformed police officers on site made them feel comfortable and safe. So, in response, they were always sending over hot dogs, donuts, or whatever to us.

I would try to pay for anything that came my way, because it felt right. But Med Ted would say, "Hey, you're gonna ruin a good thing, trying to pay for this stuff." I'd respond, telling him that I felt the need to leave some money to cover at least part of what I knew I owed. He'd frown and stare at me, then smile and shrug.

Med Ted liked to look at the magazines on the stand. They had fishing and hunting magazines, and, of course, an array of girlie magazines, as well. I'd get bored standing around there, but obviously I was the rookie and he was the senior guy, so that's how it would go down until we'd get a medical call, then we'd be off and running.

One evening, we responded to a heart attack run not far from where we were, and we came rolling up and saw the front porch light on, shining bright in the night. We got out, went up, and found the door open, all the house lights on, so we went in. A guy standing there said, "Hey, I think my mother-in-law died." He pointed to the back of the house. "She's back in the bed there."

We walked to the bedroom and, sure enough, there was a little old lady, extremely frail, thin as can be, lying there, not moving. Her mouth was open, her dentures in a cup on a side table, and there were no signs of life.

Med Ted checked for a pulse, looked at me and shook his head, and I figured he meant that we were too late, and she was gone. Then he says to the guy, "My partner here will give her CPR just in case." I stood there thinking, *what?* Ted saw my face and told me to get started. I looked at him and said, "All right," and proceeded to do as we were taught. I pinched the nostrils, held her head back, took a deep breath, blew into her mouth, and watched her chest rise. Then I followed that with chest compressions, pushing on her breastbone. After about the third compression, I heard what can only be described as the world's loudest burst of flatulence, a giant fart, way beyond anything I had ever heard before. That's saying a lot from a guy who has hung out with some heavy beer-drinking loose cannons, guys who delighted in cutting the cheese at every opportunity.

That fart took us all by surprise as it was amplified, bouncing off the walls in that little room. The next thing I know as I go to give more mouth-to-mouth breaths, this little old lady's eyes popped open and she was looking right at me, which startled me. I jerked back and straightened up in hurry. She stared at me, a confused look on her face, and I'm sure the look I returned was just as confused. Then I looked over at Med Ted and her son-in-law, who said, "Man, that's a miracle."

I leaned over the lady and said, "Are you okay, ma'am?"

She still had that confused look on her face, but she replied, "Yeah, I'm fine. What are you doing here?"

I said, "Well, you know, we thought you were, ah, not, ah with us anymore, and we were trying to bring you back, if that was possible."

She cleared her throat and said, "I'm fine, and matter of fact, I'm kind of hungry."

I glanced over at Med Ted and said, "I guess we're finished here."

The son-in-law, his eyes wide, said, "That was the wildest thing I've ever seen." Then, he said, "What do you think it was?"

Without missing a beat, Med Ted looked at the little old lady and said with a straight face, "Well, I'm not a doctor, but I'm pretty sure it was an *inFARTion*."

The son-in-law nodded like he understood the medical jargon, that infarction, the appropriate pronunciation, meant obstruction of blood supply resulting in the death of tissue. For me, I bit the inside of my lip to keep from bursting out laughing and looking highly unprofessional. As we exited, I tried to keep a straight face, and the only thing on my mind was getting back to the convenience store in a hurry and getting a bottle of mouthwash.

As I cleaned up my mouth, I was thankful the lady lived, and we had a happy and humorous ending. And I felt good that my batting average on CPR was 100 percent, one for one.

CHAPTER 14

WORKING VICE

Vice 1

Is working vice a good gig? Yes, indeed. It's considered a feather in your cap, working in an undercover capacity, driving cool cars (cars that don't look like cop cars), and being involved in high-intensity sting operations. I liked being involved with stings and thought they were fun. For example, we might have an attractive policewoman dressed as a hooker and wearing a wire. When guys solicited her, we could hear what was going and, at the right moment, we would pounce and make an arrest. Or we might go to a bar known for dirty goings-on and get propositioned by actual hookers and make arrests. The main point of such activity is, if an establishment gets busted enough times, it will lose its license and can be put out of business. Drug buys were more serious and could put us at higher risk, but, hey, it came with the territory of acting out the role and being convincing.

One vice case I worked on involved a gambling operation on the second floor of a building near the west end of Louisville. Intelligence had told us it was a large operation, lots of money exchanging hands, and apparently a couple of the people involved had outstanding warrants on them. Four of us were assigned to try to catch them betting on a championship NFL game. At the time, I was a younger "temporary" detective. Sometimes they'd grab a guy out of uniform to temporarily work as a detective, maybe to feel out the officer to see how he or she would get along. I was a younger guy, which allowed me to play a younger undercover role, perhaps buying drugs or whatever, depending upon what story we wanted to go with. For example, I could be a soldier from Fort Knox, returning from Vietnam and on the prowl for drugs. At one point, I helped the narcotics squad in this way and we got 52 indictments.

For the gambling assignment, I was riding with an older guy. The other two detectives were sitting on the house, and we watched a lot of people go in there. The game had started 20 minutes before, and through our surveillance, we were confident the main players we were after were inside and it was time to call in the uniforms and raid the place.

My partner and I were on one side of the street, and the other two detectives were on the other side. Since we were undercover, we had rented a vehicle from a local Rent-A-Wreck place and deliberately picked an old sedan, something you'd drive if you were down and out and that didn't look anything like a police car. My favorite stake-out vehicle was a pickup truck. Give me a white pickup and I could sit anywhere, especially if I put a little yellow light on top and a sign on the side. People would pass by and never think twice about it.

We were all set and feeling confident. The other two detectives told us they were going to try to peek inside the upstairs windows to see if everything was going as we suspected and the scene was ripe for a raid. So, we sat there down the block a way, watching them. One of the guys jumped up, reached, and pulled himself up to the second-floor balcony while the other guy assisted, pushing his legs up. He got up there and hopped onto a big balcony deck while the second guy, Robby, tried to do the same thing. Problem was, he didn't have anyone to push him up from below, and he had to pull himself up on his own. Apparently, his gun, which he liked to stick in the back of his jeans, held there by his belt, was starting to fall out. This forced him to stop, grab his gun, and hand it up to his partner on the balcony.

We got a laugh out of watching this Abbott and Costello routine unfold before us. Their maneuver proved to be harder than they thought, and they were a bit older than they wanted to believe. As Robby struggled to pull himself up to the balcony, they heard glass break. The guy above looked out at the street and told Robby, "Can you believe this . . . some guy is breaking into our car." He had taken a tire iron wrapped in a rag and hit the front passenger window, opened the door, got in, and was going through their stuff. Robby's immediate reaction was, of course, to dash to the car and grab the guy.

Robby quickly jumped down and was in pursuit. But he had handed off his gun to the guy on the second floor, which meant he was unarmed. Regardless, he ran up on the guy, surprised him, and yelled, "Police, hold it, freeze." He reached behind him to grab his gun, which wasn't there, and it took a moment for him to realize this. About this time, the humor of the situation vanished, we realized something was wrong, and we started heading up there to see if we could help. The street-smart perp soon figured out that Robby didn't have a gun and took his own gun and fired at Robby, one shot. It was another of those surreal police moments where my mind had trouble believing what was happening. We heard the shot, then the guy took off running, and so we pulled up with headlights on him.

I jumped out and saw Robby holding his stomach. My partner, Steve, took off after this guy who is running like an Olympic sprinter. As he was running, Steve emptied his five-shot revolver at the guy. I was back there, torn between staying with Robby or helping Steve. I had already called it in on the radio: shots fired, officer down, need an ambulance right away and backup. Unfortunately, I never got a good look at the guy to provide much of a description because I was focused on Robby.

First thing Robby said to me was, "Well, guess our cover was blown, huh?"

I laughed and said, "Ah, yeah, gunshots will tend to do that."

Then he said, "That creep shot me."

I look at his shirt and don't see any blood, no sign of a bullet wound.

He said, "Yeah, he shot me, but it didn't really hurt."

I lift his shirt and sure enough, there was a little hole near his belly button. I bent closer to get a good look at it and thought, that's the smallest bullet hole I've ever seen.

Robby said, "I think it was a .22; wasn't even loud."

I leaned back and asked if he was okay, and he said yeah. About this time, the other detective arrived from the second-floor balcony and was holding Robby's gun. I told him we had to get Robby to the hospital, but Robby didn't want any part of that. He said, "No, we've got to get this guy who shot me."

Steve came back, and he was breathing hard from all the running. He said, "I can't believe he got away."

I said, "You didn't hit him?" I knew he had fired a bunch of shots at him.

He said, "I swear I thought I shot him in the back, thought I hit him at least a few times."

We later learned that Steve did shoot five times and hit the suspect all five times in the back and the butt, and the guy ended up going to the hospital. Fortunately for him, none of the bullets hit anything vital, so they pulled out the bullets, fixed him up, and he was good to go straight to prison charged with shooting a police officer.

So why didn't the bullets do more damage? In those days, bullets were like "ball ammunition," as in the old cowboy movies where they pulled the bullet out, poured some whiskey on it to keep it from getting infected, and you were good to go. Nowadays, you have much higher firepower and hollow-point bullets, which essentially explode on impact. The shock alone of getting hit can knock you down, and I've seen guys who were wearing a vest have huge bruises where a bullet hit because the impact was like getting hit with a hammer.

We got Robby up and into the car, and I took off after calling in to the police operator and reporting that we were headed to what back in those days was known as General Hospital. By that time, police cars were coming to the scene from all directions, so Robby and I got a police escort to the hospital emergency room, then referred to as Room 9. Again, Robby insisted he was okay and that it didn't hurt, and when we got there, he hopped out of the car and walked in like nothing happened, except that he was mad we didn't get the shooter. The nurse took Robby back to examine him and get him ready for whatever they needed to do. I kept checking on him, waiting for the reality that he got shot to dawn on him, but he insisted he was fine.

Word got out quickly that Robby had been shot, and all these people were showing up at the emergency room. Knowing this, Robby called me over close and in a low voice said, "A couple females may be showing up here and you gotta keep them separated."

I jerked my head back and said, "What are you talking about?" He told me to talk to his partner, he would know what was going on. So, I'm like, sure, whatever, I'll take care of it.

They took Robby up to the operating room to work on him. Next thing you know, besides all these police officers milling around in the hallway of the emergency room, females started showing up. Apparently, a couple of them were Robby's ex-wives, a couple were ex-girlfriends, and a couple were his current girlfriends. This was looking bleak, and I had to get backup to keep a lid on this brewing domestic situation and keep it under control. Imagine being in the middle of a gaggle of women who rushed there knowing *their* Robby got shot.

Robby ended up staying in the operating room a lot longer than we thought. The bullet was a .22 caliber. The problem was, because it was a .22, the ricochet effect tore up his intestines pretty bad and made it a much more serious situation than the tiny hole led us to believe. What eventually happened was they had to perform major surgery, patch up his intestines, and cut out a section of his stomach, which put him on the sidelines, ineligible for active duty, and he had to retire with medical disability.

Robby was a great police officer and a good friend. Unfortunately, the gunshot wound haunted his body and several years later, he succumbed to complications and died.

Vice 2

At the very southern end of our police district heading to Fort Knox, there was an area with a bunch of stripper bars to attract off-duty soldiers. The scheme was to get as much money out of the soldiers as possible. One technique was for strippers who were not performing to latch on to soldiers who had had a couple of drinks and try to convince the soldiers to buy drinks for them.

"Hey, soldier, buy a girl a drink, won't ya?" Doesn't sound too sinister, until you stop to realize that when you bought a stripper a drink, the bartender would charge like maybe thirty or forty dollars for it. Or perhaps a bottle of champagne might be ordered to celebrate something, and it might cost upwards of $200, or some outlandish amount for a bottle that cost only ten dollars in the store. The soldiers, of course, were naïve to all of this and thought a drink was maybe five bucks, at most, and they weren't paying attention as the bill skyrocketed.

Then, when the soldier got the bill and his eyes popped out at the amount, he, of course, protested and wouldn't pay. At that point, a group of big mean bikers from a local motorcycle club would step in and beat the guy senseless and make him pay. The result was soldiers were being victimized, essentially being beaten and robbed, so Fort Knox asked the police department to do something about it.

In response, I hooked up with a partner and we went undercover. Our story was we were married guys from Detroit and were at Fort Knox working for Chrysler on the M1A tank. We had appropriate stickers on our car and looked the part, and we'd visit these bars and lay out our story. While there, we'd observe to see who was doing what, try to identify the manager, watch the girls operate, figure out which bikers were there, and get license numbers off their bikes. When we had everything we needed, we came back a few weeks later, made many arrests, and put a big dent in their operation. We put several in jail and got liquor licenses revoked, which was our main goal. But, even so, we had to be aware that somebody from the same group or family might apply for a license and try to reopen with the same scam later.

The bikers who operated as muscle for this stripper scam were part of a huge motorcycle club with lots of members, and they were ornery, always fighting and sometimes in shootouts with a biker club from a neighboring state. It was an ongoing thing, with constant retaliations, one side then the other, creating a never-ending loop. A likely location for a confrontation was a funeral for a downed comrade, which typically turned into a crazy scene at the gravesite, everyone dashing about hiding behind tombstones, guns blazing.

These bikers had a clubhouse that was located within the center of my beat in a place that was once a vacation spot. However, in the years since, it had declined drastically, taking on the appearance of an Appalachian "holler" in far Eastern Kentucky. (In retrospect, I can make that comparison accurately because in my first two years as a federal agent, I covered 18 counties in southeastern Kentucky; a considerable portion of my time was spent scouring the hollers.) The houses were rundown dumps, and many didn't have running water or heaters of any type, which meant they heated with a fire stove of some sort and, every winter, at least one of the houses burned down. There were Confederate flags hanging everywhere, mean junkyard dogs, rusted-out cars, and old washing machines in the yard. Surely, any decent people who had lived there were run out when the bikers moved in. One thing was certain, they all hated the police, and if we ventured in, we had to be careful.

The bikers' clubhouse was located right on the flood wall. They believed they were untouchable, and for the most part, they were until trouble came down on them in the form of a couple of runway girls from Tennessee. They were only 14 or 15 years old when they showed up at the Louisville Greyhound bus station. A biker saw them and offered them some food and a place to stay with lots of partying going on. The girls bought the story and ended up getting brutally gang-raped. They survived the ordeal, but not by much.

When the cops found out about it, lots of arrests were made. The day the bikers were scheduled to appear in court was bitterly cold, like only five degrees, too cold to ride a motorcycle. So, they had their motorcycles parked in the clubhouse, in the adjoining garage, or close by, and they drove in cars to court. While they were all at court, their clubhouse mysteriously burned down to the ground, taking all their bikes with it. The bikers weren't conscientious about keeping up with their insurance payments, so they pretty much lost everything.

The bikers pointed a finger at the police, saying we did it, and an arson investigator got hot on the case and believed the bikers, and he let us know it. Were we involved in some way? Not to my knowledge, but we all confided that whoever did it, did a good thing. Beyond that, we shrugged it off and nothing came of it.

As an aside, one of the things I learned about big bad bikers is they think they are tough when they're in a large group, sucker punching someone and kicking him while he's on the ground. But when we caught them out one on one on the street or pulled one of them over, they weren't nearly as tough as they liked to think. I guess that's why they had to belong to a gang.

CHAPTER 15

MERCEDES MIKE

In many ways, when it comes to investigative police work, success is likely to depend on how good informants are. Without that key source of inside information, cops will probably end up going from one blind alley to the next, accomplishing little despite considerable effort. In my decades of experience in law enforcement, I was fortunate to have two incredible informants who were far above and beyond the other 75 to 100 I dealt with. I've changed their names for obvious reasons as I discuss some of the cases we worked on together.

The first informant will go by the name of Mercedes Mike, a guy who drove an old Mercedes and acted like he was king of the world. Mike could go in and out of all sorts of criminal activity without anyone ever suspecting him of anything. He not only was a great informant, he also was a good person when it came right down to it.

Mike's gift, his secret to success, was a completely unassuming persona, not the least bit threatening, average looking, average size, unkempt like he had slept in his clothes for weeks. He was the kind of guy who, if you saw him on the street walking along with a Styrofoam cup, you might consider throwing some coins in it, thinking he was homeless or perhaps a hopeless alcoholic. He was the epitome of faceless America, another lost soul in the crowd trying to survive, which probably explains the ease with which he could infiltrate so many different crime conspiracies in the Louisville Metro area. He had the ability to buy drugs, guns, and stolen property, and he knew every bookie in town and which joints were running prostitutes. Mike knew who was importing any kind of contraband into the area, including not only drugs and guns, but counterfeit money, credit cards, and US Treasury checks, and he knew who was selling and who was distributing.

One thing I always wanted to do with Mike, but I could never get the higher-ups to go along, was to get enough money together to facilitate a big sting operation. I wanted to set up an office space in a strip mall somewhere with a garage around back and let Mike run it. He would buy anything and everything, all illegal, of course, then we'd trace back to the owner and return their stuff after arresting the bad guys. I knew this would work, especially with Mike running the show. He was that good. In fact, Mike was so believable, so likeable and trustworthy, when we'd set someone up in a mini-sting, after the guy was arrested and taken to jail and they were allowed one phone call, guess who they'd call? Yup, they'd call Mercedes Mike, the one who double-crossed them and put them in jail. That's quite an endorsement for how good Mike was at this business.

I used Mike while I was with the police department, and I continued to use him after I went to the feds. Even years later, when I was working on anything, I'd still call him, and we'd get together and were able to run a good tandem on the street. No matter how many schemes he ran, or how many people he duped, Mike still had high street cred anywhere he went. I could put a wire on him, bug his ball cap, hide a wire in his car—whatever I needed—he would get the recordings for me. I was amazed that he never let me down; Mike always delivered.

Mike had a tough life, and it was because of a mistake he made when he was younger. Some guys stole a car and picked him up to ride around and have fun. As they were driving down the street, the driver noticed someone following them and figured it was an unmarked police car, so he pulled over and said he needed to run into a restaurant and use the restroom. As he left the car, he told Mike to take the wheel and he could drive for a while. Mike took the wheel while the other guys went into the restaurant and took off through the back door and across a vacant field. The police closed in and arrested Mike for stealing the car. He was convicted and had a record, which meant he could never join the police department, his dream and major ambition in life.

Although Mike was the ultimate operator, he didn't like bad guys, and he liked putting them in jail. Not only that, Mike had this side to him that was pure and good, and when a guy was taking advantage of someone or hurting someone, and he found out, he came to the rescue, a modern-day Robin Hood. In particular, he'd look out for the elderly, protecting them from scams, and he had a soft spot for youngsters who might naively be pulled into a bad situation without realizing it, in the same way he had been sucked in. All in all, Mike had a big heart.

If I added up all of Mike's activities, he probably was instrumental in putting away hundreds and hundreds of bad guys—no exaggeration. Better yet, none of them had a clue that it was Mike who undid them. Through it all, Mike and I became good friends, which, of course is a big no-no when it comes to informants, but I couldn't resist because Mercedes Mike had a personality that was like a magnet, and I trusted him without question. If I could help him, I did, whether it be giving him a few bucks or getting him out of scrapes.

Because I had a lot of friends in law enforcement who worked in several different areas, I would farm Mike out to them to provide his services. One time, he set up a huge tax fraud case for the IRS, and they got a guy on tax evasion. Maybe Mike knew, but I sure didn't, that that job earned him a handsome reward, a check for $30,000. To Mike, it was like hitting the lottery. As cops, we could never reward him anywhere close to that, or even remotely adequately, but we always got him what we could. To be honest, I think his working hand in glove with us cops and putting bad guys in jail was reward enough for him and he never asked for anything, any special favors and the like.

How did Mike do what he did, and where did he get his information? Mostly, Mike would hang out in low-life bars, tough joints, looking the part of an alcoholic on his last legs. He'd befriend the bartender who was always a good source of information, and he'd keep his eyes and ears open for news. Like a sponge, he'd take it all in and remember every pertinent detail. He was especially good at hooking up with any girls in the place, and he'd take them out to breakfast at four in the morning when the bars closed, pumping them for information on what they had heard from guys drinking and bragging.

Mike had a way of getting guys to talk about themselves, and he'd keep them going by acting impressed and pumping up their ego to the point where they would boast about a crime, each detail embellished and chronicled boldly for effect. With this information, Mike was easily able to set them up for a fall.

Was Mike scared of retaliation from the guys he helped put away, including some bad actors, biker gang members, drug dealers, armed robbers, burglars, and even some politicians? Mike told me no; he had no fears, and he was glad to be able to help.

Unfortunately, the story ends with Mike disappearing. I have no idea what happened to him. Poof, he was gone without a trace. That's not unusual when dealing with people on the far end of the spectrum, out there on the peripheral edge of society. I can only hope he landed on his feet somewhere nice, a place with sunshine and palm trees, the kind of place he used to dream about.

Now that I think about it, despite Mike's bar antics, and so authentically looking the part of a barfly, I never saw him take a drink of alcohol or smelled it on his breath. Just another peculiar fact about Mercedes Mike, the world's best informant ever.

CHAPTER 16

BEWARE OF MURKY WATERS

I was the youngest member of a newly formed Jefferson County Police scuba diving team. Normally they wouldn't select a rookie for that sort of thing, but I interviewed anyway and was selected, which put me into some extensive training for open-water diving, rescue schools, and the like. Frankly, I think I got the job by default because not enough people put in their request for the eight-man team.

It wasn't a full-time job, and in the five years or so that I participated as one of the original members of the team, we did maybe 12 to 15 missions—accidental drownings in lakes, quarries, or the Ohio River, or diving to find evidence in a murder case. A typical example would be if someone used a gun to commit murder, then drove onto the bridge connecting Louisville to Southern Indiana, stopped, and tossed the weapon into the water. If someone saw them do it, we could get an approximation of where the gun might be.

One time, we went after a small airplane. The entire Ohio River was frozen solid that year, and people were not only running back and forth between Indiana and Kentucky, some knuckleheads were driving out onto the ice. In the bad weather, a plane came down on the river. Seems the pilot was showing off by dipping his wings, first the right, then the left, back and forth, and he apparently was focused on what was going on down below—the crowd of people on the ice watching him—because he didn't see the power lines up ahead. He hit the giant wires and ripped a wing off, causing the plane to dive straight down through the ice.

As you can imagine, it was extremely cold, cold enough to freeze an otherwise free-flowing river that had a considerable current. We wore wet suits, not dry (insulated suits), so when we went in, we felt exactly how cold the water was. After a while, the water that seeps into the wet suit traps heat being released from the diver's body and it offers a modest amount of insulation, but not enough, and for that reason, our time under water had to be limited. Imagine taking an ice-water shower and multiplying the intensity of that feeling many times over and you have an idea what it was like.

Regardless, we had to break through the ice and go in. It was quite memorable, diving all night into the river and, believe it or not, we were unable to find the plane. Sounds strange, I know, especially since the depth of the river was only about 35 feet at that spot. The locks and dam were a mile or so downriver, and every time they opened a lock, the water moving underneath had tremendous power and would pull with it whatever was in its path, altering drastically what was going on under the water. I remember what it felt like when the lock would open and being pulled by the river and having to dig into the bottom to stop the momentum.

Let me add that we were operating in total darkness, as black as black can be. Even on a bright, sunny day, it's dark under the water because the river is so thick with dirt and who knows what else. Strong power lights didn't help, because all they did was reflect the dirt in the water. This equates to virtually zero visibility, not an easy scenario in which to operate and get much done.

That night as we searched for the airplane, we were baffled by how hard it was. Goodness, you would think that if you can go under water and find something the size of a gun with a metal detector, an airplane would be like locating the proverbial 800-pound gorilla. Not so, and there we were, doing all we could that night, and then coming back again and then again when the weather eased, and the ice started breaking up. Even so, no luck and to the best of my knowledge, the plane was never found.

—

Another underwater system we had besides scuba tanks was this thing called a Kirby-Morgan surface supplied air system in which air was provided to us under water from a boat idling above. The air came through hoses and we'd walk around, anchored with rope that would allow us to go in circles, making larger and larger circles to cover a designated area. As I said, it was so dark we couldn't see a thing, but I could tell approximate distances by the knots in the rope that told me how far I had moved from my starting point. On one occasion when the ice had receded, we used this method as we continued to search for the missing plane.

We had communications through our helmets, but with the air surging through it was poor quality and when we talked we sounded like Donald Duck, and that's not an exaggeration. While I was down there exploring, they sent another diver. I didn't know he was coming, because they had to talk to him on a different radio channel. I assumed I was the only one in the water, and as I was moving in one direction, they sent him in the opposite direction. This meant as we both came around in our circles we met each other. Whoa, let me tell you that meeting someone under those circumstances, in pitch-black water, is jarring, especially the way it went down.

When we bumped into each other, I grabbed his arm, thinking it was the dead pilot's arm. He, of course, grabbed me back and held me. As you can imagine, I was quite startled to think I had grabbed onto a dead body, and it grabbed me back. I don't know what I probably screamed, but thank goodness, it was garbled and came out like Donald Duck. I say thank goodness, because it really scared me and I'm sure some of the words that came out were ones I wouldn't be proud of.

CHAPTER 17

THE JESUS SQUAD

Let me leap ahead more than 20 years after my stint as a cop. When I was about to retire from the Secret Service, I became aware of a haz-mat (hazardous materials) response team in Louisville that required people with a law enforcement background. I watched them operate and it greatly interested me, so I inquired and was invited to join and became an operational member of the team. Joining meant being able to successfully navigate the training gantlet and pass a series of tests that were quite challenging.

One test involved being able to function effectively while wearing a special "moon suit." It's called a moon suit because it is totally self-contained, and it looks like the kind of suit astronauts wore when walking around on the moon. The suit is critical and must be airtight to protect the wearer in a dangerous situation, like being exposed to poisonous gas. If the suit is not perfectly adapted, the wearer could die quickly, or at the least, be seriously injured. What's more, when dealing with microorganisms, such as bird flu, monkey virus, or anything crazy that might be lurking out there, the wearers could bring diseases home with them and expose their families.

When I took the certification test, it had three levels, and everyone on the operational team had to pass all three levels. Then after that, and once I was on the team, I had to recertify every year on a wide array of high-tech equipment that kept changing and upgrading as science relentlessly moved forward. Ironically, the hardest part of the test for most of us was wearing the moon suit. Sounds odd, I know, but trust me, it was challenging. Here's why.

As I mentioned the suit is totally enclosed and underneath the suit, we wore an air pack like the ones that you see firefighters wear when engaged in fighting a fire that is swallowing up all the oxygen. To be certified, we had to wear the suit and carry out a series of tasks, all while breathing with the air pack. Inside the suit, it's incredibly hot, and I did the course in August on a super-hot and humid day. I put the suit on indoors where it was reasonably comfortable, then had to go out in 90+ degrees and perform my tasks. Thankfully, the tasks are not too physically demanding. So, what's the problem?

The problem is that we were zipped tight into the suits and the zippers were in the back. That means once they zipped us up, we were trapped inside the suit, and we found out right quick if we were claustrophobic. I realize it may not sound like much, but bear in mind our only source of air was our air packs, and once our air was gone, we had to get out of the suits. This design was necessary because the suits can't allow anything to penetrate that might be harmful. Okay, so there was no way out, and to ensure that, they checked our pockets to make sure we weren't carrying knives, because some guys have panicked and cut their way out. That's not good for many reasons, including the fact that the suits are quite expensive.

This is where my experience as a scuba diver came in handy. I was used to nursing my air supply, making it last as long as possible under difficult circumstances, like cave diving in tight surroundings, where it's easy to panic. When people panic and breathe heavily, they use up the air too quickly. Again, if you have any tendencies toward claustrophobia, this was not the duty for you. I might add, people often discover they have claustrophobia when they have an enclosed MRI, where people are slid into a tight-fitting tube and the ceiling is inches from their nose and the sides press in on their shoulders.

I would get my suit on and talk tough to myself, mind over matter, and give the instructors a thumbs-up that I was ready to proceed and carry out my tasks. As I went along, my air tank was emptying, and once the oxygen was gone, I had better be out of my suit. This meant I had to be vigilant about monitoring my air supply. In truth, some of the guys taking the test did panic and this is the time to want to find out, and certainly not in an emergency situation. They flashed through all the air in their tanks in less than 20 minutes. In my case, with my scuba training, I was able to more than double that time to about 42 minutes, and my tank was very close to empty when they pulled me out. I might add, when this drill was over, and we took the suits off, we were drenched in sweat, and it wasn't unusual to lose several pounds of water weight.

After training and certification, I worked a lot of Kentucky Derby days at Churchill Downs with well over 100,000 people packed into a small area. I worked as part of a team that included law enforcement, paramedics, emergency room docs and nurses, and engineer types who were good at reading and interpreting the array of meters that measured air quality, looking for the bad juju stuff that could be released into the air to kill without warning. We would dispatch several such teams to different locations around the racetrack and the results were truly amazing.

We wore polo shirts and backpacks and walked among the Derby crowd trying to be as inconspicuous as possible. We had several strategies. One was to deploy these special devices with a transmitter that looked like a slender lunch box and we would chain them down in inconspicuous locations, and the transmitter would convey constant readings on air quality. In addition, our team would be hanging around the various entrances as huge crowds poured in. The cool thing is we had sensors that could detect any degree of nuclear radiation, and if something set them off, our pagers would vibrate. We would then approach a group of folks and gradually eliminate individuals, trying to pinpoint the exact source of the readings.

When we felt confident that we had identified the source, as team leader, I would approach the person and politely introduce and identify myself and say something like, "Excuse me, sir, sorry to interrupt you, but we are here for the safety and security of everyone at the Derby today, and I would like to ask you if you have had any sort of medical procedure in the past few days."

This, of course, would get me an odd look in return. In my experience, nine times out of ten, they would respond after a moment and tell me they had had a dye test to look inside their heart arteries, or maybe they had a round of chemotherapy for cancer, or whatever. As they were telling us this information, one of the specialist engineers would come up behind them with a wand in his hand attached to a device in a shoulder pack, and instantly be able to identify exactly what was giving us the signal. It might be, for example, a medical isotope that was perfectly legitimate, and all was well.

After that, I would thank the person for their cooperation and tell them I hoped they would have a wonderful day. A lot of them would smile and say, "Wow, you guys are on top of things, and it's unbelievable what you can detect with your equipment. I feel safe now."

The Louisville haz-mat team eventually changed its name to the Joint Emergency Services Unit. The acronym was JESU, which led me to assume that the origin of the nickname "Jesus Squad" for our unit came from that source. But as I got out and about, and especially after rubbing elbows with a lot of older, salty police officers, I came to find out that they didn't refer to us as the Jesus Squad for that reason. The old-timers said the real reason was that if our squad shows up, it's uh-oh, and something bad is in the air, and everyone close by is about to meet Jesus.

The Jesus Squad of guys and gals would gather once a month and train and review procedures. It's a great concept, and it's still around. I am now the oldest member of the squad with the longest-running tenure of more than 12 years. I've worked in a variety of capacities, and nowadays, being older, I've become less operational. In fact, I'm thinking that perhaps it's time I quit acting like I'm 25 and stand face to face with Father Time and heed his warnings. But truth is, although my mind says no, don't do it, my ego pushes me on, telling me I've got at least one more good year in me.

The value of the Jesus Unit would seem to be self-evident, and in large part it is. However, given that human nature is what it is and there always will be competition for resources, when there are long periods in which there are no bad episodes, we tend to see a lessening of concern by officials. This can be reflected in reduced budgets and a lower priority for what we do in favor of whatever is capturing the spotlight at that moment.

This can be a serious problem. For this sort of protection to be effective when it is needed most, you must have dedicated personnel who are on top of their game, highly motivated, and participating continuously in the most up-to-date training, and equipment must be updated and replaced. If you put it all together, the price tag is high for a 60-member team consisting of a variety of professionals. But then, what is the price you would put on protecting one human life, not to mention tens, or hundreds of thousands?

CHAPTER 18

Target Practice

When I became a cop, I qualified as an expert shot. I loved shooting so much, I became a concealed carry instructor, a role I enjoy greatly, and I wish I could do more of it. I especially enjoy working with people who have no bad habits. In contrast, those with established bad habits are difficult to train, and even more so when they think they are better shots than they really are and are resistant to change.

I taught criminal justice courses in college for four years at a local university, and one of the things I offered the seniors in their last semester was to take them shooting. There might be a dozen students, about half male and half female, and I remember all the guys were so fired up and raring to go, because they had guns and were hunters and assumed they would be good shooters. However, without a doubt, it always worked out that the women in the class were far superior on the range.

This may seem surprising because usually the women were completely inexperienced, and most had never even held a gun before. But that, ironically, was the secret of their success. They knew what they didn't know, and they listened to every word I said, grabbed it and embraced it, and put it into practice. The guys, on the other hand, were sitting there rolling their eyes, their expressions saying, yeah, yeah, let's hurry up because I already know how to shoot, and I don't need all this instruction. Most of the guys had developed bad habits that were hard to break and interfered with their ability to be a good shot, but I couldn't convince them of that until they got trounced by the women in class, and then they were ready to listen.

When people learn who I am and what I do, I'm often flooded with questions, particularly about carry and conceal issues. A Kentucky CCDW permit (carry conceal deadly weapon) allows someone to carry anywhere with the understanding that if they are pulled over by a police officer, they have to immediately announce that they have a gun on them or in the car. They have to honor signs banning firearms at courthouses, schools, or churches. And, of course, no one should carry a gun into a bar if they are going to be drinking.

Obtaining a CCDW permit requires about seven hours of training, usually on the weekend, followed by a multiple-choice written test, plus demonstrated proficiency in shooting (hitting a target seven yards away 11 out of 20 attempts). Applicants then complete the paperwork and in about four to six weeks, they get a notice informing them to come by the sheriff's department and pick up their C&C permits. The permit looks like a driver's license and is recognized in 37 or so states around the country.

Carrying a gun is a huge responsibility and no one wants to take another person's life, and I emphasize this repeatedly when I'm teaching a CCDW class. I realize that carrying can make people feel powerful and indestructible, but that's not a good way to approach it. Some people are guilty of what we call "printing," which means the gun is clearly obvious on their bodies, perhaps under a tight T-shirt or whatever. When you do this, you want everyone to know you are carrying, an ego trip, but it's stupid because if you do carry and it's concealed properly, it gives you the element of surprise, a leg up in a critical situation.

One surprising thing I learned over the years about shooting that confuses folks, is that when a good guy and a bad guy are shooting at each other from close range, say only 20 feet apart, it sometimes happens that bullets are flying everywhere, but no one is getting hit. This happens even with semi-automatic weapons discharging lots of shots. Seems ridiculous, not possible, not believable, especially when you consider that the shooters have some skill and have had at least some amount of training.

The truth is, it's not only believable, I've seen numerous shootouts as I described above: cops unloading their guns and bad guys doing the same, and no one gets hit. The likely explanation is that when someone is shooting back at you, it's a whole different ballgame from being proficient shooting at a paper target. In fact, when you are under pressure, it's common to violate the basic principles of good shooting. When under stress, the fight-or-flight kind, your pupils dilate, making it harder to focus on your gunsights, and instead of squeezing the trigger slow and easy, you jump on it as you try to quickly get off as many shots as possible. And with all the adrenalin flowing through your veins, you probably are squeezing the life out of your gun and the barrel is moving all over the place. Add it all up, and it's tough to hit much of anything.

How often have I pulled my gun while on duty? As a cop, I pulled my gun a lot while effecting felony arrests, and the same was true as a Secret Service agent. I've been in three shootouts with bullets flying around all over the place; scary, but I didn't realize it until after it was over. When something like that happens, it goes down quickly, which thrusts officers and agents immediately into an automatic pilot mode where training kicks in and takes over. One thing we have to avoid at all costs is tunnel vision. I mentioned the importance of this in an earlier chapter and how important peripheral vision is to stay alert, aware, and informed. You also must keep firmly in mind that once you take out your gun and pull the trigger, you are responsible for wherever that bullet goes. So, even though you meant to take out a bad guy 30 yards away, if the bullet keeps going and penetrates the drywall in a home and hits a young child, you own that bullet. A sobering thought, indeed.

Another thing for cops to keep in mind when they pull a gun in a police situation is that it cannot be taken out as a threat. I've seen this happen. A cop will pull their gun too soon, which then causes the bad guy to respond with something like, "Okay, you're a tough cop. Are you going to shoot me now? Go ahead." This can make a cop feel stupid in a hurry because they know they can't shoot him for no cause.

A fear cops have is shooting an unarmed person. This can occur when a cop is being physically attacked and beaten, and there is the risk that the attacker may soon get the gun from the cop and kill him. Then, the officer has no choice but to stop the attacker with lethal force. In a physical confrontation with a criminal, whether the officer is in good shape or not, he or she will get out of breath quickly. This, of course, makes a good case for cops being in top shape, because the more they struggle, the more fatigued they will become, and at some point, they may become so weakened that they cannot adequately defend themselves without using a weapon. In other words, the more fit cops are, perhaps the less likely it is that they will resort to using guns.

When there is a physical confrontation, it usually escalates in steps. First there is a verbal assault, exchanging words, then shouting, then touching, then perhaps a shove, then grabbing, then scuffling, then punching or kicking, then using whatever weapon is nearby, and so on. At each stage, hopefully, an officer can match force with comparable force and escalate the force enough to secure the situation. Officers certainly don't want to leap from yelling at someone to sticking a gun in their mouths.

CHAPTER 19

FINALLY, A FAMILY MAN

When I was single man, the afternoon shift worked best for me, although it sure could interfere with my social life. But I never settled into long-term relationships back then, not wanting to get serious because my goal was to become a federal agent, and I had too many boxes to check before getting there. Among them was finishing my undergraduate degree, then getting my master's. The afternoon shift allowed me to go to school in the morning and early afternoon, then report for work, and during any "free" hours, like between classes, I'd be studying. Also, getting off at 10:45 p.m. wasn't that late and it allowed me to go out with the guys to a bar and have a beer or two, or head straight home to study if need be. If I went for a beer, we'd typically go into another area or downtown, not wanting to be seen in areas we patrolled to keep up the image and all that.

With my kind of schedule of school plus the afternoon shift, it was hard to date someone who worked days and had to get to bed early. Occasionally, I'd run across someone who had a complementary schedule, but that was rare, and as I say, I wasn't into making any sort of commitment. This explains why I didn't get married, which was for the best for many reasons, highest among them I didn't become another statistic, adding to the bulging rolls of divorced cops.

I think a lot of cop divorces spring from getting married early, and well before people fully understand what the life of a cop is like. Some people get married young, soon after high school, and the idea of marriage can wear thin on a young person, particularly for cops who interacts with all different kinds of people throughout the day and face many temptations.

Younger officers tend to work later shifts, because older cops have seniority and take the day jobs. That can be rough with a spouse and children because of the conflicts surrounding job versus family obligations. What's more, cops are likely to be sleep deprived and not at their best when coping with minor irritations from the family.

I must admit there were times when I unwittingly contributed to already deteriorating family situations with my footloose and fancy-free lifestyle when I wasn't in school. I could stay up late and do as I pleased, sleep late, get up and work out, or be on the river in my boat or whatever, and married guys who saw that I was enjoying life would tag along, trying to get some of what I had. Then, of course, when they reported home, it wouldn't be pleasant, which explains why so many wives, even before they met me, didn't like me.

My lifestyle sort of rolled along and things worked well for me. When I was 26, I applied to the Secret Service, where I met an agent who told me they were looking for guys like me. I had six years of street experience as a beat cop, a master's degree, and I wasn't tied down with a family. It wouldn't be a problem for me to leave Louisville, which is what I had to do as an agent. For starters, I'd have to attend a variety of training schools all over the country, and that would take about a year. Then after that, they could send me anywhere in the world; these were obvious complications for a family guy. At the time, I was in a relationship with a woman who had a young child from a previous marriage, and the relationship had somewhat of a hook in me. But it was a quandary thinking about her as part of my future. It turned out that she was smart enough to read the tea leaves and saw the problems, which stopped things from going further.

My first couple of years as an agent, I was in Los Angeles. I didn't know anyone there and I was starting a new life on my own from ground zero, acclimating to the LA lifestyle, which, to say the least, is quite different from Louisville. Thankfully, I ended up meeting a bunch of great people and living on Manhattan Beach, the best beach in LA. On the other side of the coin, it wasn't all glitz and I was earning my money, traveling a lot as an agent and working some crazy hours. From there, I was transferred to Hawaii and that put me on another beautiful beach. No doubt I was lucky, and as you can imagine, living about 15 years with this beachy lifestyle confirmed my commitment to bachelorhood, which lasted until age 39.

When you live on a beach in LA or Hawaii, where do you go for vacation? For me, it was coming back home every year to Louisville the first couple of weeks in May for the Kentucky Derby and all the celebrations surrounding it. One year, I came back to Louisville with a pal from LA to visit an old high school friend of mine who happened to be running a restaurant with a sand volleyball court outside. This kind of volleyball was relatively new to Louisville, but there was a lot of excitement about it, and some guys who knew we were from LA challenged us to a match. I guess they thought they were hot stuff and intended to rub our LA noses in it. It was a hard-fought competition, and thanks mostly to the skill of my teammate, we managed to beat them, but just barely and on the final point of the match. It was exciting, and as it went along, we attracted more and more onlookers.

I wasn't aware, but watching the match was a group of young ladies, and my future wife, Tracy, was among them. I can't say it was love at first sight, or anything as romantic and simple as that, because it was anything but. One of the other girls with Tracy was interested in me and made a point of seeking me out, and I ended up spending time with her after the match. One thing led to another and we spent a good deal of my remaining time together before I had to return to LA. From there, we kept in touch long distance, and after a while, she made it known that she wanted to come to LA for a visit. Sure, that would be great, love to have her visit. In making her plans, she decided she didn't want to travel alone and brought Tracy with her, which, I guess depending on how you look at it, was a fatal mistake because it pushed the two of us together. I found that I was more attracted to Tracy and we seemed to click right off the bat. Not a big deal, because the first relationship hadn't gone very far.

So, I guess you could say that Tracy and I became an item, but as luck would have it, she started her successful pharmaceutical sales career by moving to the East Coast while I relocated to Hawaii. Talk about a long-distance relationship: we were about as far apart as you can get in this country. Long-distance relationships have challenges with ups and downs, and seeing each other took some doing. Thankfully, despite the distance, we could rendezvous periodically when I would catch a trip back to Washington, DC, for some training and we'd arrange to meet somewhere in the middle. At first, we weren't in what you might call a tightly committed relationship, and the odds were greatly against us. But something powerful yet intangible was operating, a glue holding us together over thousands of miles.

At one point, she came to Hawaii for a visit and, of course, loved it. From there, she was able to transfer to Hawaii with her new company. Dumb luck? Not at all. Get this, she was able to transfer even though they didn't have a position for her. It came about because she was able to convince them to give her a chance to develop a network from scratch as a pharmaceutical rep. Says a lot about her as she made the move and started working, but it wasn't easy. Far from it. Being in sales as a Caucasian woman and working in an environment that sees things differently from the way we see them on the US mainland, she experienced some rough times with discrimination from Hawaiian and Asian men, and even some of the women. But she's tough and persevered and was extremely successful, constantly winning awards, and headhunters were always calling, trying to attract her away to new horizons. One method she used to maneuver in that environment involved her considerable golfing skills. Instead of begging and pleading for a few minutes of a doc's time between patients, she was able to get five or six hours on the golf course, which showcased her personality and professionalism to great advantage.

We've been able to mesh our careers, coping with crazy travel schedules and what not, which required extreme flexibility and a dedicated partnership. We've raised three children, each taking our turn when necessary to step up and run the show. Tracy did her share of traveling, but not like I did. To give you an idea, when I retired, I did so with over two million frequent flier miles dating back to my days with the President Reagan detail and my investigative work in Asia.

After the birth of our first child, I put in for a transfer, because I wanted to raise our kids in Louisville and be around my parents and my wife's parents. But, even when I was transferred back to Louisville, I still had a hectic travel schedule that meant continued ongoing sacrifices on Tracy's part. My duties included guarding political candidates and covering national Republican or Democratic conventions. I also had to take my share of duty agent calls where someone got arrested in the middle of the night, whether for a counterfeiting charge or threatening to kill the president, which meant I had to drop whatever I was doing at a moment's notice and go anywhere in Kentucky.

Our partnership helped us overcome the stresses imposed by two demanding careers and raising young children. Anyone who has gone this route while raising youngsters knows there has to be someone there picking up the pieces, an unsung hero behind the scenes making it all possible. In our case, it was my mother-in-law. We call her Tutu, the Hawaiian word for grandmother as our oldest child was born in Hawaii. No way we could have made it and kept our sanity without her.

At the time of this writing, we've been married 25 years, and I cannot overemphasize how very blessed I am to have such an incredible wife and life partner. We still have a lot of fun when we are together, and we look forward to a wonderful future, walking hand in hand down the path God lays out for us, growing old with our family and enjoying our grandchildren someday.

PART TWO

SECRET SERVICE AGENT: OFFICE OF PROTECTION

CHAPTER 20

THE DREAM COMES ALIVE

My time and experience as a cop proved invaluable to me later as a Secret Service agent. Wherever I was located, whether it be in Louisville, Los Angeles, Honolulu, or in Australia, New Zealand, or Hong Kong, I always made it a point to get close to the local cops. Giving local cops respect was not usual for federal agents, who I guess consider themselves above and apart, and they tend to keep their distance. In fact, I was often told if I liked cops so much, why didn't I quit and become a cop again? I never understood that mindset. Why not make the most of all the worlds you inhabit? But, truth be told, I felt comfortable with local cops because in my heart I was still one of them, and I felt a strong kinship.

How did I transition from beat cop to Secret Service agent? In three words, *it wasn't easy*. The process was intense and took about a year to get started down the path. First off, I had to drive to St. Louis and take a Treasury exam, a written test to assess my general knowledge. From there, they did a drug and criminal history, a psychological evaluation, and then an in-depth background investigation on me that was amazing. They interviewed neighbors, teachers, ex-employers, coworkers and supervisors, everyone they could think of. They also tried to find people who didn't like me and asked them why.

Throughout the process, I requested that they not say anything to the police department until I looked solid, had passed everything, and it was getting toward the end of the line. Then, finally, word got out and I heard from my cop buddies. "Yeah, we knew you always intended to go with the feds, 'cause your dad was FBI."

This, of course, living in my father's shadow and potentially benefiting from that relationship, was one of the reasons that I didn't go with the FBI. But still, the thought lingered for some, I'm sure, about the possibly of me having an inside track. As the saying goes, "Who was my rabbi?" In other words, who was pulling strings to help me? The truth is, no one.

My first day on the job I was taken to a federal judge's office and sworn in. After that, they handed me a black briefcase. Being a police officer, I had never carried a briefcase, so this was new and different. It looked like a sleek Samsonite, the kind business people carry, but it was hard plastic, cheap, and the only thing in it was a pair of Ray Ban aviator sunglasses. I smirked at the classic image of Secret Service agents all in a row wearing their sunglasses.

Although I was sworn in, we weren't certified as Secret Service agents right away, not by a long shot. I had several stints of training to complete that would take many months. Most viewed such training as drudgery, but I loved every bit of it right to the end. When I was finally ready to move on, I learned that when most people think of a Secret Service agent, they think of the protection detail, essentially being a bodyguard. However, there is more to it, and agents don't go immediately from recruit training into bodyguard work. Instead, they start off as rookies in the office of investigation and are there for anywhere from two to five years. After that, they graduate to protection.

Let me interject a brief historical note here for clarification. The Office of Protection was started in 1901 after President William McKinley was assassinated by a self-described anarchist. The blatant act of walking right up to the president and shooting him at point-blank range made it obvious that bodyguards were needed. Ironically, the Secret Service was created many years earlier under President Abraham Lincoln, but it was created to do investigative work. It's ironic, because if the Office of Protection had been created at the beginning as part of the Secret Service and Lincoln had

had bodyguards, they could possibly have prevented his assassination.

The next section in this book is about my experiences on the protection unit. Although it came after my work in investigations, I'm starting with it because I know it's what people are most curious about. In fact, of the top 10 questions I get relating to my work as an agent, at least nine, and more likely 10 out of 10 are about bodyguard work protecting a VIP. Folks are interested in the exciting stuff, of course, but perhaps the most common question I get is when standing post, was I bored out of my mind?

Obviously, we must pay attention to everything that is going on around us with keen awareness. At the White House, there are alarms and cameras around that should provide warnings if something happens, but if not, we have to always be ready to act. It's what we are getting paid to do. On the day shift, there usually is a lot going on, depending on the location, and the activity is stimulating. In contrast, on the midnight shift at three, four, or five in the morning, things are quiet and slow. To stay awake and alert, coffee was helpful, and we always had a coffee machine in the down room. Agents tend to drink a lot of coffee, especially at night.

In addition to standing in one location for a prolonged period, which is challenging, if we were at the White House, we were standing on marble floors. Think about standing on something hard like marble in dress shoes for hours, and you can imagine how your legs and lower back would begin to feel as your shift winds down. We were allowed to move around a few steps here and there, which helped ease the ache a bit, but we had to be certain we were always in complete control of the area we were responsible for, so we couldn't move too far.

Adding somewhat to the discomfort is the fact that we wore suits, starched white shirts and ties, preferably bland ties, but as is true in life generally, you can get used to just about anything. A saving grace to the rigidity of our dress code was that we always dressed like the VIP. If the president was going camping, or to a football game, or a black-tie event, whatever, we dressed like him.

Okay, with all this said and despite our dedication, we are human beings, and as a human at times, we sometimes found ourselves fading, even a little. When that happened, the thing that always snapped me instantly right back to full attention was thinking about tragedies that have occurred over the years. Imagine being on duty when your VIP protectee is shot, and imagine that for a quick moment, you were not as alert as you should have been for some reason—perhaps you were fatigued, or you allowed yourself to be distracted—and that because of that, something bad happened that you know you could have and should have prevented. Let me tell you, that is one sobering thought, not unlike getting poked with a sharp stick, because you sure wouldn't want to carry a load like that through the rest of your life.

It's also important as agents that we kept our sense of humor. Unfortunately, at times what we might think was funny, didn't necessarily come across that way to others. For example, we had a saying that we had printed on a softball shirt we used when we had some free time for a game. On the front it said Secret Service, then on the back it said, *You Elect 'em, We Protect 'em, Don't Blame Us,* a favorite expression in the Secret Service. But at one point, it got us into a bit of hot water because the president at the time didn't like it and refused to let us wear the shirts because he thought it was directed at him. It wasn't, of course, but some folks are touchier than others.

CHAPTER 21

Former President Jimmy Carter

I was ready to launch as a full-blown Secret Service protection agent with the assignment to protect former President Jimmy Carter. He had been out of office three years or so, and my role was to begin on a horse farm near Lexington, Kentucky, the Friday before the Kentucky Derby. From there, the next day I would be part of the detail escorting President Carter and his family to the Derby in Louisville.

Pretty heady stuff, and to say that the thought of doing this was overwhelming would be an understatement. Put yourself in my place, a local boy, new to the job, and entrusted with the lives of a former president and his family on this, the most celebrated and important day of the year in Kentucky. Despite every intent not to be starstruck, I have to admit I was. Being up close to an internationally famous figure, an individual, who at one time was the world's most powerful man, someone I had seen only on TV, in the newspapers, or magazines, was amazing to me. What's more, I essentially held this person's life in my hands, not only as his bodyguard, but also his driver. What an incredible responsibility. But if you had seen me, you'd never guess what I was feeling, because when you are Secret Service, you show nothing, no emotion, whether you are bursting at the seams like I was or not. Eyes are focused, ears are perked, and you are always poised for immediate action.

It was a big time for me, and I intended to make the most of it. Guarding a former president was number one, of course, but a close second was attending the Kentucky Derby in a manner in which I had never done before. Being from Louisville, the Derby was always one of my most favorite occasions, and I attended every year. Occasionally, I'd be treated to a decent seat in someone's box, but this year, I'd be with the bigwigs. For those who have never been to the Derby, it's hard to explain what it's all about without experiencing it. To call it a horse race is like calling the Super Bowl a football game, and it clearly does not capture in any way its true sense. The Super Bowl, depending upon where it is played, will attract about 75,000 fans, as compared to the Kentucky Derby which doubles that amount, everyone pouring into one constricted area of town to celebrate the "sport of kings" and the greatest, most exciting, two minutes in sports, which caps off two full weeks of spirited celebrations in the city of Louisville.

So here I was, Friday, the day before the Derby, caught up with the Derby spirit and on my way to a gorgeous Thoroughbred horse farm for the protection detail. These spreads are truly amazing, more beautiful than any picture can capture. The barns are immense, the landscaping impeccable, and the interiors are opulent with gold-plated handles, glistening mahogany trim, every inch spic and span, and of such high quality you truly could eat off the floor. The horses housed there are magnificent, glorious examples of God's handiwork at its best, their care entrusted to only the most skilled and caring hands. That, and each one costs more money than I likely will make in my lifetime.

At the farm that Friday, we were treated to a walkabout tour, not for my benefit, of course. I was merely tagging along, eyes and ears focused, my role as protector uppermost in my mind, but still able to embrace the significance of the moment. After the tour, we got in the limo. I was driving, and the leader of the detail sat beside me in the front passenger seat. As we made our way through scenic Versailles (pronounced Ver-Sales in Kentucky), bluegrass country, on a spectacular cloudless day, the excitement of the upcoming Derby was palpable everywhere.

We were headed to a restaurant for dinner, and when we arrived, it was crowded, literally overflowing with people eating inside and out, and many were standing in line waiting for a table. I anticipated this because the Friday before Derby Day is Oaks Day, another famous racing day at Churchill Downs, but the Oaks race is for fillies, female race horses. In a sense, the Derby is a national and international occasion, whereas the Oaks is more for the locals. Likely, many among the overflow crowd were folks who had been to the Oaks, and there was a holiday atmosphere, the women in beautiful designer dresses, high heels, and flamboyant hats, and the men in colorful sport coats and seersucker suits.

The former president and first lady were dressed very nicely and fit in perfectly, but their daughter, Amy, stood out, and not in a good way. Amy was going through a rebellious stage, and apparently wasn't about to spruce up. She wore jeans, a T-shirt, and sandals. Quite a contrast to her mother and father, and especially a contrast to the way most of the locals were dressed.

It didn't take long for some of the people at the restaurant, who had consumed numerous alcoholic beverages, to start making snarky comments under their breath about Amy's appearance. Amy, of course, didn't take this well and became visibly upset. We decided that a couple of agents should take her back to the horse farm. From there on, it was a nice peaceful dinner.

The next day, I again assumed my role of limo driver and we took off from the Lexington farm, bound for Churchill Downs in Louisville, a drive that would take a little more than an hour. Amy looked better, which was a plus.

As we approached Churchill Downs, the excitement increased exponentially, with literally tens of thousands of people scurrying about, ranging from college students headed for a raucous time in the infield, to finely dressed ladies, their ensembles topped off with ostentatious Derby hats, each one trying to outdo the other. As I drove, I revisited

Derby memories from when I was a college student at the University of Louisville. We'd be up most of the night partying, with maybe an hour or two of sleep, then we'd all be off, walking a mile or so to the Downs, carrying our coolers and backpacks, our way of sneaking in a little liquid courage, our sights set on finding a prime spot in the infield, hopefully right in the middle of all the action.

But the year I drove for the Carters, we were in the midst of the throngs of onlookers with our police escort, the blue lights going, attracting attention, the oohs and ahhs as we drove right up to the front gate of Churchill Downs. At the entrance, everything seemed to stop, the police held the crowds back as we got out of the car, and everyone cheered and waved as we escorted the former president and his family through the crowd. Our destination was Millionaire's Row, high above the track and near the finish line, the ideal spot to watch the race.

I was in my suit, sunglasses, and earpiece, the Secret Service pin on my collar, carrying a gun, looking the part. What a blast for a newbie, experiencing all this, escorting the family into different rooms full of prominent people, world leaders, Hollywood swells and celebrities, superstar athletes—the kind of folks you read about in the newspaper or see on TV and in the movies.

What was I feeling? The lump in my throat said it all, and it told me that beyond any shred of doubt, this is where I wanted to be and what I wanted to do with my life, what I had worked for so hard and so long. It was a truly magical day, a day riveted into my memory, so clearly that I can conjure up every detail and smile broadly from ear to ear.

A final word on former President Carter. As I mentioned, we are all human and have our positive and negative traits and moments. I was glad to see that he was welcomed warmly at the Derby and was still a popular figure, even though his presidency is viewed as less than stellar for many reasons by historians. One telling feature about a dignitary is how he treats those who are lesser and serve, folks like me. I found him to be congenial and friendly to us and easy to get along with. That's not always the case and some high-ranking politicians take themselves far too seriously and fail to recognize that we are all God's children and equal in his eyes.

Years later, I went to Atlanta on temporary assignment to cover an event at the presidential library. Again, President Carter's popularity was affirmed, and at that time, he was dedicating much of his efforts to helping others, particularly building houses with Habitat for Humanity. All things considered, he was a nice man and I liked him.

CHAPTER 22

PRESIDENTIAL CANDIDATE JESSE JACKSON 1

I mentioned previously that in 1983, I was assigned to the protection detail of Reverend Jesse Jackson, who was competing with several other presidential candidates for the Democratic nomination. Jackson was an interesting and flamboyant candidate, and certainly a huge challenge for us, particularly with some of the people and locations he chose to visit, like Cuba, which was quite controversial, and then the national Ku Klux Klan rally in South Carolina. You can imagine the reaction from that visit.

Why such provocative locations? He knew he'd get tremendous publicity and press from these appearances, and when you are running for president, attention from national media is golden. As they say in Hollywood, regardless of your true intentions or what they say about you, all publicity is good because it gets your name out there. No doubt, Reverend Jackson was always trying to be seen and heard, which made us nervous and increased the difficulty of our job. Plus, at every turn, he seemed to be reaching out and tempting fate. That's fine for him if he wants to do that, but remember, us Secret Service guys are standing right next to him in the line of fire and we'd rather keep a lower profile.

An interesting and challenging aspect of that detail was that Jackson had his own security group. We called them "the bowties," black Muslin guys in bowties, and they were formidable looking, like they all could have been former NFL linemen. Turns out, several of them had done jail time, which created a problem, because it's against the law for a convicted felon to carry a weapon. Anyway, there they were, and I guess they felt the need for additional security because they didn't trust that Secret Service agents would protect Jackson properly because he was black, possibly opening him up to harm. It's unfortunate such feelings existed, because speaking for myself and every other crew member, we had every intention of guarding Reverend Jackson to the best of our ability and doing everything in our power to keep him safe.

Having two separate security details is not the best way to go about protecting someone. It's sort of like having two head coaches, and clearly, two is not better than one. The first hurdle to overcome was establishing who was in charge. At first, we engaged in some elbow rubbing contests when getting on an elevator because only so many people can enter, and the rest have to come later. But it was soon made clear that we were in charge, which devolved into a situation where we were forced to tolerate these guys. They weren't prepared or ready for anything that would require the kind of coordinated and instantaneous response we were trained for. In fact, it was possible they might get in the way and make a situation worse, which was a huge additional concern for us.

Jackson's plane was another concern. It was an older passenger plane, and when we first saw it and climbed aboard, we were a little worried about how safe it was. We knew that plane safety, things like certifying maintenance and all that, was something that could easily fall between the cracks and not be noticed right away. Even the "newsies," the press core assigned to Jackson, were nervous about flying on that plane. Were our concerns overblown? Seems not, as I was told later that this plane crashed, but, thankfully, without Reverend Jackson or any Secret Service agents on board.

Another plane-related issue had to do with refueling. We flew into Memphis for a campaign stop, but we were barred from taking off afterward because they had not paid their fuel bill from the last time they landed at that airport. Airport authorities held the plane on the tarmac and it couldn't depart, which threw off our schedule. Reverend Jackson demonstrated some agile thinking as he located the nearest Zionist Baptist Church, the kind he preferred, and had them announce a temporary fund drive at which he would appear and speak.

When we got to the first church that day, I observed his speech. It was a canned presentation he gave over and over during such events, which were frequent and commonplace as his campaign progressed. He'd modulate his voice effectively and use catchphrases like, "I'm not asking for a handout; I'm asking for a hand up." There were lots of "amens." After that, he'd hit the audience hard for cash. They passed huge buckets up and down the rows, and from where I stood, it appeared that everyone reached into their pocket or purse and came up with bills. It helped, I think, that the ushers were ominous-looking bowtie guys who stood in the aisle glaring, giving each person who took the bucket the stink eye with a clear message. I'm not sure if it was planned this way, but two more big bowtie guys were standing in front of the doors in the back of the church, so there was no easy way to exit if you were not inclined to give generously.

In fairness, Reverend Jackson likely didn't have the deep-pocketed donors other candidates had. When candidates supported by generous donors are elected, they often feel obligated to reciprocate once in office, one of the stains on how we operate our country. Reverend Jackson was one of the first to finance a campaign with lots of small donations from the little guys, and then if he had been elected, he would have been beholden to them, to people, not corporate interests. So, I guess you could say that despite a little strong-arming rhetoric to help the cause, he certainly wasn't taking a lower road than his competitors, and in fact, it may have been a step above. Regardless, he raised enough cash to pay the fuel bill, which allowed us to take off.

As I said previously, how you are treated as one who serves says a lot about the person you are protecting in terms of what they are truly like.

I never had a problem with Reverend Jackson, not one. He was always courteous and nice to us, and even though he had his own security with the bowtie guys, he made it clear that we were in charge. If he hadn't supported us the way he did, it could have made our job much more difficult and there would have been friction every step of the way.

One stop we made was in Detroit and it was bitterly cold. I was the gunman in the back of the car with my Uzi. When we upgraded to the big Chevy Suburban SUVs, we'd joke when blowing off steam about how we were "seeing the USA in our Chevrolet," a popular advertising jingle at the time. In my case, I was seeing the country backward. It's usually the younger guys who get rear gun duty, the ones with the lowest seniority, because even though we are all trained the same, it's not much fun always looking at the world going by in reverse. But, you can get used to anything, even that.

While in Detroit, Jackson had dinner at the home of Aretha Franklin, the well-known singer with such hits as "Natural Woman," "Respect," "Think," "Chain of Fools," and the list goes on and on. Five or six agents assigned to Jackson were at the house, along with a couple guys from the Detroit field office, and we all went down into the finished basement. We hadn't eaten in quite a while, because when you are on the job, you eat when you can, and you visit the restroom when you can, otherwise you stay put and wait. That's the life of a bodyguard. Now that we had a little downtime, we sure wanted something to eat. Typically, a local guy from the field office would volunteer to make a food run to a nearby fast-food restaurant, whatever was closest. Everybody would throw in some cash for the run, then later we would eat wherever we happened to be, in the basement, in the driveway, the car, wherever; that's the nature of life on the road.

At Aretha Franklin's house, our guy was taking orders for food when Reverend Jackson came down the stairs and said, "Excuse me, fellas, you guys are invited to come up and eat with us."

That's unusual, not the norm at all, and most of the guys respectfully declined. Why? I think it probably has to do with indoctrination. The longer you are on the job, the more solidified it is in your mind where your place is, and it's certainly not elevated to eating with the dignitaries you are assigned to protect. In some ways, it's like the house servants being invited to dine with the duke and duchess, a nice gesture, but it's probably too much for the servants to swallow and be even remotely comfortable.

In my case, however, as a new guy, I was thinking, hey, why not go up there and hobnob and get a much better meal than McDonald's burgers. Reverend Jackson looked at me and said, "What about you?"

I hesitated a moment, looked around at my colleagues, then said, "Well, it sure smells good up there."

"It should. It's great southern cooking; you like southern food?"

I said, "Yes, sir, I'm from Kentucky."

"Kentucky? Yeah, you'll like this food. Come on up here, son."

I liked what I heard, then I looked over at my boss for permission. He nodded and said, "If you want to go, go."

I went upstairs and sat at a table right next to Reverend Jackson and Aretha and enjoyed some good southern cooking that included the kinds of things my grandmother from Kentucky would put on the table: greens, grits, red beans and rice, and several other items. Best meal I'd had in a long time, and I ate my fill, then thanked them and left. Funny, but after that, I think Reverend Jackson liked me and seemed to go out of his way to be friendly toward me. I hope he didn't misinterpret why my colleagues turned down his dinner invitation, but maybe that was part of his taking a shining to me. Hard to say.

The next day, Jackson was scheduled to make an appearance at the University of Detroit, a small urban university, and we were in the basketball arena. At the time, we carried our Uzi machine-guns in black briefcases with foam cut to fit the Uzis and some extra magazines. We carried it "gun ready" with our left hands, and if we needed it, we could easily unlatch it and pull it out with our right hands and be ready to fire. I had one and my partner had one, and we were on a stage in the middle of the floor of the arena looking out at a raucous crowd.

The emcee who was to introduce Reverend Jackson was a highly charged and polarizing figure who made Reverend Jackson look like a snuggly kitten by comparison. The emcee was on fire that night, and in my view, he lived up to his reputation for spewing venom at Jews and white people, and, of course, the police, who in his view, do the dirty work for white people. As he went on and on with his hate-filled rhetoric, it was clear he was inciting the crowd to nearly a boiling point. Bear in mind that of the thousands in attendance, the few Secret Service agents who were white were the only white people in the crowd. Was he aware of that? It's hard to believe he wouldn't be, since we were on the stage with him and he'd have to be blind not to see us. In fact, our presence may have even inspired him. As it unfolded, I must admit feeling uncomfortable and thinking this could easily get out of hand with us as targets. The fact that I held an Uzi was little comfort with a crowd that size all worked up to a frenzy.

Honestly, I kept waiting for Reverend Jackson to intervene in some way, to try to calm things down, but he didn't. He let it play out. Perhaps he knew that in spite of the high-voltage rhetoric, we were safe, and we'd all be leaving as scheduled. And that's how it turned out. We left peacefully and were headed to our next stop.

CHAPTER 23

PRESIDENTIAL CANDIDATE JESSE JACKSON 2

Protection detail can be grueling, especially on the campaign trail, as we were with Democratic candidate Jesse Jackson. We would go out three weeks at a time, working every day for as long as we had to, which is part of the deal. Sometimes we might work an eight-hour shift, and sometimes it could double. Perhaps we were flying from Atlanta and were supposed to be relieved in St. Louis. We started at seven in the morning but might not be relieved on schedule because things changed and instead of going to St. Louis, we could end up in Dallas. If my relief was in St. Louis, I had to keep working and maybe it would be 20 hours or whatever. Didn't matter, we kept going. And who knows where our luggage might end up.

On these kinds of details in which we were protecting a candidate vying for the nomination, we didn't have near the assets we would have had when guarding the president or vice president, or even a former president, which often translated into flying by the seat of our pants all over the country. The good news was, all the days were not overly long, and occasionally we'd get lucky with a short day.

On one occasion, we were in DC, and suddenly we received a message that we needed to rush over to the White House and get a series of shots for overseas travel. Overseas travel was unusual when protecting a candidate, and especially a candidate who was by any measure a long shot, quite far behind in the polls. Why on earth would we be going overseas? No votes there, and getting votes was what Reverend Jackson harped on day and night to his team.

For me, going overseas was common, and by the end of my career, I had traveled to close to 70 countries, but such trips were well planned and never a last-minute thing like we were encountering. Since we were surprised, we weren't packed for the trip, but we all had quickly learned to go with the flow on these candidate details, no matter where they were going. There's that, and in this situation, it was all hush-hush, which heightened the intrigue.

Things got complicated in a hurry and more than a bit difficult. That is not uncommon with a candidate, someone who is not used to a security detail, and they don't think first about safety or what goes into keeping them safe. They are consumed with campaigning and that's their priority.

Word from our Secret Service headquarters, which we fondly referred to as the Puzzle Palace, was that they were put under the gun to make a decision, because apparently Reverend Jackson had made it known that he was going overseas with or without a protective security detail. To complicate matters further, the destination was Syria, right next to a war zone in the Middle East. Headquarters definitely did not want to send us there because they knew we'd be sitting ducks with only our sidearms. But, if we didn't go and Jackson got hurt, it would look like we didn't do our job, and maybe there was some conspiracy against this candidate.

Headquarters was put in a tight position and they decided to go ahead and send us. I'm sure there have been presidents who traveled into war zones with similar risks involved, but we had limited resources. This situation was different, and we were told it had never been done before. We ran over to the White House and got loaded up on shots, so many we got them in the right arm, the left arm, and in the butt. We also were given a bunch of pills to take to try to protect us. Living in the United States with all the health precautions in place, tends to pamper our immune systems and they are not in any way prepared for the challenges of a country where folks are dying of diseases we eradicated more than a century ago. Trust me when I say there are many countries in the world you don't want to be sick in, and where we were headed was one of them.

With no options, we quickly slapped together an itinerary and all that that entails, and we were off and running. Such poorly conceived ventures were referred to as dog-and-pony road shows, a rather alarming description for a protection security detail. We got our passports from headquarters; they held on to them for us because we have three different kinds. We have a normal one like everyone else, an official one of a different color, and a diplomatic passport that is also a different color. In this case, we all got our "dip" passports and flew commercial from DC to Berlin, Germany, and spent a day there. It was a nice break, cool having an opportunity to briefly live the life of a sightseeing tourist. Part of the reason for the layover was the need for considerable negotiations, trying to gain permission to allow a bunch of US Secret Service guys to show up suddenly and essentially unannounced in a Middle Eastern country.

But whatever the top-drawer folks want, they get, and apparently President Hafez al-Assad of Syria (father of the Assad in power now) wanted Reverend Jackson to visit Damascus. That was the story we were told. Then we found out that one of our American pilots had been shot down while flying a sortie over Syria. He parachuted out and landed safely but was immediately taken prisoner. This meant we were being dropped right into the middle of a POW situation and likely a diplomatic tug-of-war, as that kind of thing tends to be.

As you can imagine, there was a lot of negotiating to do. What we didn't know is how different the truth was from the story we were told, and how iffy the situation was, but we didn't find that out until after the fact. The truth of what happened, according to historians, was that Jackson did not have a meeting scheduled with Assad when we landed, and he was not invited to Damascus. Not at all. In fact, when Jackson first contacted Assad to plead for the aviator's release, he got no response. So, on his own initiative, Jackson made the decision to fly to Damascus, and once there, he had to convince a gaggle of low-ranking Syrian bureaucrats to arrange a meeting with Assad. Jackson worked some magic and got his meeting. From there, he worked some more magic and accomplished his goal. This version, in my opinion, indicates Jackson's powers of persuasion. It also scares me, because we were not operating under the failsafe umbrella of diplomatic protection as we would have been as Assad's invited guests as we had believed.

It turns out that one of the reasons Jackson was successful was that Assad wanted to embarrass Ronald Reagan, the sitting president, by releasing the pilot only to Jackson. Jackson, of course, would reap the benefit of getting this done, and all the publicity that goes with it would serve him well as a Democratic presidential candidate who might oppose Reagan in the upcoming election.

Goodness gracious, what a tangled political web. On the one hand, I guess it was good that we were kept in the dark. It helped keep our anxiety in check, even though it was still quite high. But, on the other hand, if I think about it, I could come up with a ton of "what-ifs" and with each one, I can imagine how difficult it might have been for us to respond appropriately given our lack of knowledge.

But we proceeded naively with our mission. A major priority was guaranteeing our safety when flying into the hot zone, then being picked up at the airport, and having a safe place to stay for a few days until negotiations were completed and the pilot released. All in all, I must admit, naïve as I was, I found the whole situation quite exciting as we flew in at night to attract the least attention possible. It was the kind of stuff you read about in action novels. James Bond stuff, except we were actually there.

The goal was to get in and out of this airport quickly, taking advantage of the darkness and using plain, unmarked vehicles. The pace was accelerated, and we didn't even wait for our luggage because we'd be easy targets, sitting ducks. We drove to what was once probably a high-end hotel, a typical western-style hotel that was still in good shape. No doubt, at one time, this area was an attractive spot for tourists, but that clearly was no longer the case. The hotel had a protective cement wall surrounding it, thick and 15 feet tall with reinforced entry gates to drive through. On top of the wall were sharp projections like spears to dissuade anyone from trying to climb over it.

We were told not to worry about our luggage, it would arrive eventually, and that we should go to our rooms and keep a low profile. It was painfully plain to all of us that nothing had been planned and we were working on the fly, taking whatever came at us and making the best of it. Some of us were allowed to go to bed, which was a treat, because we were exhausted from all that was happening, as well as the time zone changes. Unfortunately, the rest were on duty and had to keep going, guarding Reverend Jackson.

I got some sleep, but not much, and was awakened by the room shaking and what sounded like terrifically loud thunder all around. Disoriented at first, I couldn't figure out where I was, then I rushed to the window. I was on the third floor and looking down into the street, I figured out really quick what it was, a huge convoy, an armored division of tanks rolling right down the street adjacent to the hotel. I have no idea if the display was for our benefit, a show of force, or if they were going to the war front about an hour down the road. Seeing this convoy of what, to me, were enemy combatants, sparked me good and woke me up. Clearly, as Dorothy would say, "Toto, I don't think we're in Kansas anymore."

The noise woke everyone on the detail and soon we all had gathered at the command post in a room on the top floor of the hotel. We hoped, but were not optimistic, that our luggage had arrived. It hadn't, and we were informed that the authorities had confiscated it for reasons unknown, which meant we had nothing to change into. After learning the truth about what really was going on while we were there, the confiscation makes more sense than it did when we believed we were Assad's guests. Anyway, it was inconvenient, wearing the same clothes, especially after all the travel time. We had no basics like toothbrushes, toothpaste, deodorant, etc.

We sat around for a briefing, the usual stuff: be careful what you eat and drink, keep a low profile, stay around the hotel complex, do not interact or engage with anyone. That seemed to work well for about a day, then we couldn't help ourselves, and the boredom inspired us to be a little adventurous. One thing led to another, and it was decided that it would be a great time to buy some gold. At that time, leisure suits were in style for men and they were often accessorized with layers of gold chains worn around the neck, and in some cases, around the wrists. We had found out that gold was extremely cheap in Syria. Now, somebody had to leave the hotel and go out into the market to buy gold necklaces and bracelets and bring them back. We decided that since I was the guy who looked the least white, I should go. It earned me the nickname Omar.

We discussed this sketchy plan with one of the embassy people who told us where to go, provided directions, and wrote everything down for me in native writing, saying I was willing to pay US dollars for the best deal. Then surprisingly, he supplied me with the appropriate garb, sunglasses and an Arabic headdress. When I was ready and looked reasonably presentable, he said, "Come on, let's go," and led me out the door to the market. No doubt, my life was in his hands, and I hoped nothing bad would happen, especially since my pockets were bulging with cash.

In the marketplace, I used the note and handed it to a vendor who would point me to a stall where I began buying gold. I'd be shown a variety of items and I would point at what I wanted, which would then be placed in a plastic bag. I spent about an hour buying what I could afford, then started back to the hotel. As I walked, it occurred to me that I didn't do any arguing about price, simply took whatever price I was told and paid it.

Who knows, I might have been able to come away with a lot more gold if I had a clue what I was doing. Regardless, the guys were thrilled that I was able to return with such a huge stash of gold and for such cheap prices.

To celebrate our triumphant adventure, we decided we needed some beer, which meant Omar would again be pressed into action and go back to the market for a case of beer. Again, the embassy guy wrote it all out for me in a note. I remember standing in line with a case of beer right behind a Russian special forces guy in uniform. I could tell by emblems on his uniform where he was from. He was standing there with a couple bottles of vodka. What's interesting about this is, it was before the Cold War ended and we were adversaries, but there we were, side by side, buying booze and not paying much attention to one another and finally going our separate ways.

When I got back to the hotel, I received a hero's welcome that lasted about a minute, then we all had to get back to work while the negotiations proceeded. Finally, Syrian authorities decided that the pilot would be turned over to Reverend Jackson, which I can tell you was an incredible relief, and the news helped us to relax for the first time in a long while. It meant getting the pilot back unharmed, and for us, it meant we were now able to get out of there. But, as always, there are challenges and Murphy's Law (anything that can go wrong will go wrong) was operating at full force.

On our trip in, we flew to Berlin, then took a Lufthansa flight into Damascus. Because we didn't know when they would release our POW, we couldn't book return flights, and there weren't many anyway. Turns out, we couldn't get a commercial flight out, which required another round of negotiations to allow a US Air Force plane to come and pick us up. The next night, we were thrilled to learn that the negotiations were a success and an air force plane would pick us up the following evening.

This was all good, of course, but it meant we had to spend another day in dangerous circumstances. I might add, throughout this entire episode, we were constantly reminded of how outnumbered and outgunned we were. In those days, we carried a Smith & Wesson .357 Magnum, six shots in each weapon, while everywhere we went and everyone we dealt with carried AK-47 assault rifles. We were told that under the law of this country, if the president invited us as his guests, we are off limits, and nobody could touch us. While that was reassuring to some degree, I couldn't help but think, gee, hope all these guys with their AK-47s were paying attention to the "hands off" order. Again, realizing after the fact we were not valued invited guests, changed the calculus of the equation remarkably. I'm glad I didn't know.

Bottom line is, we all made it out of there safely. This included Reverend Jackson and a staffer, about a dozen Secret Service agents, Lt. Robert Goodman, and a few traveling journalists. When you are starving, a piece of rotting bread looks delicious. To us, we were so anxious to leave, boarding an air force plane poorly equipped for human transport seemed like a luxury airliner. That is, until we got up and going. The plane was not insulated, which means that the sound of the engines was deafening, and we had to stuff toilet paper in our ears to try to dampen the noise enough to catch bits of sleep here and there. Once we took off and were up in the air, it was either freezing cold or extremely hot through the entire flight, back and forth from one extreme to another. There were no seats on the plane as it was a convoy plane like a C-130; the infamous red webbing on each side served as makeshift seats for us.

But I must say as miserable as the 12-hour flight turned out to be, it was a godsend, getting us out of there, keeping our candidate safe and sound, and bringing an American pilot home.

CHAPTER 24

Protection Ins and Outs

When working protection, sometimes I was on the advance team, either that or working as a bodyguard, protecting the client. The advance team does, by far, the lion's share of the work, overseeing every detail from A to Z associated with the logistics of protecting someone, making sure they get in and out safely, and accomplish their task. This includes all phases of the travel plan: where the plane is going to land, where the wheels are going to chock up (meaning placing wedges against the wheels to prevent accidental movement), securing the stairs leading off the plane, determining who is going to meet the plane and who is going to guard the plane when we leave it. Then there is dealing with customs and immigrations and all the related paperwork, and all aspects of coordinating personnel, including the security escort and the motorcade, and determining if local police or military are involved and, if so, interfacing effectively with them. The advance team must determine which exit gate from the airport will be used, what the route is (primary roads, secondary roads), where to go (a safe house) if something should happen en route, and the most direct route to the nearest hospital from any point. And, finally, we had to make contingency plans, like lodging and a backup plan if anything happens, implications of weather changes, news associated with intelligence services (terrorist activities, rebels fighting the government, etc.), and health scares or disease outbreaks.

Advance work is demanding in foreign countries, especially smaller and less developed countries where it's a major challenge to get almost anything done in a timely manner. Perhaps there are fewer assets available, or there is a very small embassy, or it is far away from our location and we are pretty much operating on our own to get things accomplished. To get the job done, advance teams go in ahead of time—a few days to more than a week—and each day is incredibly intense. What's more, we have to approach our job and carry it out in a way that doesn't burn any bridges, because who knows, we may have to return. If there is bad blood, the level of cooperation could be substantially lessened, increasing the complexity of the task commensurately. Considering all that is involved with a visit, even a brief stopover, you can see how expensive the whole operation would be.

On the other hand, when we worked as bodyguards, we used to joke that we could put a monkey in a black suit and have him walk alongside the president, and he'd do a fine job. In other words, being on duty didn't seem to take much other than being there. But, of course, there is a lot more to it, and it takes comprehensive and relentless training and honing skills to react to virtually any situation. Part of our training was AOP, assaults on principal, where you go through a wide array of potential scenarios. We role-play those with someone pretending to be the protectee who could be the president, vice president, former presidents, candidates, and foreign dignitaries. It also could include anyone the president designates for protection, like the national security advisor. When training, everything is video recorded and graded, and a big consideration is how long it takes to react to a gunshot, explosion, someone with a knife or whatever, and, of course, whether the person being tested reacted in the proper manner.

Protection work also can be more generalized; for example, when agents are not assigned to one specific individual. For example, in 1984, I was assigned protection duties at the Democratic National Convention in San Francisco. I was still new to the whole game and I made the monumental mistake of packing a beige suit. I figured, hey, it's San Francisco and anything goes, including my upbeat suit. No one ever got around to telling me that Secret Service attire is always, and without question or exceptions, dark suits, black, charcoal gray, or navy blue. Thankfully, I had two other suits, but that wasn't comforting knowing how long I would be there. Anyway, I caught tons of grief for my blunder, and it took a long time to live it down. Such is the life for newbies.

At the convention, Secret Service agents were everywhere: on the roof outside, walking the perimeter, at the entrances, mingling on the floor, up in the stands, on the catwalks above, and on the so-called "stage crew," which was my assignment for 12-hour shifts, guarding the stairs on the left side of the stage (as you look at it from the audience). I thought it was a good assignment, and my duties were straightforward. No one gets up on the stage without appropriate credentials. And I mean *no one*.

As I stood at my post, the governor of one of America's largest states came walking right by me. I was certainly identifiable with my Secret Service pin on my lapel and badge on my belt, and I had my convention credentials with the appropriate watermarks and reflective tags clearly visible. The governor had no credentials showing, and as he pushed by me, I politely stopped him. His staff guy took me on, saying, "Hey, you can't stop him. This is our governor."

I said, "Sorry, but he's not allowed to go up on the stage without credentials."

"I have his credentials," the staff member blurted out, his frustration obvious. "They're in my back pocket, so it's all right. "

"No, sir, it's not all right unless he is wearing them."

The staffer stared bullets at me and said, "You don't know who you're messing with."

My smart-aleck side took over and I responded with, "You're absolutely right, because he doesn't have any credentials on him." I continued to stare right back at the staffer and added, "Unless he has an ID, he's not going past me. You want to try to go over me, go for it; take your best shot."

The staffer got up close, glared at my name tag, and said, "You know what, I'm going to have you fired."

I glanced down at my name tag and said, "It's Gitschier, but the spelling is a little tricky, so make sure you get it right."

The staffer sneered and waved a finger in my face. "I guarantee you won't be here tomorrow."

I said, "Good, I'm ready to go home. It's been a long week." Then I pointed and made it clear they weren't going any farther and needed to turn around.

Funny, but shortly thereafter, they came walking up again, both wearing their credentials. As they passed by, I smiled at them and said, "Let me know when I'm leaving, because I need to make a reservation for a flight out of here." That really annoyed the staffer, and I loved it.

CHAPTER 25

TWO FANTASY GIGS

For the most part, being a Secret Service agent working protection is boring stuff, standing around with nothing happening, but needing to be always alert and on top of the game, ready to react to anything at a moment's notice. In other words, most of the time, it was a whole lot of nothing, which is exactly the way we wanted it to be. But there could be explosive moments that arose without warning and we had better be totally prepared, ready to react immediately and effectively. There also were times when a plum assignment would fall into our laps, a fantasy gig that caused us to pinch ourselves and wonder if it was real. That, plus being paid to be there and experience it. Two such gigs come to mind.

The first was my assignment to the 1984 Summer Olympics in Los Angeles. We stayed in a hotel right on the Santa Monica Beach, and I worked the afternoon shift, which gave me the mornings off. A bunch of us who had gone through the Secret Service school together were on this detail, and we'd spend the mornings playing beach volleyball. Doesn't get much better than that.

Our protectee was a dignitary from a small country, a little guy, gruff and with an obvious Napoleon complex, everything about him brimming with self-importance. We found this amusing. His status didn't exactly add up to his being a heavy hitter on the world stage when it came to the kinds of important world leaders we had served, but he, no doubt, thought he was the top dog. On the plus side, the cool thing about guarding him was that we went wherever he went. So, there we were in the Olympic colosseum, with ringside seats for the opening and closing ceremonies, and seats right on the finish line for various events. An enjoyable experience to be sure.

On the down side, we had to protect him in the evenings after the games were over for the day. He was there with a small staff and without his wife, which in his mind opened the door for him to carouse all night and chase women, and he put considerable effort into it. It was funny watching him operate, this guy coming on to every woman he saw and immediately getting shot down, one right after another. I guess nobody told him that in LA, or probably anywhere in the United States, if you come up to a woman and hit on her with a heavy accent and a line like, "Hey, baby, I'm important. Do you want to come back to my place?" you are not likely to get too far. The problem for the night crew was they had to be with him all night long, protecting him on his quest, and this could be daunting, trying to protect someone in a dimly lit bar where everyone was drinking. Not good.

Normally, when we are assigned a head of state, we work closely with the local police. In fact, in many ways we are highly dependent on police officers and their support. This was an area where I shined as an ex-cop. I'd spend a lot of time talking to the local guys, getting to know them, building friendships, which can be beneficial, and this proved to be the case with the protectee. You see, the night shift guys were not only worried about his safety, they got tired of traipsing around all night long from bar to bar while he drank, chased women, and continually struck out. As we talked about this, I had an idea and contacted the local police to see if it was possible they could lend a hand to help him finally find a woman.

Here's what I had in mind. Perhaps a young attractive female cop, one who was experienced doing undercover work, could come on to him, play like she was impressed and in awe because he was so important, and convince him that he was finally going to get his conquest. Then, when he was smitten, she would tell him that she had some important business to attend to, but she would come to his room later for a visit. Since she wasn't certain about the time, he had to be in his room waiting for her, and it could be any time after ten p.m.

It worked, and he was ecstatic and agreed immediately, then he puffed out his chest and swaggered around like the cock of the walk, making it obvious to everyone that he was successful in his venture and was about to score big. In anticipation, he ordered huge displays of flowers, caviar, and expensive champagne, then he hunkered down and waited. Well, of course, ten o'clock came and went, but he couldn't leave his room for fear that he might miss her. This allowed the night shift guys a break from the bar scene for which they were grateful. Time passed and periodically he would poke his head out the door, craning his head up and down the hall. The guys standing post knew what was going on, but they played dumb. Word was this went on all night long, then finally stopped around sunrise.

The next afternoon, he finally came out for the day. We expected him to be grumpy and in a foul mood, but instead he was grinning ear to ear, his usual gregarious self, dropping hints to members of his entourage, and acting as if he had had the big night he anticipated. Obviously, he felt the need to save face because he had bragged so much about his manly pursuits. It was a pathetic display of the male ego at its worst.

The bottom line on this duty was I had the time of my life, experiencing the Olympics in a way that would not have been possible for me otherwise. I am thankful to the protectee for allowing me this opportunity, and I'm glad the Secret Service was able to keep him safe while away from home and his wife.

—

The second fantasy gig also inspired me to think, gee I'm getting paid to do this and have such a wonderful time. This was several years later, and I had finished my work protecting President Reagan and was again working in the investigative unit, assigned, coincidentally, in LA. This assignment was temporary, and I was loaned out to protect former President Gerald Ford, who lived in two locations, Palms Springs, California, and Beaver Creek, Colorado, right next to Vail. They needed someone to fill in for a guy over Christmas break. I was single at the time, and I guess the other agent had a family and wanted to be with them, so it worked out wonderfully for both of us, and particularly for me, because I got to spend more than two weeks in Colorado over Christmas and through the New Year holiday.

I flew to Denver, got a car, and drove to Beaver Creek. It was snowing, Christmas was fast approaching, and it felt like I was in a Christmas card by Norman Rockwell: horse-drawn carriages at night decked out with Christmas lights and all that. I was in a beautiful location that folks pay big bucks to visit, and two weeks probably would have cost me most of my salary for the year. What's more, I had a three-bedroom cabin with a cozy fireplace all to myself and situated right by the ski slopes.

I volunteered for the midnight shift, which put me on duty at 10:45 p.m., and my job was to protect the house where former President Ford and his family were staying, so I hung out there. I was off at seven a.m. and would have a great breakfast that came with my cabin, get drowsy, and sleep for about five hours, and then I would hit the slopes. The ski patrol gave us passes, so we could ski to our hearts' content. The great perk about the pass was, the crowds were huge due to it being holiday season, and I didn't have to wait in the long lines to get on the lifts. I'd jump on the lift, ride to the top of the mountain, ski down, then jump right back on and keep going for several hours. After all that, I'd come back, sit in the hot tub with a beer or glass of wine, then have a meal, get drowsy, take a nap for about three hours, get up and go to work.

Former President Ford was a genuinely nice person, and I liked him. Working the late shift didn't allow me much time to interact, but when I did, it was great. One night I had to come in earlier and spent some time with him, and someone snapped a photo of us together in front of the Christmas tree as he was making a little impromptu speech. The photo appeared in the newspaper, and I always regretted not getting a copy of it as a keepsake.

CHAPTER 26

TOUCHING

A female dignitary who shall remain nameless came to Louisville to make an appearance at a well-known local venue. It was a low-key event with a small detail of Secret Service agents. I happened to be the driver and the guy who was her acting detail leader sat beside me, always on the right front seat of the limo. He was someone I had known for years and his name was also Greg. When I met him for the pickup, he gave me a look that implied uh-oh, then he confided, "She's in one of her weird moods today." Mood or not, she had a reputation for being quite difficult and most guys didn't want to be around her, but we did what we had to do, sucked it up and kept going.

We greeted her as she exited the plane and found her to be as advertised, gruff, surly, wearing sunglasses, and staring straight ahead. She didn't acknowledge me, which was fine. I could care less if anyone I'm protecting ever speaks to me. The rule I was always taught as a bodyguard is if I was spoken to, I responded respectfully. Other than that, don't ask questions and don't try to chitchat, and that is how I always conducted myself.

The female dignitary got in the car and we drove to the venue in complete and eerie silence. Then we boarded an elevator for the upper floors where she went back into a little greenroom-type suite to get ready and put on her game face. Greg and I stood by waiting, and I'll never forget the transformation I witnessed moments later. She entered the room sullen and by all accounts angry as a cranky badger, then emerged all giggly and bubbly, warm as can be, and greeting everyone personably, then she went on and gave her brief address.

After her talk, we escorted her back down the elevator and began walking to the limo. The way out could not have been more different from the way in, her transformation from Darth Vader to Mr. Rogers complete in every way; she was smiling and chatty, cutting up with Greg, and she even asked who I was and my name. The other Greg told her I had been a friend of his for a long time, that I was from the Louisville field office, and my name was also Greg. At that, she said, "Oh, my goodness," and she put her arms around both of our waists and said, "Look at me, I can make a Greg sandwich." Not exactly typical of something we would be likely to hear from one of our protectees, but she thought it was funny and was laughing like crazy. I was like, is this for real, and if so, holy cow!

She climbed into the backseat and sat right in the middle of the seat and promptly removed her shoes and propped her feet up between us on the front seat. She wiggled her toes and asked Greg to give her a foot massage. I had a hard time believing my ears, and a harder time believing that Greg did exactly that. Amazing! So, there's Greg rolling his eyes at me while she is cooing and oohing, eating the whole thing up like a giggly teenager. Then she said, "And when do I get my Greg sandwich?" I couldn't believe what I was hearing, and I was thinking this isn't happening as I drove her expeditiously to the airport, hustled her and her detail onto the plane and out of my life forever, thank goodness.

What would have been an appropriate response from Greg to the request for a foot massage? When pressed, we might say something like, "I'm sorry, ma'am, but I'm going to have to decline because it's against policy to engage in such a manner," or words to that effect. Protectees can be friendly, but the goal is not to become friends. Anything that disrupts objectivity is discouraged, and acts of intimacy are completely out of the question. With that said, I'm not criticizing Greg. He had to work with that woman, and, unfortunately, if she wanted to cause him trouble, there are any number of ways she could do that, and at the least, she could get him transferred. So, I guess Greg weighed the options and took the path of least resistance.

I later learned from another source that this protectee's unofficial nickname was Driving Miss Crazy. This certainly reinforced that what I had witnessed was typical behavior for her. In other words, Greg was not the only one walking a fine line.

Speaking of nicknames, when someone new comes under protection, like a newly elected president and vice president, they are presented with a list of what appear to be nicknames but are actually potential code names from which they can choose. Code names allow rapid communication among agents as it's much quicker to say "Timberwolf" than to say President George H. W. Bush.

All presidents' code names are made public. Protectees are not limited to the choices they are presented if they find them unsatisfactory, and they can create a new one. Sounds like a simple and uncomplicated matter, but we had to be careful and not choose something that could convey an improper message. For example, I had heard the story that when Nelson Rockefeller was VP under Gerald Ford, his wife, Happy, was initially assigned the code name Shooting Star. Bad idea; we never would want to use the term "shooting" when trying to achieve rapid communication among agents.

So, the protectee approves their code name, then all family members are assigned a code name that begins with the same letter. Code names included Deacon for Jimmy Carter, Dancer for Rosalynn, his wife, and Dynamo for their daughter Amy. John Glenn was Iron, and Jesse Jackson was Thunder. Ronald Reagan was Rawhide, and wife Nancy was Rainbow. George H. W. Bush was Timberwolf, and wife Barbara was Tranquility. George W. Bush was Tumbler and wife Laura was Tempo. Bill Clinton was Eagle, wife Hilary was Evergreen, and daughter Chelsea was Energy. Gerald Ford was Passkey; Gary Hart was Redwood; and John Edwards was Speedway.

CHAPTER 27

PRESIDENT RONALD REAGAN

One of my first assignments as a protection agent was for President Ronald Reagan in Indianapolis. I drove up from Louisville, all primed and ready in my new navy-blue suit, starched white shirt, appropriately bland tie, and brand-new, super-shined Johnson and Murphy black dress shoes. Over top of this ensemble, I wore a trench coat. My goal was to look as sharp as I could because I was on temporary assignment, an agent from the local region borrowed to supplement the president's usual detail. I wanted to make a good impression.

Each of us temp guys was assigned a task, like to watch this door, that roof, that fence line, whatever. As low man on the totem pole, the youngest and least experienced, I was assigned to watch the runway near where Air Force One was to be chocked up when it arrived. My job was to scan the area constantly and make sure no one opened a window, popped up on the roof, or came through one of the security gates.

It was bitterly cold that day, low temperatures and howling winds, with a wind chill index in the single digits. At first, it wasn't a problem, and I stood there loud and proud and feeling good about myself fulfilling this ultra-important role of helping to protect the leader of the free world. In reality, President Reagan was pretty far away, but that didn't matter, because I would have felt the same if I had been standing right next to him.

The weather was brutal, and while the shoes I had on looked great, the soles were pitifully thin and poorly suited for standing on concrete runways. I learned that day that runways are thick, like 10 feet thick, and because of the way they are crafted, they do a good job of holding onto the cold. This meant all that accumulated cold was transferring upward through my thin-soled shoes and into my body.

If I had been on runway duty for only an hour, which is what I had anticipated, it wouldn't have been so bad. But due to poor weather, Air Force One was delayed an extra hour and a half, which about froze me to death. At that point, I couldn't care less about how sharp I looked. How could I, with my teeth chattering uncontrollably and every muscle in my body shivering and trying to create additional body heat? But it didn't do much good, because I was losing heat faster than I could generate it, and I began to worry that I might collapse from hypothermia. Not a good way to start building my reputation as an agent.

Anyway, after nearly freezing, I was finally relieved from duty. I warmed up and then almost immediately was pulled into another protection rotation in which I boarded a plane for Beeville, Texas.

—

I spent three years on the detail protecting President Reagan and his family. It was great because I got to bounce back and forth from the East Coast to the West Coast, to the Reagan Santa Barbara residence for long weekends or sometimes longer. The person I spent the most time with was Maureen Reagan, first child and oldest daughter of President Reagan and former wife, Jane Wyman. Maureen was extremely active in the coalition Women Against Violence, and many other social causes. Her involvement was powerful, because in a sense wherever she went, she was viewed as an extension of her father. This, even though she and her father might clash at times on some of her views, like abortion rights and the Equal Rights Amendment. Protecting her took me all around the world several times, as we visited country after country on our trips, especially those countries known to mistreat women.

Maureen kept us busy. There would be like 10 guys on her detail, two doing the advance work, then three or four per protection shift. When we visited a foreign country, we could tell they perceived it as a big deal, particularly in the poorer countries where she was treated in many cases better than the vice president. In their minds, she was comparable to the king's daughter because her father was president of the United States and the most powerful man in the world. They provided her (and us) the ultimate in red-carpet treatment, motorcycle escorts, stays at the palace, the opportunity to hobnob with royalty—the whole nine yards.

In addition to her taxing travel schedule, she would also spend a week to 10 days each month at the White House, and we'd intermingle with the regular full-time protection unit there. It was interesting to see their reaction when we would come to visit the White House, because we were viewed as having the deluxe assignment. For agents on White House duty, there were prolonged periods when President Reagan was convalescing from being shot, or not feeling well, and his detail had to hang around looking at walls, boring for an eight-hour shift. In contrast, we were jet-setting all over the world and we'd arrive with tans. We were also making the maximum amount an agent could make in virtually every one of our two-week pay periods, *maxing out* we called it, due to constantly working overtime. The guys stuck in the White House didn't have opportunities to get overtime pay, and they sure weren't tan, causing some friction and jealousy.

On the other hand, a few knucklehead agents viewed themselves as higher up, more important than us because they were guarding the president, and we were only guarding family members. That attitude is silly because we all come from the same place, the investigations unit, and we all would be rotating back there at some point. I might add that those guys who acted like jerks would eventually have to work shoulder to shoulder with everyone else conducting investigations, and when that happened, it was a pleasure to stick it to them in subtle and sometimes not-so-subtle ways. Don't get me wrong. Most agents I worked with were truly outstanding people. But like in any organization, there were some jerks, some do-nothing types, and those who sucked up to bosses to get ahead.

At times, I was on President Reagan's protection detail, and I always looked forward to that. President Reagan was down to earth, and while he was a serious and capable man, he didn't take himself too seriously, and believe me, I've run across a number of those who did on this job. In fact, I doubt that President Reagan ever had a conscious thought about delineating himself as part of the "big people" class while the rest of us were little people.

Here are some examples of what I mean by down to earth. One Thanksgiving evening, I was picking up Maureen Reagan at the Santa Barbara ranch, which surprisingly was not a huge ranch, nothing ostentatious as you would expect from a celebrity turned president. I walked up to the porch as the door opened, and to my great surprise, instead of Maureen coming out, it was President Reagan, and immediately I started backpedaling. He looked at me, gave me one of his prize-winning smiles and called me "Kentucky," because when Maureen introduced me to him quite a while before, she said, "This is my agent from Kentucky." He said, "Hey, Kentucky, have you seen the binoculars the navy gave me?" With that, he walked over to the side of the porch to what looked like a hood that covers a grill, lifted it up, and underneath, a pair of gigantic binoculars was mounted and tilted upwards. These binoculars were the kind the navy used a while ago to see long distances across the ocean; they were powerful.

He made an adjustment to the binoculars, then turned to me, and said, "You are not going to believe how it looks, seeing the moon and stars through these babies." He bent slightly and surveyed the heavens, then popped his head up and invited me to take a look. I did, and he sure was right. It was breathtaking. The combination of that view and standing elbow to elbow with President Ronald Reagan about took my breath away. He didn't seem to be in a hurry and I had the impression we could have spent considerable time doing what we were doing, but Maureen came out, and it was time for me to leave.

My intense feelings on this occasion weren't stirred simply because I was in proximity to such an important person, because I'd been there before many times. It was because we were in such an intimate setting, and he so quickly put me at ease and made me feel comfortable and welcome, as if I belonged there and was entitled to share this enjoyment with him. It was incredibly special. And, again, his thoughtfulness to include me when so many others would have ignored me as if I weren't there, speaks volumes about the kind of person he was.

Here is another example of his being down to earth. A close friend of mine told me this story. Those guarding the president have a command post, a place to rest and unwind when off duty and not standing at a post. Agents could watch TV, but that gets a little old, so it was common for off-duty agents to get up a rousing card game to pass the time. Apparently, either President Reagan had heard about the card games, or perhaps he was simply checking on "his boys," but either way, one time he popped his head in and asked if he could play. Can you imagine? How cool is that?

—

President Reagan's greatest pleasure in life was trail riding on his ranch, which required that agents be highly proficient riders to accompany him. To qualify, agents had to attend a two-week US Capitol Police riding school and pass a test that was extremely demanding. Most of us agents considered ourselves to be top-notch athletes, and truth is, most of us were, but when it came to horseback riding, it was tough holding our own, and most who took the course failed. For starters, we had to have had a lot of experience as serious riders, but even that was not enough. An English saddle was used, which is small and flat, unlike a Western saddle with a big horn to hold onto in front and a deep seat. Use of an English saddle makes it quite a challenge to do much of anything on a horse because the rider has less control.

In the riding school, we had to be able to ride some big horses and control them by using our knees, squeezing in a certain way, which left our hands free to use the phone in an emergency or pull our guns and shoot accurately while riding at full gallop. We also had to master jumps while riding fast, and be able to come to a dead stop, all without getting dumped. Obviously, few made it through, but when they did, they had the opportunity of a lifetime to ride with Rawhide.

One of the best agent riders was a woman who dearly loved horses and had a way with them that can only be described as phenomenal. She easily outshined most of the guys. She was not only good with horses, she was an outstanding agent in every way. Recognition of her obvious talents moved her smoothly, and deservedly, up the ranks, and, ultimately, I ended up working for her as the agent in charge of the state of Kentucky. She was so well thought of, in fact, and so universally respected that headquarters wanted to promote her to the director's staff, quite a big deal. But because of her love of horses she declined. Now, there is someone who knows her heart and has her priorities straight, and I'm honored to say that we are still close friends to this day.

An agent friend of mine told me another horse story. A couple of agents and President Reagan were mounted and ready to go for a ride at the Santa Barbara ranch. The president was busy, of course, and every moment that he could escape from the pressures of office was precious, and he was obviously anxious to get started. But they were waiting for

First Lady Nancy Reagan, and he kept looking at his watch, then at the front door, then back at his watch.

Finally, the president said, "Excuse me, gentlemen, I'll be right back." He walked purposefully to the house and through the front door, then almost immediately came back out holding what we all remember as a landline phone, complete with the wire dragging from it and part of the socket where it entered the wall still attached. He came striding out, looked over at the White House Communications guy who was responsible for all our radios, telephones, and what not. He approached him and said, "I apologize, and I owe you for a new phone," then he handed him the phone. Apparently, Nancy had been on the phone, keeping everyone waiting, and although the president had been calm and patient, it went on too long, so he went into the house and tore the phone from the wall. Moments later, Nancy came walking out, head down, and for the only time anyone could recall, a sheepish look on her face. Without a word, she mounted and off they went.

A quick follow-up about Nancy. My arrival was well after President Reagan was shot, and after that, Nancy was incredibly protective of him. No doubt, she was a tough cookie, and we didn't want to mess up around her. Agents knew this, and they always acted highly professionally to the point of being anal. I don't mean that in a bad way, but rather they minded their business down to the finest details. This meant looking sharp at all times, no matter what, being sharp and on the ball, always careful to stay on her good side. With that said, she was respectful to agents, unlike some others who took advantage and seemed to go out of their way to be cruel and intimidating.

—

My favorite story about President Reagan took place when we flew to Beeville, Texas. It was a big event involving both President Reagan and Vice President George H. W. Bush, a Texas-style barbecue at a huge opulent ranch. Because the president and vice president were together out on the road, a rare circumstance, and one of the first times this had happened at a publicized event, the protection detail was especially heavy. I was among several so-called "post standers," meaning extra guys brought along to boost the detail for this trip.

It was obviously Texas. Everybody wore cowboy hats and boots, and the steaks were Texas-sized, thick and juicy. After a while, it came time for President Reagan to eat. He stood there a moment, looked around, and said, "Well, okay, but have my boys eaten yet?" The response was, "Oh, gee, sorry Mr. President, we didn't know your sons were here." He chuckled and said, "No, I mean my boys, my agents. I'm not going to eat until they eat." Upon hearing those words, hands and feet got busy, some tables magically appeared, big steaks found their way to plates, and some of the working guys had the right timing on their rotation to be able to sit down and have a nice meal.

That was the kind of guy President Reagan was, unflappable and real. Two other tiny tidbits bolster and verify this image. While I was with the LA field office, a new agent was assigned to cover President Reagan's hotel stop. For safety precautions, we would often randomly alter our arrival points among the front door, side door, back door, or loading dock. On this occasion, as we walked through the large kitchen, the young agent got turned around and walked the president right into a broom closet. The president kept following him and, with a big smile on his face, didn't miss a beat as he said, "Do you want me to grab a mop or a broom?"

And I heard through the grapevine this gem involving another young agent who encountered President Reagan in the hall of the White House and accidentally let it slip and called him by his code name, Rawhide. This tells you how relaxed agents were in his presence, which certainly made post-standing life more agreeable. I don't mean to imply that agents were too relaxed and not vigilant. On the contrary, every agent I know would have eagerly sacrificed his life to save President Reagan's. As to that agent who had a slip of the tongue, I'm sure he about swallowed his own when the word Rawhide came out, but the president's response was what you'd expect. A little chuckle and a pat on the shoulder, then he was on his way.

In wrapping this up about President Reagan, when I was stationed in Hawaii, I was working the president's protection detail, and he was supposed to have a VIP photo session, private with just him and a big donor. I was there, along with a lieutenant from the Honolulu Police Department who had worked all week helping us agents. For some reason, the big donor didn't show up, and as we stood there, President Reagan looked at me and asked, "Kentucky, have you had the opportunity to have your private picture with me yet?"

I said, "No, sir, Mr. President."

"Well, then, come on and let's do it now."

At that moment, I glanced at the lieutenant and said, "Hey, you deserve this. Why don't you go ahead?" He beamed with excitement and I felt good about giving him an opportunity for an eight-by-ten photo of the two of them shoulder to shoulder. I figured I'd have other opportunities for more photos down the line. I never did, and I regret not having a personal picture with President Reagan.

—

After the Texas barbecue, our flight back home from Beeville turned out to be quite memorable. A bunch of us, maybe 50 personnel, were on a military flight, which of course, is a huge cost savings for the government compared with putting us on commercial flights. Every time the president goes somewhere, we have to take along a fleet of armored limos, bulletproof stages, and tons of equipment, and these would be transported on what we called car planes, the ones where the back tail drops down and a car or truck can be driven right up onto the plane.

We flew these planes around the country and all over the world. They certainly are not built for the comfort of passengers, even though they typically have passengers aboard. Small portable seats would be added and secured to the floor wherever they might fit, often right in front of a limo that was strapped down. So, there we'd sit, several of us in a row in front of series of limos that upon takeoff and landing would lurch to and fro due to the incredible momentum created by the airplane. Sitting there we, of course, hoped the loadmaster knew his job securing the vehicles and that he didn't have a rough night before, because a limo could roll right over us in our portable seats. To say it was uncomfortable would be a gross understatement.

As we were getting ready to depart from Beeville, and the plane was loaded to the hilt with everything imaginable, we expected that the captain of the flight would come out and address the group of passengers with a lighthearted message about the flight. In this case, it was a young and extremely short female who introduced herself, welcomed us aboard, and told us she would be flying us to Indianapolis. As she talked, all the guys were looking at her like she had two heads, some guys saying under their breath that their daughter looked older than her. Regardless of her small stature, she was in charge of this massive airplane.

We took off and the loadmaster told us this was her first official flight as captain. We started joking around about how interesting this flight might turn out to be and not necessarily in a good way. Well, sure enough, as we were preparing to land, we noticed the loadmaster and his crew hurrying and double-checking everything, especially the limos, to make sure they were secure. We were warned to tighten our seat belts, and we were all wondering what was going on, because we had all been on a bunch of these flights, no big deal. Finally, one of the older guys on our detail asked the loadmaster, "Hey, chief, what's going on?" He responded, "Well, I didn't want to get you guys upset, but the captain realized that she lost the flaps a while back." This meant that without flaps, we wouldn't have a way to slow down properly as we landed.

We had to divert to another airport and take the longest runway. So here we came toward the landing strip, and we were coming in fast and hot. Her plan was to set us down on the far edge of the runway and use the entire distance to slow down and hope it was enough to stop us. We watched out the windows and it was clear this was not a usual landing as we zipped along and then hit hard, bouncing up, then down, then up again, and I mean bounce. The whole time, we're all praying that our little captain can deliver us in one piece, and that the cars stay put or we're all dead meat.

To try to stop without flaps, the captain was braking as hard as she could, which caused the plane to shimmy like crazy, and in no time, the smell of burning brakes was strong and smoke seeped into the cabin. Looking around, all I could see were wide eyes and praying lips. Finally, we stopped, and crew guys popped the doors and came running in, yelling for us to get off immediately and to leave our stuff. By that time, the cabin was full of smoke and it was a relief to get out the door. When we exited, we saw a team of firefighters in their moon suits spraying foam all over the plane to prevent it from catching fire from the tire and brake heat.

As it turned out, our captain did not have enough runway, but she was able to veer off the back of the runway to a side route that was actually a street and ran the nose of the plane through a chain link fence and stopped about 30 feet from a lake adjacent to the airport. If we had splashed into the lake, it would have been dicey the way we were loaded down. When all was said and done, we cheered our little captain for a courageous effort and a job well done. As they say, it's not the size of the dog in the fight that counts, but the amount of fight in the dog, and she had a bunch.

CHAPTER 28

THREATS: BOGUS AND BONA FIDE

When a threat is detected against the president, whether written, received by phone, emailed, overheard, or whatever, an agent is expected to respond immediately. Most agents don't like messing with these kinds of cases, especially if they involve someone with mental challenges. Such cases are referred to as nut cases, which means the agent on the case is called a "nut buster"—politically incorrect, of course, but adequately descriptive.

The Secret Service has a whole division devoted to threats against the president and other dignitaries. When investigating such a case, time is critical, and we are under extreme pressure to get a report to our supervisors as quickly as possible. The paperwork is ponderous and entails about 14 pages of questions that must be answered in detail, but that's not the most onerous part. At the end and on the bottom of the last page, we must check one of two boxes. One box indicates that we deem the person to be a bona fide threat to the president, and the other indicates that we do not deem the person to be a threat. After checking one of the boxes, we must sign our names. Imagine the pressure you might feel when completing the forms and you are on record that the person is not a threat, but something happens. Even if it's way in the future, they would still pull your completed forms and question why you decided what you did. This, of course, is another reason agents would rather avoid this assignment.

When I worked these cases, I went for interviews to Eddyville State Prison in western Kentucky, a nasty place, old, dark and musty, right out of a 1950s' black-and-white movie. Prisoners often claim they are innocent, but here is the exception. It's not uncommon for a prisoner in a state penitentiary to threaten the president, own it, and be loud and proud about it, even though it could add time to their sentence. Sounds crazy, right? Not to them, because the purpose is to be charged with a federal crime and they hope to be moved to a federal prison that is head and shoulders above most state institutions. Especially in comparison to a prison like Eddyville, the federal prisons offer better facilities and food.

Regardless of the motive, we had to take every threat seriously and investigate it fully. One prisoner who fit the profile of an inmate attempting to play the system was heavily tattooed from head to toe. Even his shaved head was covered with tattoos; a spider web on the top and a black widow spider on the middle of his forehead. The whole time I was interviewing him, it was hard not to stare at the spider. Anyway, it didn't take long to figure out this guy's game and I checked the "not a bona fide threat" box.

Here is a much different case and it involved President Reagan. The threat was made by another Eddyville prisoner, and there was no doubt in my mind that it was real. The prisoner was a Vietnam War veteran in the special forces. He was an expert on bombs and explosive devices, and he had received medals for valor. He was the real deal.

When I met him, he began with what I believed was a heartfelt apology for making me come all the way down there to the prison to interview him. No problem, I told him, it's my job, but still he seemed genuinely concerned. Then he informed me that God was telling him to kill President Reagan. I was taken aback, because this guy seemed so normal: sincere, genuine, polite, and likeable. Plus, his demeanor didn't change, whether he was apologizing to me or telling me he had to kill President Reagan. He told me that when he listened to the radio, God talked to him and told him President Reagan was the Antichrist and that he (the prisoner) had been trained specifically to be an expert in warfare and he was being called upon by God to kill the Devil so that he couldn't take over the world. Chilling, watching his face and listening to his voice—as emotionless as if he were telling me about a baseball game he had watched.

We spent a lot of time talking. He told me in great detail exactly how he was going to carry this out, how he would use his training, and most of all, that he would use the utmost caution because he didn't want to hurt any innocent bystanders, particularly the Secret Service agents assigned to protect President Reagan, who were just doing their jobs. It seemed important to him that I understood he had no animosity or ill feelings toward me or any of my colleagues, but it was also important that I understood his mission from God was something he had to do, no matter what, and he would not rest until he completed that mission.

To this day, I can see that man's face and hear his voice, and it was the scariest interview I ever conducted. When it ended, we both stood, and he shook my hand. I thanked him for his time, and he wished me good luck. The whole experience was beyond eerie, knowing how serious this guy was and how dedicated he was to his mission. Obviously, I checked the box that indicated he was indeed a real threat to President Reagan. I recommended he receive an additional five years in prison, and that we be informed immediately when, if ever, he was released.

I might add, each person who is interviewed and deemed to be a bona fide threat is rated according to the degree of perceived threat. Class 1 is a mild threat, Class 2 is moderate, and Class 3 is a hard-core direct threat, someone to be taken seriously. When the president, or any protectee, comes to a particular district where there are any unconfined Class-3 individuals, Secret Service agents and usually a police officer or detective would "babysit" these people to know where they were and what they were doing every moment during the visit. Thankfully, we never had to babysit that veteran.

—

The guy who schooled me on all this threat stuff was Billy Hawkins, "Hawk." Over a beer, he was sharing one of his experiences about a guy who was mentally unstable and made a threat against the president. At the time, this guy was in a state mental institution, and typically agents went in pairs, not alone. But there are times when that's not possible for one reason or another, and Hawk made the trip by himself to conduct the lengthy interview. In the institution, Hawk had to first check his gun at the entry point to make sure he wasn't jumped by a patient eager to get hold of his gun, then he was escorted to a room where he was locked in with about a dozen patients. One patient quickly caught his attention when he walked in, a very large man with a hateful look on his face. The patient kept clenching his fist and squeezing it, staring holes through Hawk the whole time and poised as if, at any moment, he might charge like a bull. Talk about feeling uncomfortable. There was Hawk, all alone and unarmed in the midst of a highly unpredictable group of mental patients, and no orderlies or assistants nearby if something bad went down.

As Hawk kept an eye on the threatening patient, the door opened and a man in a white lab coat with a stethoscope around his neck walked in and said, "Good evening, I'm Dr. So-and-So. Are you the person here to do the interview?" Hawk responded that he was and showed identification. They sat down at a table and began the interview about the patient who had threatened to kill the president. Things seemed to be going well. Hawk wrote feverishly, trying to record every detail, including the doctor's diagnosis, his prognosis regarding the potential threat level, and information on whether the patient was on meds and if so what kind, if he was violent with other patients, etc. The whole time, the doctor was using esoteric terminology that required frequent interpretation.

The process was moving toward conclusion when the door opened, and two orderlies entered the room and came over to the table. Hawk told them they were about to finish up. Then one of the orderlies said to the doctor, "What are you doing down here?"

The doctor responded, "Just helping out this Secret Service agent."

The orderly smiled and said, "Yeah, well, you are needed upstairs, and you-know-who has a problem and you're the only one who can fix it."

With that, the doctor jumped up and told Hawk he was sorry, but he had to leave.

Hawk was bewildered and made the plea that he was almost done with this laborious task and couldn't he please have another few minutes to finish up.

At that point, one of the orderlies said to the doctor, "You know you're going to have to give back that lab coat and stethoscope." Hearing that, the doctor lowered his head. An orderly took him by the arm and said, "Come on, we have to take you to your room."

By then Hawk, of course, realized that the whole time he had been interviewing one of the patients pretending to be a doctor. Ironically, the patient made more sense and answered the questions in greater detail and with more medical authority than the actual doctor who showed up later to be interviewed.

CHAPTER 29

MAUREEN REAGAN: AFRICAN ODYSSEY

I mentioned earlier that when working President Reagan's detail, I spent most of my time with Maureen, his eldest daughter. This was the late 1980s, and she was quite an activist and seemingly always on the go. On one trip, I was assigned to the advance team, responsible for essentially everything that happened during her visit to six countries in southern Africa.

I related earlier many of the duties involved when doing advance work. It's quite demanding and exacting, but especially so when entering a developing country rife with terroristic threats. We also had to coordinate with the US embassy in each country, and complete endless reports to keep those who need to know in the know; at times, it felt overwhelming. But I took the challenge and stayed one step ahead of Maureen and her entourage, preparing as best I could to make sure she was safe and that her mission would be successful.

Notwithstanding all the advance work needed, on many occasions with Maureen, we did not receive much notice. Ideally, we'd get a couple of weeks to do our planning, but one particular time, it was only a few days. One of the main things that has to be done when visiting countries where the medical resources are nearly nonexistent, is for us to go to the nearest military base and undergo a long series of shots and take a basket full of pills in anticipation of an attack from mosquitos, or encountering a lack of sanitation that is hard for us to imagine in the United States.

Knowing we were headed into hostile territory, we also were matched with other Secret Service agents of a similar age and blood type to cover the potential need for a blood transfusion in an emergency. It was meant as a short-term effort to keep someone alive until military transport to a fully functioning hospital was available. When I was matched up with a guy who was known as the "party guy," I wasn't too happy about what might be flowing through his veins, and the thought that his blood might at some point be comingling with mine. But, it was what it was, and all I could do was hope I didn't need his blood.

We went to the military base for our series of shots, often as many as six or more. Military medical folks are not exactly like your doc at home. They don't care if patients are comfortable and they are not worried about customer complaints, so we might get three shots in one arm and four in the other. One of the worst was what's called a gamma shot. It's supposed to go in the hip, but more often than not, it ended up on your rear end. The contents of the shot needed to be refrigerated to preserve it, and in the best circumstances, it would be removed from refrigeration and allowed to warm up to room temperature, but in the military, that never was the case. The shot came directly from refrigerator.

We were told to bend over and grab our knees and that it might hurt a little bit. Being told "it might hurt a little bit" is not something you want to hear when you are about to get a shot, and especially a shot from one of these military medical types. The needle was long, and when it penetrated the skin, it felt like it had a square head, not pointed, and because the stuff was so cold, it didn't pass through the needle easily. It would take a good minute or two, which felt more like an hour, to push the plunger all the way down. The result was the point of insertion instantly swelled up bigger than a golf ball. This misery was compounded by the fact that soon we would be taking off on a long air force flight and sitting on a sore rear. I mention all this detail because folks have the impression that being a Secret Service agent is glamourous. We are surrounded by the world's who's who, and therefore, surely, we must partake in at least some of all that that entails. To some degree, that's true, but for the most part, the behind-the-scenes activities often greatly overshadow any glamour that might come our way, and a gamma shot serves as a perfect example.

My advance team partner and I took off and spent our first night in Brussels, Belgium, where we were able to recharge our batteries briefly before taking off early the next morning on a flight to Johannesburg, South Africa. I anticipated maybe a three- to four-hour flight. Wrong! It was 10 and a half hours, the flight that never ended with my rear end screaming at me the whole way. Since I couldn't sleep on the flight and didn't get a lot of sleep the night before, I was exhausted when we arrived. Thankfully, there was nothing for us to do there other than wait three or four hours for our next flight on a tiny airline no one had ever heard of with one pilot and no co-pilot, a substantial cause for concern. But when in Rome, you do what they do in Rome.

We took off and noticed the pilot was flying low, barely off the ground over a desert with no signs of civilization. I thought, man, if this plane ever goes down, there is no way anyone will ever find us. But we made it and landed near a game preserve out in the middle of nowhere as the sun was going down. Normally, this would not be a problem, except in this case, the pilot literally had to fly back and forth over the runway to scare off the animals lurking there. After a few passes to clear the runway, which was little more than a wide dirt path, we landed with quite a thump. Welcome to wherever.

With all that was going on, we forgot that we had had little to eat in a long while and we were famished. But we knew we couldn't grab anything that came along in these countries because it's easy to get sick, and then we would be of no use to anyone. In anticipation, thankfully, I had stocked up with cans of tuna fish and giant jars of peanut butter, no refrigeration required. Plus, when in Brussels, I picked up several loaves of hard bread to go with my peanut butter. These items were my lifeline and I depended on them on many occasions.

A couple of jeeps came tearing out onto the runway to pick us up. They were from the anti-poaching unit, guards who try to protect animals on the preserve from poachers killing them and selling body parts for profit. The US government had hired these guys to act as bodyguards and guides for us.

We drove to the game preserve, which turned out to be the kind of place where folks would fly in and take pictures of animals, not a place where they could hunt and kill them. It was surrounded by deep jungle, a place where animals could feel safe and hide. Visitors wanting photographs had to wait until the animals decided they needed a drink of water and ventured toward a nearby river; this typically was at dusk or dawn. One strategy was to take tourists in a four-wheel drive vehicle upriver and put them in a raft that would then flow downstream past the drinking animals. A wide array of animals might show up, including giant eagles. To attract them, people would throw fish from a boat and the eagles would swoop down from out of nowhere at amazing speeds and skim the fish right off the top of the water.

Since we were in the middle of nowhere, the only power for electricity was gasoline-powered generators, which were shut down at about nine at night. This allowed us to sample some adult beverages, mainly banana beer, which has a high alcohol content, and some of our guys ended up with quite a buzz. Fortunately, we weren't working until the next day.

The anti-poaching guards patrolled the outer perimeter of the grounds while we covered the inner perimeter around the buildings. We posted our guys with big powerful flashlights and Uzi machine guns. As the advance agent, I briefed them and told them that not only were we concerned about "two-footed" attackers, but they also needed to be on guard for "four-footed" attackers, who would be delighted to have them for dinner.

I figured this type of warning might help the midnight shift stay awake.

When the lights went out, I made one final pass to make sure everyone was on their perimeter post and that all was well. I walked up to one of the guys, and as I spoke to him, he froze, staring out into nowhere. I said, "What are you doing, John?" He responded with a finger to his lips and pointed into the darkness. I looked but couldn't see anything and told him so. He said, "Yeah, but wait till I turn this light on." When he flipped his light on for a second, we could see what appeared to be about a hundred pairs of eyes staring back at us from the brush. I chuckled as I walked away, confident there was no way he'd be nodding off.

Several hours later, one of the guys we called Agent Orange had consumed too many rounds of banana beer and had to get out of bed and relieve himself. He earned his nickname from agents who had served in Vietnam. You see, he had trouble with women and apparently was trying his best to make a good impression by taking suntan pills. Unfortunately, instead of sporting a golden tan, the pills turned him orange, and his orange glow stayed quite a while, cementing his nickname for the rest of his life.

Agent Orange got up and had to go, but there was no running water or bathrooms. He made his way to the outhouse, which had wooden seats. The wood had a split in it that had never been repaired, and this agent, with his beer-bulging bladder, sat down on the split seat.

Now, going back to when I briefed the guys about all the predators, I also included special remarks about the variety of lethal snakes that likely were lurking nearby, including "five-steppers," "three-steppers," and "one-steppers." They, of course, had never heard of these snakes and asked me what I was talking about. The labels indicate how many steps you would have before the venom paralyzed you and you fell to the ground.

No doubt the snake talk made a lasting impression on most of the guys, including Agent Orange in the outhouse. When he sat, the split wooden seat grabbed his rear end. Thinking he had been bitten, he let out a loud bloody scream and stumbled from the outhouse, trying to run with his pants down around his ankles. Obviously, he didn't get far before falling face first to the ground where he started flailing around in the dirt. The noise woke everyone up, and we all triggered our bright flashlights and headed toward the noise. At the same time, the guards on duty with their machine guns came running, also trying to figure out what had happened.

When we all got there, Agent Orange was on the ground screaming that a snake bit him on the ass. That was alarming, of course, because in minutes he could be dead. One of the guys started yelling, "Someone do something or he's gonna die." With that, they were all asking me what we were going to do. I responded, "I'm sure not going to suck the poison out." This got everyone laughing, including the poor guy on the ground. Then, with a little sleuthing, we were able to piece together what had happened and that he was attacked by a toilet seat and not one of the lethal snakes. It was a light moment in an otherwise nerve-wracking assignment.

—

As point man for the advance team, I had to always be thinking ahead, so I left early the next day to get things set up for our next stop. The country we were headed to was different from the last in that it had some infrastructure. I was surprised by all the fairly large buildings as I looked down from the window of the much larger plane, about 50 to 75 seats, as opposed to the puddle-hopping eight-seater I had flown into the last country. To board this larger plane, I had to reroute back through Johannesburg, a brief and refreshing return to civilization.

As I watched from above, I was impressed with the size and seeming sophistication of the city that was our next destination. But my impression quickly changed when we landed and drove through the city. I realized that the buildings were nothing but empty shells, the entire area reduced by hard times to virtually nothing as compared to a past when it was an obviously thriving metropolis. The buildings had been gutted and anything of value removed, leaving a façade somewhat like a movie set. Another thing that caught my eye were the Russian Migs, fighter planes, a reflection of the protracted cold war between the United States and Russia that was still ongoing at the time. Admittedly, seeing the Migs gave me a flash of discomfort, but I had to focus my mind and keep moving forward.

I went to the local US embassy, where I received a briefing by a couple of marines, then I started on my advance work. I made my way to the home of the leader of the country and was stunned to see a fabulous palace, such a remarkable contrast to the shells of buildings in the city. Not only that, I learned there were seven more similarly splendid palaces throughout this small country. This struck me as strange given the destitute nature of the people living there, barely able to stay alive, and yet this leader lived in such opulence.

I went up the driveway and encountered the palace guards all dressed in their finest attire with their fluffs and spears, mimicking the pageantry of the British Beefeater guards. (By the way, the Beefeaters earned their name because when they were warders at the Tower of London, part of their salary was paid in chunks of beef.)

When I came around the corner, I encountered dozens of new Mercedes Benz vehicles, so new the plastic covers were still on the seats. They were being washed, so I asked the guy who was hosting me what the deal was with all these new expensive cars. He told me it came from US tax dollars that were donated to this poor country for food and medicine and such, but instead ended up in corrupt pockets.

It's not my place to question the nature or purpose of whatever mission I'm on, but it was painful to see the incredible contrast between immense wealth and abject poverty existing literally side by side. Worse, it was being supported by US funds, money so entirely wasted with no one checking to see that at least some portion of it was being used for intended purposes. But then, I'm not a politician and I have no idea why we were there, or how in good conscience we could allow ourselves to be hosted by someone who so blatantly stole and squandered donated funds earmarked for humanitarian efforts.

I was happy to leave that country. Two down and four to go.

—

Our next stop required that we board a tiny four-seater plane with a pilot that looked, at best, like he was in the 10th grade. I tried to be subtle, but I had to ask if he really was our pilot. He was, and when we took off, we flew right above the treetops, so close I don't know how we missed scraping some of the taller trees. But we didn't, and I had to hand it to our boyish pilot; he seemed to know what he was doing. Either that, or he was real lucky. The flight pattern was quite challenging, and the pilot kept cutting it hard at tight angles as he followed a meandering river basin below. It got so rough at times, I wondered if he was trying to make me air sick because I had annoyed him by asking if he was my pilot. If so, he was succeeding, and I finally had to ask him why he was doing this, flying in this way.

He smiled and responded that he should have explained the whole situation to us, but he was afraid we'd cancel our flight. Hearing that was disconcerting to be sure, then he went on to explain that one of their planes had been shot down the previous week by guerilla fighters, so they were told to fly barely above the treetops and follow the rivers where the guerillas couldn't set up and shoot missiles at the plane. I swallowed hard at the news, but there was nothing to be done other than ride it out.

As we approached the airfield, it was another wide dirt path and we had to make several passes to clear off all the animals. When we landed, instantly we were surrounded by thousands of folks in native dress, some of them making a strange, but melodic sound by clicking their tongues in unison, while others offered a sort of African yodeling. Whatever it was, it was meant as a peaceful greeting. We climbed out of the plane and were met by a UNICEF (the United Nations Children's Emergency Fund) truck that took us to a camp with more than 50,000 refugees, most of whom were old men, women, and young children trying to escape the ongoing war between the government and the guerillas.

Although I had been briefed about what to expect at the refugee camp, seeing it was overwhelming: nothing but a vast sea of people and no infrastructure or support of any kind. One tiny comfort was to see some food that was available in bags with the American flag stenciled on it. The food was a white powder, specially prepared and loaded with vitamins, minerals, and protein, that when mixed with water made a nutritious paste. Not sure how it tasted, probably bad, but for people who are starving and for whom that was the only thing keeping them alive, taste was of little consequence. I'm glad to say that on this occasion, we got it right and our tax dollars made it to where they could do some good.

Here and there were M.A.S.H. units (mobile army surgical hospitals). I give a lot of credit and I am grateful to groups like Doctors Without Borders who volunteer, giving up a year of their lives, risking all to provide medical care and save countless lives. It was truly inspiring, and as the people began arriving to receive treatment, one of the first to catch my eye was a woman. She walked slowly, her strides tiny and more of a shuffle as she carried everything her family owned wrapped up in a blue tarp she had slung over her shoulder. That level of poverty hit me hard.

I scoped out the M.A.S.H. units to get a feel for the route we would be walking and what we might encounter. I stopped a nurse and asked her if, when we toured in two days, we could come through the same door I had just used and if we could speak to this child or that one over there. In response, the nurse pulled me aside and told me the two children I had pointed out wouldn't be alive in two days. That startled me and all I could think to say was, "Really?"

She nodded and said, "Yes, these kids will be replaced by two others. They are dying faster than we can treat them."

That sure was a smack in the face, but it got worse. As I walked back toward the airplane, I saw a mass grave that apparently had just been dug. It was nothing more than a huge pit where relatives were dropping off loved ones and covering them with dirt to keep diseases from spreading more than they already were. I will always remember a man, probably a grandfather, carrying a young girl toward the grave, the anguish so evident on his face. I say grandfather, because in this huge group the only males were old men or young boys.

—

After that, I had to move on to the next country on our African tour and do the advance work with Timmy, another agent. Problem is, we had to fly whatever airline was available, and thank God, that country wasn't too far away, only a few hours. But, despite the short distance, we had to do a layover and wait for another flight the next day. So, to pass the time, Timmy and I visited the hotel bar, a tiny bar that served nasty beer. One thing we noticed is that each time we ordered a beer, even though it was the same nasty beer, it came in bottles of different shapes and colors with no labels. I finally asked the bartender; he told me they got their bottles from Europe, cleaned them, and put their own local beer in them. Hmm, that's interesting, and I let it go at that, not wanting to know how they cleaned the bottles and how sanitary they might be. We closed our eyes, partook, and got a slight buzz.

The only other guy in the bar was a short African with a heavy accent. A happy guy who was quite drunk and who kept buying us drinks. We intended to have only one, maybe two beers, but he kept sending them down to us. After a while, we declined his beers and offered to buy him a drink. This led to us sitting together and becoming buddies. He kept referring to Timmy as Dimmy and telling him he was the nicest guy he ever met. We had told him we were American businessmen there to close a deal. He told us he always wanted to visit America and all the things he wanted to see. As time passed and it got late, I kept saying thanks for the beers, and that it was nice of him, but we had to get to bed because we were flying out very early in the morning.

As we were easing our way out of the bar, I heard a loud noise. It was the little man; he had fallen from his bar stool, crashing through nearby chairs and onto the floor. Luckily, he didn't bash his head on the stone floor. We ran over and pulled him up, trying to wake him. I asked the bartender who he was and how we might be able to help him. The bartender didn't know him, but he knew the man had taken a room at the hotel. We looked in his pocket for the room key, found it, then carried him to his room. I opened the door, and we brought him in, took off his shoes and laid him on the bed. With that, we bid him goodnight, but he didn't hear because he was still passed out. I tossed the key on the table and we left. Walking to our rooms, we got a laugh out of it, but didn't give it any more thought.

The following morning, there was a knock on the door and it was Timmy. He told me we had a problem. A big problem. I asked if they had canceled our flight. He said, no, the problem was that he still had his gun on him. He had locked it in his suitcase and meant to put the suitcase on the air force plane with Maureen, but instead he had the suitcase with him. Uh-oh, that meant we were going to have to board this little airplane with Timmy carrying a gun. Not good. The embassy was too far away to get their assistance, and Timmy would need his gun in the next country.

We had to get going and catch the plane because we were expected to do the advance work for Maureen's next visit. We decided we'd have to smuggle the gun onto the plane. The thought made us both nervous, because we were in a backward, impoverished country with all sorts of military guys walking around with AK-47 rifles, and we were flying into another country from this one. As we walked across the tarmac to our plane, we were stopped by a military guy who told me to raise my hands. I did, and he patted me down, then he asked for my passport. No problem. Then I turned and looked back at Timmy and he had this horrible look on his face. It was rug-cutting time and he knew it.

Timmy raised his hands for the pat down, and the guy found the gun tucked into his belt in the rear. This caused the guy to start shouting, which brought a flock of other military guys on the run, guns raised. An airline officer butted in and told us we couldn't be carrying a gun, which, of course, we obviously knew. My mind was squirming back and forth: Should I stay with Timmy and get arrested with him, or fly out, try to get someone in authority to intervene for Timmy, then proceed with my job? I decided I couldn't leave Timmy on his own, and I started pleading our case. Then I reached for my Secret Service credentials and my diplomatic passport, but before I could pull them out, I heard this guy yelling from a distance. I turned around and at the top of the stairs to the plane was a guy in a captain's uniform and it's our little drunk buddy. He's yelling, "Dimmy, Dimmy, what are you doing?" Then he starts yelling at the military guys in some foreign dialect and they backed off. He tells them, "Dimmy's my friend, and he can fly in my airplane with his gun." He motions us to come up the steps.

As I was standing there, my jaw dropped to my chest; I was thinking this little drunk guy who fell off the bar stool four or five hours ago is now our pilot on this airplane. Timmy and I looked at each other and our looks told the story. What's worse—going to some horrific jail in this country and then likely being tried for terrorism, or getting on this airplane and flying out with our little drunk pilot? We chose the latter and got on the plane, Timmy with his gun. Once we were on the plane, the pilot said, "I knew you guys weren't businessmen, because *I Spy* [an old TV show] was one of my favorites."

A funny coincidence among the many, as it turns out, one of our pilot's jobs was to bring in all the bottles from Europe for the beer. So, breathing a momentary sigh of relief, but scared of what was to come, we tried to settle in and relax. As the plane taxied, I closed my eyes and prayed like never before. Miraculously, we took off and had a smooth flight. What's more, our little drunk pilot escorted us like royalty through customs in the next country, getting us through, gun intact. I have no doubt, there was divine intervention operating on several levels that day.

—

The trip to one African country is particularly memorable. I was not on the advance team, which was something of a break for me. When we arrived at the airport, members of the advance team who had been in the country came on board before we deplaned. It wasn't safe to talk outside, and we weren't close enough to the embassy, so by default, the plane was the safest place for our orientation. The advance team and the CIA agent told us that, due to an unexpected event, there was a great deal of turmoil in the country, and we were not to treat this as a normal visit (as if our previous visits had been what I would call "normal"). Anyway, they wanted all machine guns out of the cases ready to go, and we were instructed to stay on high alert, which meant a serious 360-degree, "heads on a swivel" mind-set as we traveled to the hotel.

Under no conditions were we allowed to leave the hotel. Big trouble was expected over a defector in hiding that the United States was protecting and was desperate to get out of this country. You can imagine the tension and apprehension of having President Reagan's daughter there, and the fear that, in retaliation, they might try to attack us and kidnap her and use her to exchange for the defector. This necessitated ultra-caution, including requiring that Maureen's visitors come to the hotel, rather than her going out to meet them. Thankfully, the hotel appeared to be more of a fortress than a hotel, surrounded by a high brick wall with jagged metal poles sticking out of the top.

I was told I'd be working the noon to midnight shift, and that we'd be getting out of the country quicker than expected. This meant cutting our visit to only one and a half days, and we had to start prepping to get out of there. As part of the preparations to leave, I was to supervise the motorcade route from the hotel to the airport. The motorcade would consist of an armored limo brought in from a US embassy in Africa, plus a trailing car. Maureen would be in the limo accompanied by agents and more agents would travel behind. I was instructed to scout the route the next morning before my shift. In fact, I was told to examine two different routes, going out on one route and returning on the other.

I met with my team in the hotel lobby and was surprised to see the limo pull up out front with a follow-up vehicle behind it. It struck me that they were being vigilant about this scouting trip, much more than usual, but with the stakes high, I figured it was a good idea to rehearse as closely as possible to real-life conditions. I was informed that the driver from the embassy would drive the limo and not one of our agents. This was because he needed to keep a close eye on things as the limo tended to overheat in the African temperatures and that he would know best what to do to avoid that. Curious, I glanced at the limo, but with tinted windows, I couldn't see anything inside.

Our supervisor jumped in the front passenger seat of the limo. I did the same in the trailing vehicle with one of our agents driving, and two agents in the backseat. One thing that struck me as odd was that the briefcases containing the Uzi machine guns were in the trailing vehicle, rather than stored in our command post in the hotel, which was manned 24 hours a day. Thinking this was an oversight, I made a mental note to be sure to take the guns back later to where they belonged.

We started on the primary route from the hotel to the airport, and we planned to come back on the alternate route. In case something happened that created an emergency, we would already be familiar with a different route to the airport. Although this was a practice run, and Maureen was safe in the hotel, we were warned to be on the highest alert. So, off we went to the Entebbe International Airport. It was the site of a famous incident that occurred on July 4, 1976, when Israeli commandoes successfully carried out a heroic counter-terrorist hostage rescue mission, in which they saved more than a hundred people who had been flown there after a skyjacking.

We entered a manned security gate, and as we passed through, we heard from the limo that we should stay close and we did. But instead of heading toward the airport building, we went in the opposite direction, out onto the tarmac. Okay, perhaps we are going to where the air force plane was to be chocked up, but there were no air force planes in sight. We proceeded out to almost the end of the runway and sat with our flashers on. I figured we were waiting for airport security to come and meet us and take us to wherever they wanted us to go. Moments later, I heard a plane landing, a C-17 US Air Force cargo plane, and as it was landing, the limo in front took off at a high rate of speed and appeared to be following the cargo plane.

Since I was told to follow the limo, that's what we did. The plane was charging down the runway with the limo behind it and we were close behind the limo. "Strange" is the word that came to mind. Then the plane veered off the main runway to the side. The limo stayed close behind, and as we approached, I got a call telling me to keep my distance and stay back about a quarter of a mile. Now I'm thinking this is getting weird, especially since this was supposed to be nothing more than a scouting run to check out routes to the airport.

As the plane slowed, the rear gate opened, and a ramp came down. To my surprise, when the plane stopped, the limo drove up the ramp and onto the plane.

What was going on?

From a distance, I saw the limo stop, the doors fly open, and they popped the trunk. Then, in a flash, the doors and trunk were closed, and the limo backed down the ramp of the plane. Seconds later, the cargo plane was moving down the runway and took off. The looks we exchanged in our car told the story. Then it dawned on us that the defector had been in the limo and we pulled off getting him to the airport and out of the country to a safe place for debriefing by pretending that all we were doing was a practice motorcade run. Smart move. Mission accomplished.

We followed the limo back through the airport security gate and took the alternate route as instructed back to the hotel. We certainly didn't want to deviate from our original plan even though the steps we were taking were no longer necessary. At the hotel, the limo stopped and out came the CIA agent who had briefed us on our arrival, along with a couple of guys who looked like they could handle themselves pretty well, probably former special forces guys contracted by the CIA. They said, "Thanks a lot for the help."

I'm thinking, uh, yeah, sure thing, any time; glad to play a part.

Then they added, "By the way, you guys have to leave today as soon as possible, because there could be retaliation for what we just did, and it could get ugly in a hurry."

I replied quickly, "Roger that, we're ready to get out of here."

—

As we finished up our African tour, we couldn't help but notice how similar the countries were that we visited: the abject poverty and little hope contrasted with the lavish wealth of the few in power. It would be easy to get caught up in this tragedy playing out in front of us, but I had to stay sharp. I had to concentrate on my duties because we never knew who the good guys were and who the bad were. Worse, the tide could shift in either direction instantly, depending upon what was going on at the moment. There were no uniforms, nothing to identify who was who. Having experienced good and bad government forces, and good and bad guerillas fighting for what they believed to be a noble cause, I found it hard to have confidence that we always were in the right place and trusting our lives to the right people. Sounds a little strange, I know, coming from me, someone assigned to do advance work for the protective security detail, but that's the simple truth. And, I suspect even the CIA, who greeted us and briefed us on what to expect, were often shooting from the hip, as well.

All in all, this Africa trip was highly instructive and inspiring for me in many ways. I am thankful for the experience, which renewed my appreciation for how profoundly blessed we are to be born and raised in our wonderful country. I was also thankful for the dedication, energy, and tireless work of Maureen Reagan and her staff, and the efforts and resources of the United States to help these people in any way possible.

CHAPTER 30

PRESIDENT GEORGE H. W. BUSH

A memorable and eventful protection assignment was when President George H. W. Bush traveled to Japan. I was the advance agent and was aboard the Air Force One flight taking President Bush from Tokyo to Kyoto. It was at the end of a grueling ten-day extended tour that took the president through 16 time zones. To say the least, he was fatigued, but when we arrived in Kyoto, he played some vigorous tennis with the American ambassador. When it ended, he came back to his room and made the comment that he wasn't feeling well. After all he had been through, his doctor advised rest to recover and before proceeding with his diplomatic duties, including a state dinner, but President Bush wasn't going to shirk his duties under any circumstances. We were warned that he might not make it through the dinner, and we certainly kept a keen eye on him.

Poor guy was doing the best he could under the circumstances, posing for VIP pictures from photographers and trying to answer questions from journalists, but it was clear he was wearing down quickly. At one point, while posing and trying to smile, he abruptly turned away and threw up in a garbage can, and when he did, he got vomit on his tie as he bent over and it swung forward. His vomiting certainly wasn't humorous, but I had to chuckle when they put out a request on the Secret Service radio asking if any agent had a maroon tie to lend to the president. One guy quickly responded, "Yeah, yeah, I have one." He saved the day, earning in the process bragging rights for coming to the president's rescue.

Next up was the receiving line before dinner in which President Bush had to smile and shake hands with an endless array of dignitaries. I'm not sure how, but he made it through. As for me, I had to coordinate with the Japanese police, which meant heavy negotiations on every item because they were always difficult to get along with. Despite my best efforts and applying every negotiating ploy I knew, they ended up allowing only three Secret Service agents into the large room where President Bush was having dinner. The rest of the detail was kept outside all the doors, ready to respond. There were several Japanese police inside the room, but we couldn't trust how they might respond to a challenging situation.

Knowing what I knew about the president's condition, I was uncomfortable with this arrangement, but there was nothing I could do about it, and I knew from experience that arguing wouldn't do any good. This was frustrating because I usually got along great with authorities, and particularly the local police in almost every other country, but not these guys. With the Japanese police, we called it "three sucks and you're out" negotiations. This meant if you asked them for something like a motorcade alignment or asked to place a tactical team here or there, or assign snipers to the roof, we knew if we got one suck (the lips pursed to make a quick sucking sound), we were probably going to get it done. A double suck meant it was going to be tough to comply with our request, and a triple suck meant it ain't happening.

At dinner, President Bush got through the second course of raw salmon and caviar (imagine eating that if you were feeling ill as he was). When the third course of grilled beef arrived, he pushed his chair back from the table and fainted, his chin falling to his chest. That, of course, was alarming to us, but worse, as he slid to his left, it was obvious he was going to fall out of his chair. At that point, one of our guys, a Secret Service agent, fought through the crowd, pushing past the Japanese police, all of them useless and frozen in place like mannequins, which is exactly what we feared could happen. The agent came to the rescue, vaulting over the table and catching the president before he fell.

We lowered the president to the floor as the White House doctor came rushing up to help. At this tense moment, the president's eyes opened, and typical of him, he told his doctor with a grin, "Roll me under the table until the dinner's over." I loved it and nearly burst out laughing. Moments later, the president got up, still alarmingly pale, but ready to move on, smiling big as if nothing had happened.

Long story short, a national catastrophe was avoided, and he recovered rapidly once we got some fluids in him. You can imagine the field day the media had over this event, including Dana Carvey spoofing President Bush on *Saturday Night Live*. Even so, the president always took such ribbing with good humor, able to laugh at himself, an admirable trait.

On that same Japan trip, as in all overseas trips, we traveled with two Air Force One planes that are identical in every way except for a slightly different tail number on each plane. We flew in on one plane but had to fly out on another. We were told that when they went through all the safety protocols, they didn't like the way one of the engines was acting. As always, extreme caution was exercised, and the decision was made to switch to the backup plane.

After we boarded, President Bush turned to his detail leader and asked, "Why did we switch planes?"

This amazed everyone because the two planes are perfectly identical in every way, and other than the slight difference in the tail numbers, there was no way to tell. But President Bush was a hero pilot during World War II, and we figured that maybe in his DNA, he had a sense for such things. With that, the president studied our faces and a slight smile began to form at the corners of his mouth. He could have let this dangle, and let us speculate about his additional sense, but he didn't. Finally, he grinned and said, "I know because my favorite pen is not in my office desk drawer." Then he added, "And I knew none of you guys would ever touch it, so there was only one explanation that made sense."

We took off and flew in country to another destination to meet with the emperor. We were escorted to an incredible palace, a special place that not many folks have ever entered, but we were permitted to go with the president after we all took off our shoes. I had a funny feeling standing next to the president and taking off my shoes. It reminded me of warnings from my mother to always wear clean underwear and socks without holes, because you never knew when you might be in an accident and end up in the hospital or have to take your shoes off beside the president of the United States. Fortunately, my socks were intact, and my mother would have been proud.

When leaving the palace, cloud cover was low, and it was too foggy to helicopter the 15 or so miles to the airport, so we had to drive. We would prefer not to drive 15 miles on narrow winding roads, but we had no choice. On the way through the countryside, we saw an incredible sight. Lining the road, mile after mile for the full 15 miles, were uniformed Japanese police officers. I have never seen so many officers in a row in my life. I guess they wanted to make sure we made it to the airport without the slightest chance of an incident of any kind.

—

On a different occasion, I was in Taipei, capital city of Taiwan, with George H. W. Bush, who was by then a former president. It was not one of my favorite places to visit, a real hassle getting in and out of the airport and horrible traffic from far too many cars and motorbikes—a zillion of them everywhere we turned, zigzagging in and out of traffic, paying no attention at all to what was going on around them. We'd pull up to a red light and stop, and they would gather around us like a cluster of gnats, hundreds of them gunning their engines and waiting to peel out as soon as possible, the exhaust from all the bikes pouring out and polluting the air.

The former president was invited to play golf, a game that he loved. As an aside, he and his son, George W. were the two fastest golfers I have ever seen, or could imagine seeing, and I've seen a lot of golf and worked security for PGA tours. They literally would jump out of the cart, address the ball quickly, swing, get back in the cart, and were off. They played not only fast, they both were very good golfers, keeping the ball in play and turning in decent scores, all while covering the course in three hours or less.

Two lower level staff members from the embassy were dispatched to accompany former President Bush on his round of golf in Taiwan. As it turned out, these two guys were hackers, and that's being kind. I'm not much of a golfer, but on any given day, I could have beaten either of those bozos easily. They would hit the ball into the rough, then go and hit the ball back to the rough on the opposite side, back and forth, back and forth. I can't imagine how many balls were lost that day, but the count would have been astronomical. Poor President Bush, he was doing a slow steam, wanting to play his game, not as fast as he would with his son, but at least at some reasonable pace. Instead he spent most of his time standing around, waiting on these two knuckleheads who didn't have a clue what they were doing. As my colleagues watched us, they were saying, oh, boy, he's going to be in a terrible mood later after the agony he is experiencing.

The neat thing about this is I was walking fairly close behind the former president, while two other agents were in a golf cart a little way back. Because he was so bored, he ended up turning to me and talking to me throughout the round because there was no one else to talk to. I'd watch him hit, then he'd ask me, "What do you think, a five or six iron?" or whatever. As it turned out, it was a really mixed experience for me. On the one hand, I was on this golf course in the middle of nowhere, saddled with two knuckleheads who should never be allowed on a golf course. But on the other hand, I had a few hours all to myself to chitchat warmly with a former president.

—

Hong Kong was one of President Bush's favorite destinations as he was ambassador to China in the mid-1970s. When he was there, he always seemed to be in a great mood. Plus, he was one of those people who had a keen sense of humor and could pull it off with a straight face. On this trip, he was the former president, and we were staying in the penthouse on the top floor of a gorgeous hotel right in the thick of things in downtown Hong Kong.

I was the lead agent, and as we were leaving his room, he looked over at me and in a serious voice said, "Marshall, I cut this out of a magazine and I thought you might want to share it with the boys, maybe help them out a little bit." He handed me a folded piece of paper and I thanked him.

He called many of us Secret Service agents "Marshall." Over his eight years as vice president, four years as president, and all the years since then as former president, he must have had hundreds of different Secret Service agents protecting him, and it was impossible to keep track of names, so he defaulted to calling us all Marshall.

We walked toward the elevator and as we waited for the doors to open, I unfolded the piece of paper in my hand, curious about what it was. I looked down and read an advertisement in English out of a Hong Kong magazine for tiger penis soup. The ad was real, no doubt, and in all my trips to China, I knew they tended to do things a bit differently and often ate exotic meals, considerably unlike what we have in the United States. According to the ad, eating tiger penis soup increased virility and gave men harder erections.

When I finished reading it, I lifted my eyes and saw former President

Bush looking at me from the corner of his eye, a sly grin on his face, then he gave me a quick wink. I'm sure he didn't want his wife to see it, so I quickly folded it up and put it in my pocket, knowing I'd share it with the guys later. As I said, he had a great sense of humor and we had to be on our toes to catch some of his best stuff because his delivery was dry.

—

Here is one of my all-time favorite memories while serving on a protection detail, and it involves former President Bush and his wife on another trip to Hong Kong.

We were staying in a high-rise hotel after a busy day. It was late, and all was quiet as expected, then an agent saw a break in the door to the Bush suite. It had been opened a crack from the inside, and the agents on duty got nervous because it was 1:30 a.m. They called me to report it. I was still up at the time, so I came charging down the hall. Breathing hard, I'm standing there thinking about what I should do. What were my options? Do I possibly unnecessarily awaken the former president and his wife in the middle of the night because their door was ajar? Could it be caused by a change in air pressure and the door was not securely locked? Should I use the house phone to call them rather than us all rushing in and scaring them? Could it be something about the former president's health? As I was pondering what to do, Barbara Bush came out the door. Highly unusual as there was no place to go, especially dressed as she was in her robe.

I said, "Ma'am, is there something I can help you with?"

I felt somewhat relieved, but there was still the possibility of a problem lurking in the shadows and a second shoe dropping.

Mrs. Bush stopped and glanced up at me with that deep, all-knowing look of hers, shook her head slightly, and replied, "No, son. George is asleep, and I didn't want to disturb him because he has had a demanding day and more of the same tomorrow. But I sure wanted to, because joy of all joys, I found out that we have a brand-new granddaughter, and I needed to tell somebody about it."

I smiled and nodded, as if to confirm that she, indeed, had told someone. Then she stepped toward me, opened her arms wide, and gave me a big hug. She held on, her arms pulling me in, and I thought, wow, this is amazing. I hugged her back, not in the least self-conscious, which surprised me. So, there we were, an unlikely pair hugging in a hotel hallway in the middle of the night. Then, a moment later, she eased her grip, stepped back to arms' length and said, "Thank you." With that, she turned and went back inside the door.

It was a strange and wonderful moment that made me feel warm inside. As strict and formal as the Chinese are, especially around dignitaries, my Hong Kong police colleagues were awestruck by the whole thing.

CHAPTER 31

PRESIDENT BILL CLINTON

I was assigned to Hawaii, the office in Honolulu, and Bill Clinton loved visiting there while he was president. He loved playing golf, and for several reasons, I used to get a kick out of following him around the golf course, even though it was a lot of work on our part. In advance of his game, we had to make all the preparations, including closing down part of the golf course and assigning agents strategically, with plainclothes guys, uniforms, snipers, K-9s, you name it. Our goal was to give him as much privacy as possible, while still protecting him to the max. On each hole, we'd send a couple of guys, one on each side of the fairway standing in the rough, about 200 yards from the tee to watch the flight of the ball. Their job was not to track the ball, but they knew where it was.

That night, the Clintons were at a fancy formal dinner with the governor of Hawaii who had played golf with President Clinton earlier in the day, and they were talking about their golf game. As they talked, Hillary Clinton was sitting nearby listening while the president was pontificating about how well his golf game went. Finally, I guess she could no longer contain herself. She leaned forward and spoke loud enough to command attention. "Bill really likes playing golf, especially with his best friend."

She let that hang a moment, and everyone looked at her, wondering what she meant. Who was his best friend? The president finally asked her what she was talking about. She responded with, "You know, your best friend, Mr. Mulligan."

All golfers know exactly what this means and everyone, including us agents, broke up in belly laughs. President Clinton, on the other hand, gave Hillary a look that, if looks could kill, would have wiped out a small town.

Hillary had launched quite a zinger at her husband, and it's fair to say that it didn't necessarily seem to be purely in the spirit of good humor. A mulligan means a second chance, a do-over when there is bad luck of some sort, often governed by the golfers themselves. In this context, Hillary was, of course, referring to her husband's well known self-determined mulligans, his decisions about which strokes counted and which to ignore.

—

I was again in Hawaii with the Clintons for Hillary's birthday. We took off in a helicopter from Honolulu to the big island of Hawaii to a posh resort, nicely secluded with cabins spread about, and we, of course, had the area secured in advance. Hillary's staff was throwing her a little party, and the president, Hillary, and Chelsea were there, plus the staffers. One thing that was striking about the event was the trepidation among staffers because they couldn't determine the kind of cake that Hillary liked.

You'd think being in paradise and surrounded by profound luxury and sharing it with family members would be cause for celebration and there wouldn't be a care in the world. But, frankly, everyone knew from experience that Hillary could be tough on her staff, and that was her reputation. But now, in retrospect and thinking about this more deeply and objectively, my sense is that Hillary Clinton is a perfectionist, who drives herself relentlessly with incredible demands. In turn, because she expects so much of herself, it's natural that some of those expectations would spill over to others, especially those closest to her. This could cause resentment. In my case, I never had a problem with Mrs. Clinton.

On another occasion, there was an amusing scene as they set up a scenario where President Clinton would be photographed jogging along with palm trees lining the road, an ideal setting. He ran maybe about 60 or 70 yards, as we followed him in our cars. After running this distance, he veered into a McDonald's restaurant and ordered a Big Mac, fries, and Coke, and we all poured in behind him. I guess the lesson is what you see in the press or on TV isn't always what it appears to be.

President Clinton was a regular jogger and the staged scene described above was intended to convey that to the public. Unfortunately, he also had a voracious appetite for unhealthy foods and apparently seemed to think that jogging protected his heart from the relentless assault of all those Big Macs, fries, and ribs. Not so, and his diet caught up with him, causing him to undergo quadruple coronary artery bypass surgery in 2004. That wakeup call caught his attention and he became a vegan and lost 30 pounds, which he credits for keeping him alive.

—

I vividly recall two experiences in Hawaii with President Clinton, one very positive, the other not so much. The first story is about two hikers who were lost in the mountains and the rescue efforts to try to find them before it got dark. I was close to members of the Honolulu Police Department SWAT team and had done quite a bit of high-level training with them over my six years there. I considered many of them to be good friends, and two of them went up in a helicopter to search. They were in a large basket hanging from the helicopter, a precarious position to be sure, but these two guys were fun-loving thrill seekers and they were in hog heaven. While in flight, something malfunctioned with the helicopter, might have been the little rotor on the back, and it caused the helicopter to start spinning out of control, which caused the basket to swing wildly, throwing the two police officers out to their deaths.

A real tragedy on several levels. I lost two friends, plus the Honolulu

PD always strongly supported us agents on our protection duties, going out of their way to make our life easier, and I felt a huge debt to them. The accident happened a few days before President Clinton arrived for one of his visits. He arrived right after the funeral, which of course, was quite difficult for the families. Each officer was married and had small children, ages three to six. When the president arrived, it occurred to me that it would be a comforting gesture if he would take a moment and speak to the two young widows, saying something about the valuable service their husbands provided and how appreciated it was.

To try to make this happen, I spoke to Clinton's head staff guy and asked if he would consider saying something to the president about it. I hated asking the staff for anything because of the ongoing natural friction between the staff and Secret Service agents, and the constant butting of heads. This is always the case, regardless of who the president is. The staff seek photo opportunities and want the president to press the flesh with the public and be seen as friendly and fully accessible, while agents worry about security issues and the risks involved when he is exposed. But, I sucked it up and asked the staff guy, and he immediately blew me off. I persisted and told him we needed only a few minutes of the president's time, and no matter how brief, the gesture would be highly significant.

The president was visiting a huge army base on this trip, talking to generals and such, and I collared the staff guy again, and told him that the widows and children were in one of the rooms down the hall, and if the president could just poke his head in and utter a few words, amounting to about 10 seconds, that would be great. Well, apparently, my efforts paid off and this was mentioned to the president.

He walked up to me and said, "Is this where the deceased officers' families are?"

I responded, "Yes, Mr. President," and I opened the door to the room and the president entered, along with his head staff guy.

President Clinton was great with the families, and you'd think he had all the time in the world. In fact, he told the staff guy to step outside because he was going to be there a while, which annoyed his staff guy who was chewing nails and staring hatefully at me. The children had several leis made of flowers. In Hawaiian culture, it's common for children to refer to adult friends as "uncle," so they were calling the president "uncle" and having him bend forward, hugging him, and placing leis around his neck. It was beautiful to watch, and I was so appreciative, and if big bad Secret Service agents ever cried, that would have been the moment.

One of the kids asked the president if he could see the plane, Air Force One. President Clinton looked over at me and said, "You take care of that, agent. I want them to get a tour of the plane, and I'll get there a little early."

True to his word, he arrived early, and took the families on a personally guided tour of the airplane. When it was time to go, he stood at the top of the stairs with the families, waving at the crowd, and pictures were taken that appeared on the front page of the Honolulu newspaper. This was President Clinton at his best, and from that day, I always felt deeply indebted to him for doing that.

I mentioned a second experience with the president that was not so pleasant. This was on a different visit to Hawaii. At the time, I was close to members of the Honolulu full-time SWAT team who worked temporary assignments on some protection details with me. In addition, I got close to members of the Honolulu PD motorcycle unit. I always had a motorcycle and enjoyed riding a Harley Davidson, a big old hog. I'd ride with a group, as many as a dozen HPD officers, on Sundays. These relationships blossomed as well, and eventually, some of the members worked on the police motorcycle escort for my protection details.

On this occasion, we had had a hectic and very full and long day with President Clinton. On such days, I always tried to release the HPD motorcycle guys as early as I could once I knew the protectees were in for the night, because they had to travel some distance to get home, and we had to reload and do it again early the next morning. I finally was able to release the motorcycle guys well after midnight, but before they left, I asked a staffer about the itinerary for the next day, and specifically any plans for the morning. But I couldn't get an answer, because I guess he couldn't get an answer. I kept bugging him because we had to know to get set for the next day, and I couldn't let the motorcycles guys go before we got this information. Finally, the staffer informed me that the president would be going for a jog at seven in the morning. That meant the motorcycles had to be there an hour earlier, just in case. I hated to tell them, but their response was, "No problem; that's okay, Greg. That's the job."

That night we all got only a few hours of sleep, then were up and on the job again at six, ready for duty. The appointed time arrived, seven a.m., and no president. Then it was eight, then ten, then noon, then on through the afternoon with nothing going on, then finally at seven p.m., we got word that the president wouldn't be going anywhere and was in for the day. Secret Service agents are always around, we are housed nearby, and we can switch on and off with others. The motorcycle guys, however, didn't have that luxury, which meant they sat there waiting for 13 hours on very little sleep because no one alerted us about what was going on.

I realize it seems like a small thing, and for the most part, it was. But it would have taken only a few seconds for his staff to set things right, to avoid needlessly inconveniencing an entire group of fatigued, hard-working and dedicated professionals.

—

Here are two more examples of the ups and downs of serving during the Clinton presidency. The first case was a ceremony commemorating the end of World War II, and it was held in Hawaii. President Clinton was to make the rounds of all the military bases, and for such occasions, the military does extensive planning, and nothing is left to chance. An important wrap-up meeting was to be conducted to ensure all was in place for President Clinton's arrival and participation in the event. The meeting was held at a nice hotel near Waikiki Beach. From a protection perspective, a presidential visit, and especially on a big special occasion, is as big as it gets. If it's overnight, it's bigger, and if it goes for three or four days, as it would on this occasion, it's humongous.

In attendance at the meeting were the local police, firefighters, sheriff's office, a lot of high-ranking military brass, and of course, the Secret Service detail. Quite a group. A critically important part of the planning process was knowing the president's itinerary, especially arrival times. It was no secret that President Clinton was famous for never staying on schedule and for being late, often really late, which, of course, clashed badly with military precision when planning.

At this meeting set for seven in the evening, it was expected that as lead agent on the Secret Service detail, I would know the president's itinerary, and, in fact, everyone kept asking me, because that was the starting point for everything else. I hadn't been informed, which was typical, and this meant we had to wait for Clinton staff members to show up with the news. Having worked with his staff, I honestly wasn't optimistic that this would go well, but I hoped for the best, which seemed increasingly more naïve as we moved beyond the starting time for the meeting.

Making high-ranking military officers wait is not a good thing, and I could feel the temperature of the room rise minute by minute. Finally, nearly an hour late, these two knuckleheads from Clinton's staff stumble into the room drunk, wearing flip-flops and tank tops, badly sunburned, and they could hardly complete a meaningful sentence. I glanced over at a two-star general standing beside me, and he was livid, boiling hot. He looked back at me and frowned. Without a word, his eyes scanned the room, stopping at each person gathered there, everyone spruced up in dress uniforms or suits and looking spiffy, then his eyes landed on the two staff members. Under his breath and obviously keeping a lid on his frustration and repulsion at what he saw, he mumbled something I won't repeat here.

On the positive side, President Clinton and his staff could surprise us in the most endearing ways. An another occasion, I was working with a one-star Air Force general that I liked and respected greatly. It so happens we were on a golf course, and as we walked, I carried out my instructions to guide him toward a little tent that was set up on the side. He gave me a questioning look, but went ahead and entered, and when he did, President Clinton entered the tent from the opposite side with the general's wife. He greeted the general warmly, and with that captivating gift he had of making people feel that they were the most special person in the entire world, he congratulated him and pinned on his second star. I was deeply impressed at the cool way he carried that off, so creative and certainly memorable. Bravo to you, President Clinton.

—

One thing about being a Secret Service agent was the never-ending array of new experiences. Part of the planning process for the ceremony commemorating the end of World War II involved transporting our advance team to a Navy ship that would be in Pearl Harbor. The only way we could do our advance work was to go out to the ship, which at the time, was a couple hundred miles off shore in the Pacific. This involved landing on an aircraft carrier, the USS *Carl Vinson*, a Nimitz-class super carrier. I boarded a plane and took off for a flight of an hour or so to the ship. Soon I could see the fleet below. I say fleet, because aircraft carriers always travel with extreme protection, including destroyers, battleships, and submarines.

As the plane approached the fleet, naively I expected that we would pass over the ship, then circle around and gently make our descent. To my great surprise, as we approached, the pilot literally dropped the plane out of the sky, cutting power and allowing us to freefall. It felt like flashing over the top on a fierce roller coaster and then going down 10 times faster; I had the unnerving sense that at any moment I was about to be flung out. No words were said, but I think the pilot was having fun with me as he cut it back hard to the left into a "U" turn and as he straightened out, bam, he hit the deck of the carrier. The impact was incredible, then I felt the deck cable grab the hook underneath the plane, which brought us to a dead stop; the feeling was akin to having your intestines yanked out of your body.

In general, I don't have the strongest stomach around, and this got to me. As I got off the plane, I was horrified to think that I might lose my breakfast. This called for some serious self-talk: Man, I can't lose it in front of these sailors and look like a weenie and have them laughing behind my back at the big tough Secret Service guy messing up the deck.

Not sure how I did it, other than simply willing myself to keep my food down, and it worked, but I'm sure I looked pale and iffy for a few hours. Regardless, I kept working, no excuses.

When I began feeling human again, I was able to appreciate the magnificent ship with six thousand crew members on board, a floating city. The deck was impressive with all the planes and helicopters and such, the crew members dressed like Fruit of the Loom characters in different colors—purple, green, red, blue—and each color with a specific job to do, all of them scurrying around like ants. Below deck were five or six more levels. It was a maze, and once you make a couple of turns, you have no way of knowing where you are, front or back, left or right. As you can imagine, this complicated planning for where the president would board, where he would go, and so on. And things were made even more complicated because when the ship arrived in Pearl Harbor, the show was on and there was no opportunity for a dress rehearsal. We had to get it right the first time.

When I boarded the plane to leave the ship, I was told I would experience a lot of g-force when the plane took off from the deck. I looked and thought there was no way the deck runway was long enough to get the plane up in the air, but I put myself in God's hands and hoped for the best. The pilot revved up and told me to put my head down and cross my arms over my chest to prevent my head from snapping back. Finally, after revving it to the max, they released it and, for several seconds, we exploded forward, the adrenalin rush incomparable. We actually dropped below the deck when we hit the end of the runway and were right over the water, then we took off and gained altitude for the trip home.

Before joining the FBI, my dad was a football coach at U of L and a top recruiter. Among his recruits was Johnny Unitas. In 1979, Johnny chose my dad to deliver his introduction to the Pro Football Hall of Fame in Canton, Ohio. Quite an honor.

Like father, like sons. My dad, Frank, my older brother (also named Frank) and me (# 85) during our football-playing days at the University of Louisville. My dad was a star quarterback at the University of Louisville and was inducted into the U of L Hall of Fame.

My look as a store detective and later as an undercover cop. Pretty convincing, huh?

My police mug shot—it was useful if anybody checked to see if I was an undercover cop. Jefferson County Police Department

Graduation day from the police academy
(1977). I couldn't wait to hit the streets.

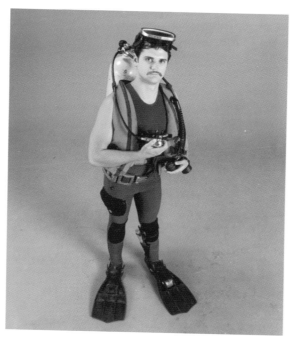

I was the youngest member of a newly formed Jefferson
County Police scuba diving team. Emergency dives into a
frozen Ohio River in the middle of winter are as scary as that
sounds. Recruitment poster, Jefferson County Police Department

**KENTUCKY
TRAFFIC ACCIDENT FACTS
1979**

You know you've made the big time when you appear on the front cover of the *Kentucky Traffic Accident Facts* magazine.

The Jefferson County Police Department
Jefferson County, Kentucky

A Challenge.
An Opportunity.
A Diverse Career.

A police-recruiting poster shows the many hats cops can wear, including beat cop, EMT, SWAT, motorcycle, canine, dive team, and my favorite, undercover.

Recruitment poster, Jefferson County Police Department

New York City, working out of a 9/11 US Secret Service command post

New York City, working with the Counter Surveillance Unit for the first anniversary of 9/11

Slugger from Australia (on my right), Chan from Hong Kong (on my left), and I worked on numerous international million-dollar credit card cases together. Thanks to our mutual trust, we avoided a lot of red tape, and we arrested and prosecuted numerous international fraud criminals.

It was the assignment of a lifetime: Secret Service detail agent for Pope John Paul II on his visit to the United States. His specially designed vehicle was referred to as the "Popemobile."

I helped protect Pope John Paul II at Papal Mass in St. Louis with more than 100,000 turbo-charged people in attendance.

Pope John Paul II went out of his way to thank his security detail.

I seized the opportunity to kiss the Pope's ring, much to the surprise of everyone in attendance, including Vice President Al Gore and his wife, Tipper.

Finally, a family man and a dad

It's a rare occasion that I get the opportunity to relax and unwind with my daughter, Madison.

The Gitschier family is complete. At the time, it was quite a juggling act with two demanding careers, crazy schedules, and raising three youngsters. It would have been impossible without my wonderful mother-in-law; she was the glue that held it all together. We call her Tutu, the Hawaiian word for grandmother, as our oldest child was born in Hawaii.

Wow! How time flies. One minute the kids are toddlers, and the next they are asking for the car keys. I am a truly blessed and lucky man. Left to right: Brandon, Madison, Greg, Tracy, and Gregory.

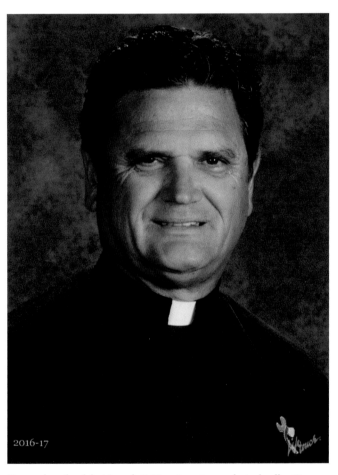

2016-17

It was a long haul, but I made it. Here I am in my clerical collar, Deacon Greg Gitschier.

In my role as deacon, I help celebrate Mass. In this photo, I am
assisting Archbishop Joseph Kurtz at a televised Mass of the Air.

The St. Patrick archery team qualified to compete at the world championships. I helped
them raise money for their trip, and they surprised me at Mass with a check to Kids
Cancer Alliance. Let me add a big thank-you to Jennifer Lawrence, who signed a bow
that was raffled off to raise funds.

A teenage Jennifer Lawrence poses with Patrick, one of our Kids Cancer Alliance campers. Patrick was nicknamed the fighting Irishman, because as a youngster he had survived seven onslaughts of cancer, and each time, he miraculously survived.

Jennifer Lawrence with Patrick seven years later at a U of L basketball game. Patrick was in the crowd, and when they announced that Jen was in attendance, he sent me the earlier picture by phone. I showed it to Jen and she recognized him immediately. She was so excited, and she insisted that I go and get him and bring him up to visit with her.

In my role as bodyguard for Jennifer Lawrence during her annual Christmas hospital visit with children suffering from cancer

I have helped protect the two owners of Vineyard Vines, Shep and Ian Murray, for the past five years at the Kentucky Derby. We have developed a very close relationship, since they donate many Vineyard Vines items to support our Kids Cancer Alliance camp every summer. Photo courtesy of Scott Henson

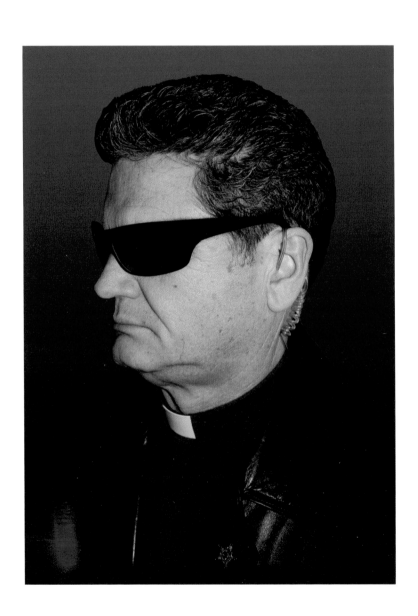

CHAPTER 32

PANIC IN THE PROMISED LAND

Throughout an agent's career in the Secret Service, even when he or she has finished a stint of full-time protection work—being a bodyguard every day for three to five years—then goes back into investigations and works counterfeit money cases, threats against the president, or big fraud cases, the agent can still get called back into protection work at any time. "ROTA" stands for rotation; an agent is told not to make any personal plans for a particular month because he or she is on call and likely on a protection assignment. We know in advance when our ROTA months are going to be.

On one of my ROTA calls, I was assigned as shift leader for National Security Advisor Sandy Berger; he was regularly briefed by all the intelligence agencies on the state of the world and what threats are anticipated. He required Secret Service protection because his job included dealing with terrorists. On this occasion, I flew to Israel with President Clinton on Air Force One and Advisor Berger was included under the umbrella of President Clinton's security detail. We arrived at the airport early in the morning, maybe about two or three o'clock, and motorcaded into Jerusalem.

It had been a fatiguing flight, and I looked forward to grabbing some sleep, but I had to be alert on the drive, which was barren and uninspiring. The landscape in the dim light was full of rocks and not much greenery; *harsh* was the word that came to mind. Since we were traveling at an early hour, there was very little traffic and we made good time to our hotel, where we were told to grab some sleep. But it wouldn't be much because we had an early morning briefing lined up.

When I woke up, I was groggy, a natural state on this job, so I immediately sought out the strongest coffee I could find, then started to make my way to the briefing location at another hotel. It was a nice day, sunny and clear as I made my way through the modern section of Jerusalem, not the old section often shown on TV. This part of the city looked like any other large city around the world, cosmopolitan with all the hustle and bustle.

As I walked, two teenage girls, probably around 18 years old, were coming toward me. They looked like typical teenagers in America, with one exception. As they walked by me, I noticed each had a sling over her shoulder and in the sling was an M-16 rifle. I thought, wow; that's unusual. As it turns out, it was. Later, I was informed that since the US president was in town, everyone was on standby. In Israel, everyone does a stint in the military, so I assumed the two teenagers were likely to be National Guard-type folks.

At the briefing, we were told we were headed to Bethlehem and the Gaza Strip, the place featured on TV quite frequently, over the next two days. Typically, news stories involved some conflict with the PLO, the Palestine Liberation Organization, and attacks on Israeli soldiers who would respond in kind. I looked forward to the visit, notwithstanding the risks involved, because it was a first for me. Also, I'm a history buff, and I was surrounded by history.

I had a few hours to kill before I had to go into work that afternoon, so I decided to do a little sightseeing in downtown Old Jerusalem. I was only another tourist tooling around the shops and such. I headed toward the Wailing Wall, one of the city's most famous tourist locations. As I strolled along, someone must have brushed up against me at some point and sensed or detected that I possibly had a concealed weapon. I didn't know that I had been fingered, of course, and as I was leaving the Wailing

Wall area, I noticed two police officers walking toward me, then a car cut me off, and two additional officers came up behind me.

They were official looking and they meant business, so my hands went straight up. I told them I was with the US delegation, part of the Secret Service, and I showed them my credentials. They took my stuff and called it in. Then I was told someone had reported that I might have a gun. I told them I did indeed have a gun, because I didn't want to leave it in my hotel room. The lead officer looked me up and down, then finally told me it wasn't a problem. I responded, "Great job. You guys are professional and I appreciate what you do." That was it. As I walked away, I thought how different it was to live under constant threat as they do, and how everyone was tuned in to the relentless potential for danger, versus how naïve and trusting we are in the United States. I like our way of life better, and we all should appreciate how blessed we are and how good we have it.

My sightseeing was sandwiched between meetings and typical security preparations for the next day. We were to be part of the detail that took the president from the helicopter landing zone in a motorcade into the Gaza Strip and PLO territory. Everything, as always, was planned to the smallest detail, but even more intricately in this location, and we were whisked through all the border checkpoints like clockwork. It was a gorgeous, bright, sunny day with blue skies, and everyone was apparently given little American flags, because as we came pulling in, everyone was waving flags at us. A cool welcome.

We ended up spending the day there, and it was uneventful: everything proceeded as planned. At the end of the day, we were to go to an arena with President Clinton and the national security advisor for a meeting with Yasser Arafat, leader of the PLO. At the time, he was probably the most infamous of the Arabic leaders, known to be the main terrorist in that part of the world. But we were his guests, and we felt like guests.

We made our way into the arena. We planned to leave before it got dark outside. While there was sunlight and Israeli jets were flying close overhead, all was well, but that could change immediately. In the darkness, we'd lose our ability to clearly see what was going on, and we'd lose our military support. The speeches went on and on and on, and the next thing we knew, it was getting dark. But in our position, we couldn't interrupt the president and tell him to hurry up and leave right away to ensure his safety.

The president stayed much longer than we expected, and it got dark. We needed to get out of the downtown area as quickly as possible. The whole idea was to get the president in the car and zip out of there and through the various checkpoints as fast as possible, and on to the landing zone and the helicopter. From there, another crew would have to pick up the cars and bring them back to Jerusalem, because I was assigned to fly on the helicopter.

Finally, as we contemplated the multitude of things that could go wrong, we got word that the event was wrapping up. One of the guys on the CAT team came over to us and told us they were a man down in strength and needed a fill-in. CAT is the counter-assault team, essentially the presidential SWAT team; they have special forces training that prepares them for any kind of attack from anywhere. Now, these guys are what we call high-speed, low-drag kind of guys: extremely well trained, in great shape physically, and good shots, and anyone who stepped into the fold with them would be expected to hold his own.

As it turned out, they asked me to fill in and help cover one side on the rear of the motorcade as it pulled out. My friend was a supervisor with those guys, and I told him, no problem, happy to do it. I asked, what's the plan? He said that the second-to-last car before the PLO police car was a white van, and when it slowed down, the doors would be open, and we were to run and leap into the vehicle, then slam the doors shut, and roll out with the motorcade. This was not unusual, and we had trained to do this exact thing many times over the years.

I was covering my left flank when the president came out and everyone was rushing around, nervous because it was dark, and anything could happen. As the cars pulled out, we were looking away from the cars to cover behind us. As they moved along, in my peripheral vision, I could see the white van slowing down, and as it slowed down, sliding doors on both sides of the van slid shut. Apparently, the driver, who was one of their guys, assumed we had already jumped in, and he took off, leaving us there.

My friend and I looked at each other with expressions of *this is not a good situation at all.* As we watched those taillights disappear into the darkness, we knew we were up the creek and had to do something fast. We both slipped our machine guns (MP-5s in those days) under our suit jackets, but since we were dressed in suits and looked like Secret Service agents, we stood out in the massive crowd like neon signs in a coal mine and had to get away as quickly as possible.

We headed to the back of the arena, trying to lay low and figure out a plan. One of the female staff members from Arafat's office recognized us and told us, you know you can't be here. We're like, yeah, we know that, and we know that being stuck in a foreign country unfriendly to the United States, having no passports, and carrying machine guns is not a good thing.

We were desperate to figure out what to do, and about that time, here came a white Suburban around the corner, so we ran out and stopped it. Arafat's aide told us we couldn't take that car, but we jumped into the backseat anyway. I remember that the car was brand-new and the backseat still had the clear plastic on it. We told the driver to take us to the soccer field, which was the loading zone where the helicopters waited for departure. We were mere minutes behind the motorcade, but we knew that once the president was onboard, they weren't going to stay around long.

We told the driver we needed to get going, but he told us he couldn't. I said you must drive now, to which he replied that they would shoot at him if he tried to drive through the blockade. We basically hijacked his car and I told him not to stop for any reason, just keep driving.

As we drove toward the blockade, I could see the driver's hands trembling as they clutched the steering wheel, but to his credit, he didn't slow down. We approached the blockade, my heart in my throat, wondering how we'd explain all this if we got stopped. Fortunately, I guess we must have looked official because they didn't stop us, and we drove around the blockade. We sped up from there and made it in the nick of time to the loading zone. The first chopper had already taken off, the second was getting ready to leave, which left a third and fourth sitting there with the big rotor blades turning.

We jumped out of the car, thanked the driver for the lift as we departed, and then we had to run as fast as we could across a muddy soccer field at night in our dress shoes and suits because we sure didn't want to miss our ride. By the time we got to the 'copters, the second one was gone and the third was revving up and ready. As we approached, we saw the chief on the helicopter give us a signal with his fingers slashing across his throat, meaning we couldn't board. He pointed to the fourth 'copter, so we dashed around underneath the spinning blades to that one as the third one took off. This was our last shot.

As we approached, the loadmaster stopped us and told us he couldn't take us because the 'copter would be overweight. We said, "Look, we've got to get on this chopper, one way or the other. We have nowhere to go, no place to stay and we can't be here." He apologized but emphasized the need to adhere to the weight limit and that he couldn't put everyone on the helicopter at risk. There were probably 15 people in the chopper, sitting in a line on each side. The thing was loaded to the max.

One of the agents was assigned to the liaison division, which meant he was essentially herding and babysitting congressional delegates (senators and members of congress); they were known as "co-dels." Now, when a politician goes overseas, they'll take other members of Congress with them. Not sure how much work they do, and these people on the chopper had big shopping bags filled with items from shops in the Palestine area. To our surprise, the liaison agent suddenly stood up and told the group that two of them had to get off because it was more important to take us, two Secret Service agents. A bit stunned, they all looked around; no one wanted to get off. Now, here's the catch. They had gotten to the arena in a motorcade that took three or four hours, but now they were jumping on the 'copters for a quicker return trip.

At issue was the fact that my friend and I had two immense liabilities. One: we didn't have our passports with us. And, two: we were carrying machine guns. There was no way we were going to be able to pass through all the checkpoints on the way to Jerusalem, some 50 miles away. When we were stopped at the first checkpoint and they discovered us, we would be yanked out of the car and taken who knows where. After that, who knows what might have happened, but it was a mess that could easily escalate into an international incident.

On the other side of the coin, the co-dels didn't have a problem, other than they wanted to avoid the several-hour drive over bad roads and multiple checkpoints, and they preferred taking the helicopter. So, it boiled down to their willingness to experience some discomfort versus our being exposed to extreme risk. Amazing what people will do to avoid discomfort, and it became a standoff when none of the co-dels stood up.

I could see the look on the agent's face and it was clear the selfishness of the co-dels was getting under his skin. So, he told them in no uncertain terms that he was only going to ask one more time, and if two of them did not get up and walk off the helicopter, he would personally take them off. He added that my friend and I were trying to do our jobs and protect them, the American delegation. He said what I think is the greatest line I have ever heard from a bodyguard: "We are here to protect your ass, not to kiss it. So, get off this @#$*% chopper now."

It worked and two of them stepped down and ended the incident, which could have gotten ugly. My friend and I boarded, sat down, buckled our seat belts, then took off for the 30-minute flight back to Jerusalem. It was beautiful at night from the air, and especially beautiful to us after what we had experienced. I've always felt indebted to that agent, who had an outstanding reputation and, in my opinion, was one of the legends of the Secret Service.

CHAPTER 33

PRESIDENT GEORGE W. BUSH AND VP DICK CHENEY

I didn't spend much time with President George W. Bush, as it was later in my career and my duties had changed somewhat, but the time I did spend in his presence was quite pleasant. Presidents Reagan, Ford, George H. W. Bush, and George W. Bush were honest-to-goodness nice people who treated everyone around them with respect and as equals. That's saying a lot when you consider you are talking about the president of the United States, but it's true. Each of these fine gentlemen had only one face and it was the same one you saw on TV, at photo opportunities, press conferences, or walking down the hall in the White House. The same was true for Laura Bush, a nice, high-quality woman who was always courteous and respectful to everyone who crossed her path, no matter his or her station in life. Clearly, I was blessed to spend most of my protections detail time with such high-quality folks.

Right after 9/11, I was involved with what was called a counter-surveillance unit (CSU) that was a smart move on the part of the Secret Service. Our main job was to keep track of anyone who might be watching us while doing our advance work for a presidential visit, because we thought during the year after 9/11, the terrorists might try to hit us again. At this time, President George W. Bush was coming to New York City, and a female agent and I acted like we were a couple of tourists walking about and taking pictures, keenly alert to see if anyone was watching us as we did our advance work. At other times, we kept an eye on everyone, particularly staff members. For example, if the president's staff was in the hotel lobby and talking too loud on the phone or with other staff members about sensitive issues, or if they happened to leave behind any papers, it was our job to intervene discreetly. I liked this type of work and volunteered for it often.

I enjoyed my trips to the presidential ranch in Midland, Texas. It was a huge, 1,600-acre spread, but like the Reagan ranch house, the Bush homestead was quite modest, and you would never guess it was inhabited by the most powerful man in the world. The ranch was loaded with cattle that belonged to someone leasing the land. Gazing out at the massive herd reinforced the fact that we were, indeed, in Texas. At night, if we looked up in the sky we could see what looked like stars moving in circles, but actually they were our air cover protecting the president from anyone trying to invade his space from above with any type of aircraft. I thought, gee, that must be a boring assignment for those jet-fighter pilots, all of them alpha-dog jocks, flying around in big circles all night long protecting the president's residence far below.

George W.'s way of relaxing and blowing off steam was clearing brush and using a chain saw. Similarly, President Reagan enjoyed vigorous and challenging physical work, like chopping firewood, and both could work for hours. But we worried about the potential for an accident when watching that chain saw in action. Chain saws can kick back, or the slightest distraction can cause the user to misplace the saw and get cut, and with a chain saw, no cut is minor. Plus, we were quite a distance from the nearest hospital.

This required having highly trained medical staff on hand, and not run-of-the mill paramedics. Air Force PJs, para-rescue jumpers, were used—guys who jumped out of helicopters and went behind enemy lines to rescue downed pilots. Not only were they super paramedics, they were also tactical fighters. A good friend of mine, in fact, received a Silver Star, the second highest commendation awarded in military service, for his efforts to rescue other special forces guys. Just an awesome group, incredibly well trained, brave, and real gentlemen besides.

One time when I was at the Midland ranch, George W. was preparing for his morning run. Now, let me tell you, he ran at a blistering pace, and typical agents couldn't keep up with him. In fact, we learned early on when he was campaigning for president, that the guys who tried to run with him couldn't keep up no matter how hard they tried, especially carrying a gun and radio. This meant we had to go out and get men we called rabbits, athletes who ran track in college.

On this morning, the rabbits were out there warming up at sunrise, the typical time George W. preferred to run, and a scout team went out in advance to secure the area. Even though the run would take place on the ranch, we had to make sure no one had breached the perimeter. Unlikely, but anything was possible, and we always had to keep that in mind. The scout team was in a typical Secret Service black Suburban, and because they were on a ranch in Texas, they kicked up a bunch of dust, which lingered quite a while. So, here came the president for his run, and he looked at this looming cloud of dust, knowing he couldn't take off and run into it while breathing deeply. This was the first time I ever saw him visibly upset, as were the supervisors, who chewed out the agents in the SUV because they should have been out a half hour earlier and not right before the run. But, George W. didn't say much, and he let it go quickly, which says a lot about him. The kind of schedule presidents keep, whether at home or at the White House, is jam-packed from morning to night, every minute is valuable, and wasting time when it comes to rare moments of relaxation and recreation is not a small thing, especially for the agents who caused it.

As far as getting an up-close-and-personal glimpse of what's inside a president, George W. came to Louisville one time and toured the Louisville Slugger Museum and Factory. I did the advance work, and it was a fun event. No doubt, President George W. Bush was having the best time, clearly in his element as someone who loves baseball, deeply absorbed by all the exhibits, grinning and laughing like a kid in a candy store. They crafted a special bat for him with his name on it, and also manufactured PowerBilt golf clubs and equipment, and a personalized golf bag. Unfortunately, someone misspelled his name, but they caught it in the nick of time before they gave it to him, saving all kinds of embarrassment.

—

I had an encounter with President Bush's vice president, Dick Cheney, that allowed me access to him in a personal way. Vice President Cheney didn't come off as the soft and cuddly type. In fact, most who have watched him on TV might say they've never seen him smile and that he is much more apt to snarl. I admit that that was my expectation. In 2000, I had been assigned as the head of the small Lexington, Kentucky, office, and during my time there, we had the first vice presidential debate between candidates Cheney and Senator Joe Lieberman at Centre College in Danville, Kentucky.

My job was to take the lead and prepare everything to ensure the safety of the event, a task that took months of meetings and working out all the logistics, including motorcades, venues, you name it. Each candidate had their own protection detail, and it was my job to coordinate efforts with them and make sure we all got along for the greater good.

When Mr. Cheney arrived, I was introduced to him by his detail leader. This, of course, is the necessary and obvious exception to the rule of not speaking unless spoken to, and I had no idea what to expect. Predictably, he didn't smile as he looked me square in the eyes and said, "Agent, you don't know me." He paused a moment, and I thought, uh-oh, here it comes. Then he said, "And I don't want you to think that I am ever being rude or disrespectful toward you or any of your colleagues, but I am a quiet man who doesn't say a whole lot. I am deeply appreciative of the great work the Secret Service does, and I know you will do a fine job. So please don't take offense that I don't often speak or interact with many people."

Taken aback by his gracious words and demeanor, I swallowed hard and said, "Yes, sir, I understand completely."

I passed along his message to all my guys not to see him as rude, but rather quiet and reserved. And he was, for sure.

The debate went off without a hitch, and it was a great event that put Centre College on the map. All the national news big shots were in Danville to report and comment. Historically, many experts have said that it was one of the best vice-presidential debates in history, and perhaps this is because of the outstanding behind-the-scenes work of the Secret Service. Just kidding. When we do our job well, few people know we are there and we attract as little attention as possible; that's the way it should be.

I was honored to be part of it, and I was delighted to meet Vice President Cheney and come away knowing that his TV persona does not accurately portray the classy gentleman he is. But, then, that's often the case, but in reverse. On TV someone might be all smiles and goodwill, then off camera, they morph into their real self, taking advantage of those around them, speaking down, putting down, never conveying a kind word or any sense of appreciation for those who make their life comfortable and convenient. Please know, I'm not talking about us, the Secret Service agents who serve. We don't expect anything other than the opportunity to do our job. No, I'm talking about all the dedicated "little people" who serve, and the daily interactions we observe that involve them.

CHAPTER 34

THE UNITED NATIONS

Throughout the Secret Service, we know not to ask for time off in the second week of September because we will be inundated with requests to protect heads of state coming to the United Nations for their annual meeting. Typically, there will be 100 or so requests to protect foreign dignitaries on their visits to New York City. All are automatically offered Secret Service protection, but some decline and bring their own details. This is a gray area. The protection details for some dignitaries might be composed of thugs who do what they please inside their own country, no matter how brutal, and that's not what we want on our streets. Thankfully, the decision making is out of our hands. It is a State Department issue. They decide who can carry and under what circumstances, and perhaps permission is granted to allow only one member of a foreign protection detail to carry, or whatever.

Each time the UN meeting rolled around, agents who weren't on a full-time protection detail (president, vice president, former president), were pulled in to work for somebody who was visiting. Imagine the magnitude of staffing required with 100 visiting dignitaries and at least a dozen agents for each detail. Typically, I enjoyed my UN assignments, meeting and getting to know agents from other countries, creating friendships that last to this day. But, there were exceptions.

One UN assignment stands out among the many I participated in as most memorable. My VIP protectee was a visiting president. He was a large man, bald, jovial, and very personable. As the acting detail leader, I spent a lot of time with him and I liked him. The security crew he brought with him was another story entirely. I don't mean to make fun of their lack of sensitivity or preparation, but they needed to spruce up a bit when they hit New York City, which meant they had to go shopping for suits. I'm not sure how they went about it; perhaps they sent one guy and told him to buy a rack of suits and attempt to convey what kinds of alterations to make. However they went about it, they ended up with a bunch of identical black pinstriped suits, but the alterations were not completed and most had cuffs that were pinned or stapled. They obviously didn't pay any attention to sizing and all the suits were ill fitting to a comical degree.

It was September, pleasant early fall weather, but they thought it was cold, being used to much warmer weather, and they wore these big puffy winter coats, which topped off their ensembles. They also apparently rarely showered, and when we were standing in a hallway for prolonged periods or in a crowded elevator with these guys, the odor about blew us away. In fact, in the area outside my protectee's room, the strong odor became so foul that one of my guys went out and bought a bunch of Christmas tree car deodorizers and hung them on all the doorknobs up and down the hallway. That helped a little, but not nearly enough, so I went out to the drugstore on the corner and bought some Vicks VapoRub and had everyone apply some inside their nostrils to try to override the smell. This was a trick I learned as a cop when we had to conduct searches in nasty places with burnt flesh or decomposing bodies. But there was little we could do other than try to convey a message through an interpreter that your guys were staying at a first-rate hotel, the Waldorf Astoria, where the water was free and so was the soap and shampoo, so please encourage them to take advantage and get in the shower.

Typically, official trips were scheduled for no longer than a week, but afterward, the dignitary might decide to do some sightseeing. This could mean visiting Washington, DC, or going to their embassy if they were a large enough country. Some wanted to go to Chicago, Dallas, Los Angeles, or even Disney World. Regardless of the itinerary, we were obligated to keep them safe for an additional week or more.

I'm usually very accommodating and easy to get along with when working with other security teams. In fact, I often go overboard in this way, and it's certainly not typical for me to get my nose out of joint and get irritated with someone, but it can happen. It did with the head of the security detail for this VIP. This guy was small in stature, a scrawny little jerk with an attitude who liked to let everyone know he was in charge. Worse, I had to work closely with him to coordinate our efforts.

We didn't get along from the get-go. I guess he felt threatened by my authority because back home he was the top dog and whatever he said was the law. That kind of person can't tolerate not being in complete control, and they don't play well with others. For example, when we'd get on an elevator, he would make every effort to elbow me out of the way, but I needed to be close to my protectee, which means I had to elbow back, and sometimes it wasn't with a gentle nudge. When we got in the car, he always tried to beat me to my seat in the limo, the front passenger seat, but I wasn't about to let that happen. You get the picture: this guy was a real pain, nonstop from beginning to end, and we quickly developed strong animosity toward each other.

The scrawny guy was the only one on his security detail allowed to carry a gun, but he was not allowed to take it into UN meetings. On their second day at the UN, we were, as usual, pressed against each other on the elevator, and I could tell he had a gun on him in the back of his ill-fitting suit. He got around it the day before by walking in with his president as the one staff member allowed to accompany the country's dignitary through the VIP entrance that had no metal detector. But now that I knew he was carrying a gun, I wasn't going to let him do it again. I went to the uniformed sergeant in charge of overseeing everyone coming into the UN building and told him that, despite several warnings, this guy had a gun on him. He said, okay, he'd check it out.

I went around the metal detector with my Secret Service credentials, but this guy with the gun had to go through normal channels, and sure enough, the gun set off the alarm. The sergeant was immediately on the scene and made it clear through the interpreter that the gun was out of bounds. This, of course, was not news to the VIP's security guard, but he played like it was. He was shown a heavy-duty metal box with a slot on the top. To unload his gun, he had to place the barrel in the slot and leave it there while removing the magazine.

He was told what to do. His gun was an old Russian 9mm that was not well maintained. What's more, the little turd didn't even have a holster. Instead he stuck his gun down the back of his belt like some street punk. When he went to pull his gun out, he apparently had his finger on the trigger and it went off; he almost shot himself in the butt. Oh, my God, talk about panic, responding to a gunshot inside the UN. They grabbed this guy and face-planted him on the ground and not gently. To be honest, I stood there trying to hide my grin, getting the biggest kick out this jerk getting his comeuppance.

Of course, word got around superfast and Secret Service headquarters called me within 10 minutes wanting to know what was going on. This was coming from the top floor, so clearly it was no laughing matter. They wanted to know why my protectee was around a gun that was fired. I explained, keeping a straight face, and it seemed to satisfy. The next day there was a picture hanging in the command post of me walking with my protectee into the UN, and there was a lot of funny, irreverent stuff written below it on the bulletin board. Many of the comments referred to the article with my picture on the front page of one of the sections of the *New York Times*. In the picture, I'm holding my earpiece, listening intently as if in disbelief and looking like I'm talking into my sleeve. The caption below says, "He did what?"

Things finally got so bad with this man that they boiled over. On an elevator, three of the guards kept pushing against me. Not sure what point they were trying to make, other than they were throwing their weight around in front of their president and perhaps making a feeble attempt to intimidate me. I put up with it until I had had enough. I hit the button and stopped the elevator, then I turned to them with some choice words and told them if any of them ever touched me again, I was going to lock them up. That got their attention and it got so quiet you could hear a pin drop.

After the fact, I thought, I'm supposed to keep my cool under any circumstances, and there I was, right next to my protectee acting out in that way. So, when we got off the elevator and into the Secret Service limo, I apologized for my behavior. As I said, he was a jovial guy, and it was apparent that he wasn't offended in the least. In fact, he appreciated my approach, and on the spot, invited me to his country to teach his bodyguards how to act professionally. Pretty cool. I was flattered, but I told him I had other duties I needed to attend to. But this got me thinking that if the scrawny guy found out about his invitation to me, it would push his insecurities and jealousy over the top, and he might act out to compensate for his inadequacies.

But the story doesn't end there. Months later, a CIA guy sent me a message and told me to look in the *New York Times* on page three. There was an article about the scrawny security detail leader, the one I had clashed with. I know this sounds unbelievable, but he had assassinated his president, the same jolly big man we had been protecting at the UN, and afterward, the guard was immediately killed by one of the other bodyguards.

Typically, in a situation like that, the guy who leads the security detail is contracted by people who want to overthrow the government, and, of course, he assumes he will receive a great reward for his efforts. However, the newspapers reported that this assassination was not part of a coup, but rather a heated dispute over money. Hard to say what the truth was, coup attempt or not, but the result was two deaths, one quite unfortunate.

I was reminded of that bodyguard recently at a Secret Service convention in Louisville by a younger guy who had received a national award. I sought him out to congratulate him and he surprised me by saying, "I know who you are, Gitsch." I asked if we had met before, and he said, yeah, but that I wouldn't remember.

"You were a detail leader at the UN one year when I was assigned as a brand-new agent to New York City," he said. "The story got out about you and the guys wearing huge overstuffed coats that looked like the Michelin Tire Man in 60-degree weather and acting like it was 60 below."

He went on to retell the story about how I handled the guards in the elevator and how great he thought it was, then he said it had been retold a thousand times and everyone always loved hearing it. I guess you never know when something you do can live on and create part of your legacy without you knowing it, even though at the time it might have seemed like a big mistake.

—

In 2001, it was time for another United Nations gathering, which meant that agents were again brought in to protect the visiting dignitaries. My protectee was from a small African country and he was having some health issues, so he came in a few days before the UN meetings, and we flew him to the Mayo Clinic in Minnesota to have some high-tech tests done. While there with our protectee, we took extra precautions and wanted to keep him away from the public, so we ended up housing him in an assisted living facility nearby, which catered to retired priests and nuns. It was a safe place, peaceful and quiet, and we kept a low profile. Because it was full of religious folks who had dedicated their entire lives to serving

God, my guys nicknamed it Heaven's Waiting Room.

Our visit ended, and we packed up and were about to leave the hotel to go to the airport to fly to New York City when we got word on the radio to stay put. We were confused and went upstairs to our command post where a TV was playing. The date was September 11, and we saw that a plane had hit one of the World Trade Center towers. We were stunned along with the rest of the country, but doubly so as we realized that our Secret Service field office was in the second tower. If we hadn't detoured to the Mayo Clinic, we might have been there. Then, moments later, another plane hit the second tower and watching it was like someone punched me in the stomach. At the same time, I felt the strong presence of God, protecting me as he had done so many times in the past.

The day before had been a Sunday and I went to Mass as I always do wherever I am. It was a nice old cathedral, quite large, but there were few people in attendance. The poor attendance was particularly noticeable because of the size of the church. The next day, after the planes hit, I wanted to go to Mass to pray for the victims and their families. I worked the night shift and was off duty, so I walked to the same cathedral I had visited the day before. This time, however, I couldn't get anywhere near it because the crowd had filled it to overflowing with thousands gathered outside. Interesting, I thought, that on Sunday, the Sabbath, hardly anyone attended Mass, but on Tuesday, less than 48 hours later, thanks to the 9/11 attack, the place was mobbed. A shame, I thought, that it takes a tragedy to bring us together in ways that should be natural for us as human beings.

From a Secret Service perspective, I marveled and regretted that there were no agents on board those planes that hit the towers and other locations. This was unusual because so many agents were being brought in from all over the country to guard dignitaries visiting the UN and the odds favored that on at least one of the flights, one or more of our guys would have been there. It's such a shame, because when the terrorists stood up and brandished their razor-blade box cutters at the passengers, we would have acknowledged them enthusiastically with our semi-automatic .357 handguns. Unfortunately, it wasn't to be.

CHAPTER 35

THE POPE

In my first year on the job as a Secret Service agent, I remember one of the senior guys telling me about his experience being on the Pope's security detail when Pope John Paul II visited the United States. The guy had a picture on his wall of agents standing on the running boards of what we called the Batmobile, the follow-up car to the main car, typically the presidential limousine, but in this case, it was the Popemobile. Being on the running boards is important when it comes to security, because if anything happens, the guys standing there can jump off and be an immediate presence to go on offense and take on an attacker or be on defense and cover up the dignitary in the car.

I would always gaze in awe at the picture on the wall any time I was in his office—the Pope in the United States with huge throngs of people lining the roads and cheering. As Secret Service agents, we protected world leaders for a living and we weren't easily impressed, but this did not apply to the Pope. The first time I saw the picture, I knew I wanted to be on the Pope's security detail next time he visited, but I was told it's hard to be selected for this honored duty because everybody wants to do it. Even so, this was always in the back of my mind.

In 1999, I had 15 years on the job, and a memo came out saying anyone interested in applying for the security detail for Pope John Paul II's upcoming visit to the United States should submit their name right away. I was excited because this was my big chance after all the years of waiting. I put in for it. I didn't have any sort of inside track, no one at headquarters who was going to speak up for me, no inside voice, no one in a position of power and influence.

I knew the competition would be keen with only six positions on each 12-hour shift, noon to midnight, and midnight to noon. Despite believing the odds were close to zero, I got a call telling me that out of the hundreds of agents applying, I had been one of the few selected. I was stunned and felt like I had learned I held a winning lottery ticket.

But it was real, and I got a reporting date to undergo a week of specialized preparation at our training center in Maryland. Typically, the thought of undergoing an intense and incredibly demanding week of training, especially with several years of active duty and experience under my belt, would not be welcomed news, but this was different. I was excited to go and couldn't wait to get there.

At the training site, I was instructed on the specifics of this extraordinary visit. Clearly, the brass wanted everything to go smoothly; no detail was overlooked, and no assumption went untested. On this type of detail with the six of us, one agent drives the main car, in this case the Popemobile, and a shift leader is in charge of the follow-up car. Of the remaining four, there is someone in position one, on the running board next to the Pope on his right side in the back of the limousine, and someone in position two on the opposite side. These two positions covered the back doors of the limo. Positions three and four were forward, covering the front doors of the limo, essentially forming a box around the Pope.

In training, we had a lot of drills, everything imaginable, with an emphasis on taking out a would-be perpetrator. A lot of it was videotaped, with us driving and experiencing challenges to see how we'd react. We went through a teargas and biochemical course because, at that time, bioweapons were a major concern. It was a long and intense week, and when it was over, the shift leader was the one who decided the six positions on each shift. Once again, through what I can only explain as divine intervention, I was selected for position number one closest to the Pope.

I was beside myself, elated that I was going to be right next to the Holy Father, on his right side during his visit, such an incredible thrill for me that words fail to describe it adequately. I detected more than a bit of jealousy among the troops, and from one guy in particular, a former Catholic. What's more, after talking about it, it so happens I was the only practicing Catholic on that shift. He said things like, "You can't have Greg right there in number one, the key spot, because he'll spend the whole time trying to kiss the Pope's ring and won't be of any use as far as protection is concerned." And he called me a "ring sucker" as we verbally jousted back and forth. Regardless of how anyone felt about it, I was selected, and I was going to make the most of the experience.

The Pope arrived in St. Louis, and we were there to meet his airplane, which was named, correctly in my opinion, the Good Shepherd One. We got there early, of course, to work through details of the airport arrival, arranging the motorcade to leave from the Archbishop's house in St. Louis. We secured the perimeter around the house and all was set for him to go, and we'd be with him.

We knew that the Pope was bringing along members of the Swiss Guard, the guys you see on TV all dressed up in fancy uniforms and positioned throughout the Vatican. There also were three or four guys wearing suits who traveled with the Pope. We were used to blending in with other security teams, sometimes easily, sometimes not. Thankfully, the Pope's guys were skilled professionals of the highest quality, and nothing like those guards from the Congo.

At the briefing a couple days ahead of time, there were several hundred personnel in the room. This included the uniform division with their metal detectors and canine officers for bomb sniffing and such, and counter-snipers. These were expert marksmen who would figure out where a sniper would likely set up and they would set up opposite those locations to take them out. And, of course, we had hundreds of post standers, regular agents who got pulled for this detail requiring that lots of vacation days were cancelled during the Pope's visit.

All in all, it was a huge operation. Along the parade route, we had agents on the roofs and stationed around the buildings, securing areas once they had been swept for bombs. Local police and other federal agencies manned the route, and in the background, poised and waiting, were various SWAT teams from the military and FBI. It's an understatement to say that we were heavily fortified, but we felt the need to be because of the trouble going on around the world, and we knew it could strike anywhere at any time. Beyond that, we certainly didn't want to risk the Holy Father being harmed in any way, especially on American soil.

What I remember most, among all the amazing things to recall, was wherever we traveled, there were unbelievably big crowds despite it being a frigid January day. I think there could have been two feet of snow and ice, and everyone still would have shown up for this historic event, lining the roads for many miles. They were all waiting for an opportunity to catch a glimpse of the Pope as he went by, waving to his left, then his right, and as he passed, people would scream, cry, and throw rosary beads. As I watched while standing on the running board, I had to pinch myself to make sure I wasn't dreaming. I know it was cold, very cold, but I didn't notice. With all the excitement and exhilaration, I actually felt warm. That's how football players go out and play in short-sleeve jerseys in bone-chilling weather. They are so pumped up, they don't feel the cold.

I also had to be careful and remind myself that I was on a security detail and had to keep my eyes sharp and my wits about me, looking for possible bad guys in the crowds. But, I'll admit it wasn't easy pulling myself back time and again from getting caught up in the festivities. It was especially meaningful to me as a practicing Catholic. It couldn't get any better than that.

From the motorcade, we had to move the Pope into a hockey arena where the youth got to visit with him. Then it was time for the big Mass in the stadium where the St. Louis Rams play. The stadium filled up quickly and the overflow crowd was placed in the convention center connected to the stadium; 117,000 people participated in the Mass. Quite a crowd, not counting the many tens of thousands of folks lined up on the motorcade route. It was quite a logistical challenge to file everyone through metal detectors and check purses and pockets before they could enter the stadium and vie for a seat.

When the Pope entered the arena in the Popemobile, the uproar was deafening, everyone on their feet, screaming at the top of their lungs as if experiencing a never-before-felt joy of the spirit. The sound was so incredibly loud, I had to turn the volume on my earpiece way up, and still it was hard to hear clearly. I've never been to the Super Bowl, but I imagine in the waning moments of a tight game with everything on the line how loud the sound would be, but even then, it would not come close to what I was hearing. Plus, there was the added stimulus of flashbulbs going off constantly and the shift leader yelling instruction through my earpiece. The frenzy is hard to appreciate if you weren't there, but the crowd was so juiced that some folks got caught up in it and did things they never normally would do, or even think about doing. One thing stands out—I saw people holding their babies out at arm's length to get them closer to the Pope, and this included people in the upper decks, holding babies over the railing. Just imagine! You might recall the public outcry when Michael Jackson did the same thing from a hotel balcony and it was caught on film. But no one seemed to notice or be upset, except me, and when I saw this, I gasped, and remember praying, dear God, please protect those babies.

We drove slowly around the edge of the football field. I was alongside, walking with one hand always touching the Popemobile. My job was to look away from the vehicle and scan for any potential threats, so touching the vehicle kept me in contact and I knew instantly how fast it was going.

As we moved along, we were showered with rosary beads, and I remember thinking the greatest risk to my safety that day was getting hit in the eye by a stray bead.

Not only were the stadium seats filled, but chairs were set up on the field, virtually in every place you could think of, and as we drove, we came across a section on the field with a lot of handicapped children in wheelchairs, their parents standing behind them. It was a gripping scene, with mothers wailing, the tears flowing as they helped their children focus on the Pope, no doubt with hope that a miracle might occur.

After circling the field, we pulled up to one of the end zones and a huge stage with an altar. The Holy Father left the Popemobile and was helped up onto the stage and to the altar where he was surrounded by bishops and cardinals. As this was happening, our detail split up and assumed clockwise positions around the stage in front of the altar. In my position, I was about 15 feet in front of the altar facing the crowd, the Pope behind me conducting the Mass, and it occurred to me that I was the last line of defense for the Pope. A heavy thought, indeed.

In the Pope's sermon, he talked about being pro-life and against abortions, and he emphasized that you cannot be pro-life and yet be in favor of the death penalty. This gave me pause, because as a cop working in bad areas, I had seen lots of bad things go down, and as a result, I always felt comfortable with a death sentence. Some people, by virtue of their heinous crimes had, in my opinion, forfeited the right to keep living. But after hearing what the Pope had to say about it, I felt like it was a message intended specifically for my ears, and I realized I was wrong about the death penalty, and from that point on, my stance on the issue changed 180 degrees. By all means, lock up the bad guys and never let them out, but I could no longer justify taking a life for a life.

As the Holy Father's visit to the United States was ending, we lined up inside the building, getting ready for the Pope to board his plane. We learned that the Pope wanted to thank his security detail. I was first in line. When he approached me, I knelt and kissed his ring, and I have a great and treasured picture of this moment. All the guys on my shift who had made fun of me for being a ring sucker, all did exactly the same thing. To top it off, the ex-Catholic guy, after kissing the Pope's ring, shook his hand, and when he finished, he examined his own hand and said out loud to no one in particular, "Did you feel that? Unbelievable!" I might add, I got a picture of this guy kneeling and kissing the Pope's ring, which I reminded him of quite often afterward.

When all was said and done, and I returned home, I felt like a changed man. My brief personal encounter with the Pope affected me more deeply than I imagined, and it was instrumental in setting a future course for me as a servant of God.

CHAPTER 36

PRIVATE BODYGUARD

After retiring from the Secret Service, I stayed active and one of the things I enjoy doing is public speaking. I have addressed groups of all types, but I especially enjoy young people, where I emphasize the importance of making good choices and staying close to God as they navigate the challenging teenage years. When I make a talk, I have a brief bio I send along to guide the moderator when introducing me. The bio summarizes the things I've done in my career: guarding presidents, heads of state like Queen Elizabeth, the Pope, and all the rest. At the end, I indicate that I have been a private bodyguard for folks like CEOs of major companies, the mayor of Louisville, the two brothers who started and own Vineyard Vines (hugely popular clothing and accessories among 15- to 30-year-olds), and others, including Jennifer Lawrence.

When I started working as a private bodyguard, I found it to be pleasant and rewarding. A big part of that is I get to choose who I work for, which makes a huge difference in how I feel about it. I'm certainly not going to sign on to protect the types I wrote about earlier, or some political figures who treat underlings like peasants and worse. On the contrary, I can be selective, and my first job guarding the CEO of a major international corporation afforded me the opportunity to work on some of the Summer and Winter Olympic games. All told, our security team worked in China, Russia, Italy, Greece, London, and Vancouver.

My role was not so much as a "walk along" beside the VIP, but rather being in charge of the advance work, then I would be at the site when they arrived. When big stuff is going on, it can get hairy when it comes to traffic, parking, dealing with the threat of terrorism, and all that, so it can be a challenge to get people in and out safely. On the upside, it afforded me a bird's-eye view of everything that was taking place, and when bodyguards are with a person of stature, we get the best of everything. This included all-access passes to go behind the scenes, and in some cases, we had meals with US Olympic athletes, chatting with them about their experiences and expectations.

I worked for five years protecting the mayor of Louisville. The way it came about, I met the mayor and one of his security guys told him, "Hey, Mr. Mayor, Gitsch is the guy who used to train us on the Louisville Police dignitary protection team."

The mayor looked me over, then responded, "How come you're not working for me?"

I told him I had retired and was sort of feeling my way. Next thing I knew, I was being interviewed, then immediately hired as part of his security team. This gave me a firsthand look at how things are done, how deals get made, and the ins and outs of good old-fashioned Kentucky politics.

When people learn that I work for a mayor who is a Democrat, they often assume I am as well. I'm neither a Democrat nor a Republican, never was and never will be one or the other. I'm an independent, and I vote the person and not the party. Similarly, when I worked as a Secret Service agent, I could care less what party the VIP was from. The kind of person they were and how they treated those around them was much more important to me. Let me add that it certainly isn't necessary, and often not the case, but when we had a high level of respect for the person we were protecting and willing to give our lives for, it made bodyguarding even more meaningful.

I have purposely kept this chapter short, because I know readers are dying to get to Jennifer Lawrence. Here goes.

CHAPTER 37

Jennifer Lawrence

I have known the Lawrence family a long time. Jen's mother, Karen, and I went to high school together. She was a cheerleader and I was a football player of some note, good enough to be a team captain, selected all-state, and play in the all-star game. Then at the University of Louisville, where my football career flamed out, Karen continued as a cheerleader. At one of the homecoming dances, it turned out that neither of us had a date, so we went together as friends. Then, she met her husband, Gary, a guy I knew from U of L. I also knew Jen's older brothers, Blaine and Ben, who as young men, worked at their parent's summer camp that my children attended, and later my children worked there as well.

We had lost touch before reconnecting at our 25th high school reunion and she told me about her daughter, Jen, who had done some modeling in Louisville, but was now going back and forth to New York City.

Jen has a warm personality and wonderful sense of humor. I mean she can be really funny, and it's obvious wherever she went that the photographers fell in love with her. People told her she ought to be an actress because of the way she captivated people and held their attention. After a while, she moved in that direction and began her move up the ladder, starting with bit parts, and then starring in some episodes of a TV series called *Medium*.

Karen moved to New York City to be with Jen who was still young and needed a chaperone. After *Medium*, Jen landed a recurring role on the *Bill Engvall Show*, a TV sitcom in which she played the smart-aleck teenage daughter. Next, she got a role in the movie *Burning Plain*, where her talents were immediately apparent, and she made a huge impression. Her next movie, *Winter's Bone*, another dark movie like the first one, won her wide acclaim, showcased her talents, and introduced her to the public in a big way. She played the role of the teenage daughter of a crack addict in destitute surroundings in the Appalachian Mountains. The movie was filmed in Missouri. I believe they wanted to shoot it in Kentucky, but for some reason, they couldn't.

When the movie *The Burning Plain* came out in Louisville in 2009 and Jen was here for the opening, I worked as her bodyguard for the first time. I remember Karen telling me about the movie before I saw it, and she said it was very dark and not easy to watch her daughter play the role. When I saw it, I was blown away. I knew Jen had talent, but her performance was amazing, and I knew the sky would be the limit for her.

I had the opportunity to guard Jen on a movie set in Canada where there were some security challenges but had to decline because I had prior commitments. I turned Jen over to a friend of mine, a female and former Secret Service agent. Afterward, we talked quite a bit about it, because I was curious to learn what I had missed, and frankly, I wished I could have followed through and worked on the movie set.

What did I miss? Well, on a movie set, actors and actresses work hard for long hours. They might be up early in the morning for makeup and a fitting, then work all day and into the night. Bodyguards must be there every moment, which means there's a lot of sitting around. The feedback I got was that being on the set was exciting, but after several 14-hour days in a row, it morphed into a grind that was considerably less exciting. What's more, there isn't any down time for bodyguards. They must transport the protectee to the set, then while shooting, always be nearby in the shadows. They try not to attract the attention of the director or appear to be a distraction or in the way; they don't eat food meant for the cast and crew. During the day, they might escort the protectee back to their trailer when necessary to change clothes or whatever, and when the day is over, they take their protectees home and when they sleep, the bodyguards eventually get to sleep, but are up before the protectees are and ready to go.

The level of security is much less than that used when protecting a president or head of state. With a president, there are three rings of protection, but on a movie set, it's more relaxed and typically there is security around the perimeter, but that's it. The attention is much more focused on staying on a tight schedule, because movies cost a fortune to make. Every moment is expensive, and they don't want to lose any time dealing with security personnel and related issues that might arise.

As far as Jen goes, the reports I received told me that she is the consummate professional. A true compliment to her talents is that directors give her a lot of room to interject her own lines in places where she thinks they will be more effective than the script. Given Jen's personality, this makes sense.

Early on in Jen's career, around the age of 18 when she was working on TV, I was very involved with a summer camp called Kids Cancer Alliance. The group helps families who have a child with cancer. Jen's mom, Karen, knew of my passion for this project, and she brought Jen and her dad up for a day. Jen had her hair pulled back, wore a T-shirt and cutoff jeans, a ball cap and sunglasses, and she looked just like the other teenage counselors. We spent the day touring the camp from top to bottom, and afterward, we had dinner, then sat back to relax. As executive director, I had some discretion and I decided to play a video I had of Jen on her TV show. No one at the camp knew who she was, and I didn't let on, other than asking the audience if they watched the TV program, the *Bill Engvall Show*. A bunch of hands went up, so I said, "Well, then, I'm surprised none of you said hi to our good friend, Jennifer Lawrence, who stars on the show." Then, of course, when they realized who she was, they all freaked out big time.

I asked Jen to come up in front of the group. Now, this is interesting because Jen obviously is such a well-known public figure, but she doesn't like standing in front of people, which is not a secret because she says this all the time. When she's up there, she gets nervous, but she got up there as a teenage girl talking to other teenage girls. She started talking about things she hates, everything from going out on a bad date, to people getting on her nerves, to having an outbreak of acne at exactly the wrong time; the girls in the audience absolutely loved it because it was Jen being Jen, genuine without the slightest pretension, as if she were simply one of them, but she was also Jennifer Lawrence. I always appreciated her doing that, giving the counselors and kids a fantastic memorable moment.

One time I took a picture of Jen with one of the younger campers, Patrick, nicknamed the fighting Irishman, because as a youngster he had survived five onslaughts of cancer and each time, he miraculously survived. Some years later, Jen came home to Louisville and was invited to a U of L basketball game at the Yum Center. People who aren't from Louisville perhaps don't know how big basketball is in Louisville and the state of Kentucky. It is a monstrous attraction, every game sold out with more than 20,000 screaming fans in attendance. Jen was in the athletic director's private box, and I was outside in front of the door. During a break in the action, the camera found Jen, put her picture on the big jumbo screen above the court and announced a big welcome to her. She's always been a big U of L fan, and she waved, and everyone went nuts.

Down below, Patrick happened to be at the game and he sent me a text. He had my number as I'm close friends with his parents; his mom was on our board of directors of the Kids Cancer Alliance. His text said, "Hey, Mr. G., are you with Jen?" I texted back, "Yeah, she's up here in the A.D.'s box." He asked if I would show Jen the picture I had taken of the two of them many years earlier, and he forwarded it to me on my phone. I took the picture to Jen and said, "Don't know if you'll remember this young fella, but several years ago he was at camp when you came and . . ." Before I could finish my sentence, she said, "Oh, my God, is that Patrick?" I said, sure is, and she asked me to bring him up to the box. I told her that wouldn't be easy getting him through all the security checkpoints between where he was and the box, to which she replied, without missing a beat, "Greg, I know if anyone can do it, you can, so please go get him."

Dutifully, I went down and bluffed my way from one checkpoint to the next and brought Patrick back up to the box where we took a new round of pictures of the two of them. So cool how she recognized how important that little encounter would be to him.

When Jen comes to town, I am her bodyguard, but the degree of my involvement can vary greatly. At times, I may pick her up at the airport after a commercial flight, or if her visit is low-key, the family will pick her up. I was happy when they didn't need me much, because it meant Jen was going to have a relaxing visit with family, and particularly with her brothers' children. I know how much she really enjoys being an aunt. She also came back to town to be in a couple of family weddings, and at such times, we do our best to be discreet and keep it as quiet as we can. But such events are a huge challenge, in terms of both security and privacy. The problem is that everyone feels entitled to a selfie with Jen, or they want to chat with her or shove a camera in her face while she is eating her salad. My job is to be nice but firm and try to give her some privacy to enjoy a few family moments without too much hoopla.

For public appearances, I was pressed into action doing advance work. On occasions where no one knew we were coming, the planning wasn't terribly taxing. But when the public knew she was coming, advance work became important to ensure her safety, and getting her in and out in a timely manner. For example, every year at Christmas, she visits Norton Kosair Children's Hospital, and with my connections with Kids Cancer Alliance, we spend a lot of time with youngsters who are battling cancer.

She'll spend several hours there, giving each child her individual and undivided attention, then sign a big poster with a personal message to them. We take lots of pictures during such events, and my main job is to carry rolled-up posters, Sharpie pens, and a small pack of tissues. Sometimes Jen has to stop and collect herself after being with some of these children who are fighting various forms of advanced cancer against terrific odds.

We made our way from room to room, after getting permission to visit each kid because of HIPAA laws. We emphasized to every family that we didn't want any fanfare or publicity, and we asked them to not text or tweet or put anything out on social media for two hours about what was going on, so that we wouldn't have to contend with a massive crowd. There was that, and if other kids throughout the hospital knew we were there and visiting, they would be upset that she didn't come to see them, which would be impossible, of course, because there are so many.

On such visits, as you can imagine, watching little faces light up is precious, and every one of them has a story worth telling. I think my favorite Christmas visit story was when we walked into a little girl's room as she was playing a game on an iPad, and she was totally involved in it. Her mom knew we were coming and was expecting us, and you could see by her expression that she was blown away that Jen was there.

The mom said to her daughter, "Hey, look, sweetie, look who it is, your favorite actress." The little girl didn't respond, wouldn't look up, so the mom kept at her. "Look who is here to visit with you. Please don't be rude; look up and see."

Finally, the message seemed to have resonated with her, and the little girl looked up all wide-eyed, and said, "Oh, wow, Miley Cyrus?"

Well, the look on Jen's face was priceless. She laughed real big and said, "Well, I guess that put me in my place."

I've said this before, and it's worth repeating here. When someone reaches a lofty perch with high status, like a president and other VIPs, or in Jen's case as an internationally famous movie actress, the trait I so admire and value is their remembering who they really are, one of us, not separate and above. Jen's response was so delightful and revealed who she is, a humble, down-to-earth person who has been blessed extraordinarily and is thankful for her blessings; she doesn't take any of it for granted.

Most recently, we had an event that was heavily advertised and required a lot of advance work. It was a ticketed fund-raiser event for the Jennifer Lawrence Foundation, which "assists and empowers charitable organizations that fulfill children's vital needs and drives arts awareness and participation." Kids Cancer Alliance receives generous funding from the foundation.

The event was held at the Frazier History Museum in Louisville, and we had eight meetings in which we planned out all the details, including the hiring of off-duty police officers. It was a huge happening, and Jen was going to be there two nights in a row. The first night was set up as a pajama party for more than 100 kids who were invited to spend the night at the museum in their sleeping bags. But, before the sleepover party got going, we brought Jen in to meet a special group invited for a private encounter. Each charity organization that the Jennifer Lawrence Foundation supports could send two kids, and that's who made up this special group. Let me tell you, it wasn't easy picking only two kids for this out of all the children Kids Cancer Alliance serves, but the staff did a great job and selected the kids who most needed an emotional boost at the moment. After the private meeting, Jen went out and addressed the entire group of kids. Organizers had planned to let her take three questions, but the questions poured in and she graciously answered every one as if it were the only one asked, and it kept going.

The second night was for adult donors to the foundation. First, she had dinner with about 35 folks, then after that, she went upstairs to the main staging area and mingled with several hundred, welcoming them, thanking them, and making them feel special as only she can do.

Jen and I have a great working relationship. She is comfortable with me, and we operate more like two friends and not as a protectee and bodyguard. I'm constantly vigilant, of course, and do my job and then some, but we try to keep things free flowing, while ensuring her safety and guarding her privacy to the extent possible.

PART THREE

SECRET SERVICE AGENT: OFFICE OF INVESTIGATIONS

CHAPTER 38

DISAPPEARING ACT

The Secret Service was created under President Abraham Lincoln to do investigative work. During the Civil War, the Yankees had counterfeited Confederate currency, and vice versa, and something like one out of every three dollars in the United States was counterfeit. This meant that to safeguard the economic security of the country, now and in the future, Lincoln needed a highly trained force to find and break up these counterfeit operations all over the country. In the TV series, and later a movie with Will Smith and Kevin Kline called *Wild Wild West*, the two stars played government agents working directly for President Ulysses S. Grant. And it's true that agents would put their horses on a train in Washington, DC, and take off to destinations across the country.

Eventually, the agents—referred to as operatives—developed a reputation for being very good at their job, so other presidents began using them in different kinds of investigations, including getting the lowdown on their likely opponent in the next presidential election. This was in the late 1800s. This practice was stopped to preserve the Secret Service as an honorable, bona fide law enforcement agency.

Today, the Secret Service has a large investigative branch, specializing in counterfeit US currency and treasury checks, stolen checks, and basically anything involving financial fraud, including more recently, counterfeit credit cards. A little-known fact: Secret Service agents were asked to start the FBI. Most FBI agents I know don't like hearing that.

Enough ancient history. During the late 1980s, when I was assigned to the Los Angeles field office of the Secret Service, I caught a squeal, what we used to call a complaint. It was a counterfeit case occurring near the University of Southern California in downtown Los Angeles. In daylight, this looks like a decent neighborhood with nice houses, clean streets, well-tended yards, and palm trees, but looks can be deceiving. Lots of alleys run behind the houses, and at night, this becomes a dangerous and sometimes deadly area. Gangs were catching on and memberships was starting to grow in the 1980s. The Bloods and the Crips, the most noteworthy gangs at the time, were each trying to gain a foothold into various crime syndicates.

It didn't take long for me to figure out that people who were passing counterfeit twenty-dollar bills, also were likely selling them, and my job was to determine the players, including the printers, the ultimate prize. In those days, the government made bills with an offset printing press. Today, things are much different. Bills are computer-generated with intricate images and hard-to-reproduce aspects, making them much harder to duplicate convincingly.

I did my surveillance and took photos and videos of the house we believed to be the central focal point of the operation. There were lots of people coming and going at all hours for no apparent reason, other than to purchase phony twenty-dollar bills. We put together an operational plan for the counterfeit squad, including a list of suspects with mug shots, known associates in that area, cars registered to these people, etc., and we noted that counterfeit bills were being passed freely from one criminal to the next. In other words, they were ripping each other off, demonstrating the adage that there is no honor among thieves. When a criminal makes a purchase, whether it be drugs, guns, credit cards, contraband, whatever, counterfeit bills can be used because the deal goes down fast and there is little or no opportunity to count stacks of bills and less time to examine the bills for authenticity, making the buyer easy prey. This, of course, breeds more crime, given the desire to get even.

Once we determined exactly how we were going to proceed, we used a surveillance van, which actually was a new van made to look old and beat up, rusted with holes in it, one headlight or taillight out, a piece of junk on its last legs. Making a new van look this way takes talent. We were fortunate because in LA, there's no shortage of folks who can make things appear any way you like; their talents are used extensively in the movie industry. As bad as the outside of the van looked, the inside was nice: new and plush, carpeted, a restroom with a water supply, a receptacle for dry ice to help cool the interior of the van, storage for extra weapons, tools for serving search warrants, etc. There was also video-recording equipment. In those days, vans had roof vents, and inside the vent we put a periscope, a zoom camera, and telescope, enabling us to watch what was going on across the street, take pictures, and do video recordings for evidence to be used in court. No two ways about it, the van was about as geeked-up as you can get, and I had a ball playing with all the stuff on board.

Since I knew the players, the bad guys, I was in the van with my partner for this assignment. We called him Bear, a large African American gentleman, a guy I had worked with several times over the years. We had become good friends and that friendship persists to this day. He was a former professional football player, large and he could handle himself well. He and I were in the back of the van, and we had a third agent on our team nicknamed Speedy Gonzales, a politically incorrect label, but accurate because he was a fast and nimble Hispanic guy who ran marathons at a blistering pace. (I use agent nicknames here and elsewhere in the book, for obvious reasons.)

Speedy drove the van into the targeted neighborhood in the daytime and parked it, then got out and walked down the street where a "cool car" picked him up. A cool car was anything ranging from a pickup truck to a minivan to a convertible, or even motorcycles, whatever was available from the lot of cars or bikes we had seized recently because they were used during illegal transactions. Kimo was driving the cool car, in this case a sleek IROC Z28 Camaro and he picked up Speedy, while Bear and I stayed in the van. Guido was nearby in a Mercedes working surveillance. We informed the LAPD what we were up to in case something bad went down and we needed quick support and backup.

It was a hot day and we were in the van baking in spite of the dry ice, watching people coming and going, taking pictures and all that. In our side portholes and the rear window were two-way mirrors. Also, the van had a wall separating the back from the front seat, and it had a peephole we could see through to the front of the van. From these various vantage points, we had to be vigilant and aware of what was going on all around us: front, sides and back. We were keenly aware that we were stuck in a surveillance van in a rough neighborhood.

Later in the day, a guy seemed unusually interested in the van, because it had been sitting there a couple of days. He walked up to us and checked all the door handles. They were locked of course, something we always do no matter where we are or what we are doing. He then tried to look inside, not knowing that a foot away we are staring right back at him. He looked in the mirror and started picking at a zit. Bear and I were so close we had a hard time not laughing. Then he started looking around to see if anyone was nearby. Seeing no one, he pulled out a screwdriver from his long-sleeved T-shirt and it looked like he was going to try to pop the lock on the side sliding door. We had to think fast, so as he messed with the lock, I unlocked the same door and slid it open. Bear grabbed him by the neck and jerked him into the van like a feather sucked into a vacuum cleaner. I immediately closed the door and locked it. If anyone happened to be watching at the exact moment he was taken, they likely would have believed he was abducted by aliens because he disappeared in an instant.

Bear threw him down on the floor and he got a good whiff of my Hoppe's gun-cleaning fluid as he looked up into the barrel of my 12-gauge shotgun. He was terrified and wet his pants as he told us he thought we were hit men for somebody and that we were going to execute him on the spot. Once we assured him that was not the case, and that we were the police, we cuffed him and told him we would duct tape his mouth if he uttered one word. Soon the stench from his pants was getting to us, so I grabbed a plastic trash bag, cut two holes in it for his legs and duct taped it over his clothes and around his waist, trying to contain the smell as much as possible. He sat there in the trash bag until it got dark enough that we could hand him off to a couple of our guys without blowing our cover.

Ultimately, it all worked out well. A few days later, we got a search warrant, served it and recovered a bunch of counterfeit twenty-dollar bills. We also confiscated anything that looked like it had been purchased with the phony bills, including cars, motorcycles, gold chains, TVs, whatever. The main player in all this realized that he was looking at some serious federal jail time, so he immediately ratted out his partners, telling us he bought the money in the warehouse district from someone working a printing press. That allowed us to move forward with the next steps and nail the printer, the ultimate prize when it comes to counterfeiting cases.

—

When funny things happen on the job, they often happen in the midst of what could be highly dangerous circumstances, and agents can't appreciate the humor until after the fact and they are in a safe environment with their buddies enjoying a brew. This story revolves around an agent nicknamed Ricardo who was with Dan and me when we served the warrant relating to the counterfeit twenty-dollar bill case.

Ricardo's nickname came from the famous Mexican actor Ricardo Montalbán, a dashing leading man in movies and on TV, known for his regal and commanding presence. The agent Ricardo worked with us as a member of our crew. He wasn't a bad guy, but he was pretentious, quick to tell people he was Castilian Spanish, not Mexican Spanish, emphasizing that he was from the upper crust. Like Ricardo Montalbán, he was always dressed to the nines in expensive three-piece suits with matching vests. He also prided himself on using perfect grammar and he delighted in correcting our use of Mexican Spanish.

When it came time to serve the warrant, we were informed that a film crew from a British TV station was granted permission to follow agents around, and the higher-ups figured ours would be a good case for them to film. So, there we were, doing our job with a three-person TV crew on our heels filming every move. We didn't have a problem with it, and we knew it wouldn't have mattered even if we did. Whatever, go with the flow. We gave them bulletproof vests and some pointers, like stay back and give us plenty of room to operate, because we had no way of knowing what was on the other side of the door we'd be knocking on. Hopefully, we'd be catching the perps off guard and our mission would go down without the need for a lot of action.

As we approached the house, we assumed that Dan and I would take the lead as we both went through the LAPD SWAT school and we were comfortable making the entry and being the first two through the door. Dan was a Vietnam vet and a certified badass, and I always felt comfortable with him by my side. If necessary, we'd use a barricade rammer, hit the doorknob, and get through the door. If I went left, Dan would go right. It was preferable, however, to simply check the door to see if it was locked. Hopefully not, and we could simply turn the knob and walk in.

We were all set when Ricardo decided that with the TV cameras filming us, he would take the lead, and he jumped ahead of us. Dan and I exchanged a look, but neither of us said a word. We approached the door in our stacked formation the way we were taught, staying away from windows and being ultra-cautious. Then Ricardo did something monumentally stupid. He drew his gun, raised it, and turned his back to the door, something a SWAT-trained professional would never do, and he kicked the door like a mule, backward. We were shocked to watch this because protocol dictated that first we would check the door to see if it was unlocked, and second, we would announce our presence with a search warrant.

The door turned out to be one of those cheap doors, essentially hollow with a thin veneer covering, and when Ricardo kicked it, his foot went right through it. Ricardo, in his fancy suit with his gun raised, was trapped with his foot through the door and he couldn't get it out. Funny, to be sure, but now it was an officer safety issue, so Dan and I rushed to the door and checked it. It was unlocked, and we pushed it open a little and started yelling to anyone who might be there that we had a warrant. As I swung the door open, poor Ricardo had to hop on one leg backward and we rushed past him, covering the rooms.

This was a supremely embarrassing situation for Ricardo, especially since it was all caught on film and looked more like a skit from the *Three Stooges* than a sophisticated law-enforcement operation. But, all in all, it turned out to be a good thing because after that, any time Ricardo decided to mount his high horse, we had the perfect antidote to quickly knock him off.

—

Let me wrap up this chapter with a side story about that well-equipped van we used for our surveillance work. On another occasion, I was working with Bear and a female agent. She was a good agent and a good person, likeable, effective in her own way, and a good shot, but at times, she could be out to lunch, which earned her the nickname Spacey. Anyway, Bear and I always kept an eye on her to make sure she wasn't waltzing into trouble without being aware of it.

One night after completing an operation, we had her drive the van home. Bear and I assumed that she knew what we believed everyone on the squad knew: the van was never to be brought into the federal building. We had a separate lot for all the cool cars like our van that we used for various operations. It was important to have a separate lot so that someone up to no good couldn't watch the federal building and see what cars the feds were using. The cool car lot was some distance away and it was locked securely to keep people from stealing the cars. It was LA, after all, and it's quite embarrassing when someone steals an unmarked official vehicle, and especially one outfitted with lots of expensive equipment.

The female agent was not aware that the van should not be taken into the federal building, and as she drove in, she either didn't see or ignored the numerous signs stating the clearance height. The high-tech and expensive periscope on the van's roof increased the height quite a bit, a formula for disaster in the low-clearance garage. As she entered the garage, she called me on the radio. I was upstairs with Bear processing a prisoner we had just arrested, getting mug shots, fingerprints, and all that, which is why she was driving the van back alone. I heard the call come in on the PA system, so I went to the radio and she asked what parking space in the garage should she put the van in. Hearing this and fearing the worst, another agent yelled out, "Who let Spacey drive the van?"

As soon as she said "garage," I panicked, picturing in my mind what was going to happen. Sure enough, because of the low clearance, when she drove into the garage, she hit the main water pipes of the fire suppression system, rupturing them, triggering all the fire alarms, and calling every fire department in the area. Still on the radio, and this is the honest-to-gosh truth, she asked if there was a fire in the building and what was going on. I told her not to move from where she was, to turn off the van and sit there until I arrived. With that, I took off running. It's a huge building, and by the time I got to her, the water, gushing from the ceiling, had already started covering the basement floor. As she sat in the van, I had to find the emergency shut-off valve and try to get things under control before the fire department arrived.

It took a while for her to piece things together, and I tried not to say too much, knowing how embarrassing the whole thing was for her. The good news is, the periscope on top of the van still worked.

CHAPTER 39

MOSES

I spent a lot of time in Hong Kong before the Chinese takeover in 1996. I remember going to bed one night with the British flag flying over the city and waking up the next morning under the Chinese flag. Before the takeover, Hong Kong was a British colony, and their police department was called the Royal Hong Kong Police. The department was comparable in size to the New York City Police Department, about 33,000 officers back then, and it's probably much larger now.

I worked closely with the Royal cops over about a five-year span, busting counterfeiting rings. When US currency was being counterfeited in a foreign country, they'd fly in a guy like me and I'd help them set up the overall mission, plan the investigation, arrange surveillance to determine the location of the plant where the money was being made, try to do some undercover buying—all the things required to catch the bad guys. In those days, US paper money was all green and black, and it was much easier to counterfeit than it is today.

One counterfeiting case was quite memorable. I was working with a Royal cop who knew an informant I'll call Moses. Moses told the cop he wanted to work with a Yank, an American, but he made it clear he didn't want to work with the CIA or the FBI and would only work with someone he could trust. So, the cop from the Royal Hong Kong Police Intelligence Unit referred him to me.

A lunch meeting was arranged for the three of us; about halfway through, the Brit got up and said he had a meeting. He told us he wanted to introduce us, me and Moses, and whatever happened happened. Then he took off. That left me and Moses on our own, and we talked about a lot of stuff, feeling each other out. It was a chess match of sorts, me trying to figure out why he did what he did, his motivation, goals, and most important, whether I could trust him. A key piece to all this was that we had a mutual friend, the Brit who brought us together. He thought highly of Moses and that carried a lot of weight with me.

We met a few more times, and after a while, I felt comfortable with him, and I think he felt the same. Moses liked to drink wine and eat cheese, and we'd have these long lunches, quite enjoyable, but also quite unusual for me to kick back like that in the middle of the day. Moses looked like he might have been an immigrant from Asia. He didn't look anything like Mercedes Mike, my key informant in the United States, but they were similar in many ways. Both were likeable and unassuming, not in any way threatening, nothing to distinguish either of them—the kind of person you'd look right through on the street and not remember a thing about him. His bland persona helped him fit in anywhere without being noticed, an important characteristic. Moses was highly intelligent and well educated, and if I closed my eyes while talking to him, I'd swear I was talking to a British lord, someone from Parliament; he was proper and formal in his speech.

Moses told me about some of the cases he had worked, and I told him what I was interested in: any sort of protective intelligence that might influence the safety of our president, past presidents, stuff like that, plus, of course, counterfeiting. That's where we clicked because the thing that interested Moses the most was counterfeiting, especially credit cards. He was aware of the Chinese gangs that were counterfeiting those cards, and he agreed to work on that for me and get some feelers out, including going into any country I wanted, if necessary. I asked him if that meant he could go into mainland China and work a case. He said, yes, all he had to do was pay off the police wherever he went, and he had contacts all over.

Moses told me he could even go into North Korea. I'm sure my jaw dropped, as everything I know about North Korea indicated it was pretty extreme and dangerous. He said, yeah, you have to watch your back, but they're like anyone else. They take bribes and provide information.

The North Koreans counterfeit a lot of American products, everything from Harley Davidson leather jackets to Disney merchandise, Marlboro cigarettes, and even Jack Daniels whiskey. They also like to counterfeit drugs, mass producing prescription drugs. Not the real drugs, of course, but they look just like them, same size, color, and markings—masterful placebos.

One of the cases we worked on was a massive American currency counterfeiting operation, and we figured out that the bad guys were coming to this huge building to buy bills. Hong Kong has gigantic buildings everywhere, and we couldn't figure out who owned them, how many people might be working or living in them, or anything about them because they don't have the laws we do to be able to trace such things. This afforded protection of sorts for crime syndicates because they could hide any involvement with these properties.

Our target building was in the middle of a highly industrialized area with lots of similar-looking buildings, and the Hong Kong police were set up for surveillance across the street. They felt confident that the printing press was in this building, but they couldn't do much overt snooping because it would tip their hand to the Chinese triads, criminals who run the show. They weren't making any progress, so I came up with a scheme. I told them that an offset printing press sounds a lot like a washing machine, and if they could get me into the building, I'd dress for the occasion and walk up and down the halls and listen for the machine and possibly hear it if it was anywhere near the hallway. It wasn't the greatest, most sophisticated plan in the world, and I don't think they were too impressed, but it was the best I could come up with.

Then, I got lucky. As Moses and I sat staring at the building, I saw that a lot of the windows were covered with cardboard, aluminum foil, paper, whatever—anything to block the light. As I continued looking, I thought I recognized something, so I borrowed a camera with a zoom lens and focused in on it. On one of the windows was this yellowish, golden-looking paper covering it, the kind of paper used for printing presses. Bingo! I was excited, but I didn't tell anyone because I wanted to milk this and get some mileage out of it. We had a meeting to plan our next move and I said if we were going to follow through with my washing machine plan, I had a feeling and I wanted to start on the seventh floor. You can imagine the looks I got. I, of course, didn't mention that the window in question was on the seventh floor, and I had counted the windows from the side of the building and knew exactly which room it would be in.

It's hard to believe the counterfeiters would make a bonehead mistake like that, but I guess they figured no one would be likely to recognize the printing paper. But when Secret Service agents go through training, one of the things we had to do was to see where real US money is being made and walk through the process in detail, watching the engraving and printing processes, observing them sizing up the paper before putting it on the machine, and then visiting the company that provides the paper. Because of that experience, I knew what the printing paper looked like in its raw form.

Sure enough, we walked up to the seventh floor and I walked right to the door and told them this is it, this is the target. I loved the incredulous looks I got as they couldn't believe this was possible. But I was right on and we busted these guys. The response was priceless, and the word spread quickly that American Secret Service agents are amazing with their powers of observation and their investigative skills. Well, I let this go on for a little while, then I spilled the beans over a pitcher of beer. We all had a good laugh, and as they liked to say, I really took the piss out of them with that one. In Hong Kong and Australia, piss means beer, so if one of your coworkers called you up and said, hey, let's get out and get on the piss, it means going out for some beer. Or if they told you they got pissed last night, it meant they got drunk. Don't know the origin, the rhyme nor reason behind it, and no one was ever able to explain it to me.

Moses did good work and we paid him as much as we could. And like Mercedes Mike, his goal, what motivated him, was catching bad guys and putting them away. He was also a thrill junkie, loved the thrill of the chase, loved to outsmart guys who thought they were clever. Over time, our relationship blossomed, and it was one of those relationships I highly valued. Law enforcement owes a great deal to guys like Moses and Mercedes Mike who put a ton of bad guys in jail. The cool thing is, none of the ones they helped bust had a clue how it all went down.

Years later, Moses moved to the United States, and he called me and wanted to meet. I hooked up with him and his family, took them to dinner, and we had a ball catching up with stories about old times, especially the one about the paper in the window. I was glad to see him leave that dangerous life style and settle down with his family in this country.

CHAPTER 40

SUPER NOTE

I have always had a fascination with all things surrounding counterfeiting, maybe because it's so challenging, like a high-stakes chess match. Anyway, I was in the right place at the right time and in the thick of things on the Super Note case. It was a top-secret case, and the most important counterfeit case at the time involving the highest executive offices in the country, including the president. The Super Note case involved expertly counterfeited $100 bills, and it rocked the system to its foundation. The case was so important, in fact, it's the reason we have more color on every one of our large bills today.

Frankly, a shakeup was long overdue as the US system went 80 years without any significant changes in how we printed money. We used only three colors, two greens, one black, and some of the ink was pressed into the paper and some of the ink was raised above the paper. Obviously, when a country uses the same printing process decade after decade, it doesn't take long for criminal technology to catch up. The Super Note case changed all that. Not only did the Bureau of Engraving and Printing add color to paper money, but also instituted several additional security features over time.

I was working out of the Honolulu field office, which was responsible for covering all of Asia. I was working the case in Manila and meeting with some of the bigwigs at the Central Bank of the Philippines. When I walked in to attend my meeting, I was approached by Margie, an older woman who asked if she could speak with me. I said, "Sure, ma'am, but first I'm heading to a meeting, and afterward I'll stop by your desk." This was a fortuitous meeting, because she showed me a $100 bill that she believed was counterfeit. She had shown it to another agent, but he couldn't find a problem with it. That didn't satisfy her, because she had a gut feeling that it was counterfeit.

I took the bill and examined it and looked for all the fine details that can give a bogus bill away, including using all the letters and numbers printed on the bill, like the date it was made and in what city and so on. But like my predecessor who had examined it earlier, I didn't see a problem, no hint it was counterfeit. Nothing caught my attention, and I was used to seeing high-quality counterfeit bills from my days with the counterfeit squat in LA.

I told Margie I doubted it was counterfeit, which disappointed her, so I asked her why the bill had made her so suspicious. She didn't have an answer, only a feeling for some reason arising from her 30 years of experience dealing with paper money. Not wanting to ever leave any stone unturned, I told her I would, if she agreed, send the bill to Blackie, an expert in Washington, DC, in our counterfeit division and let him look at it under a high-powered microscope. He could do all kinds of tests with chemicals and whatnot on the paper and the ink. She loved the idea and was thankful, so I packaged the bill and sent it off. Honestly, I didn't expect anything to come out of it and I didn't give it another thought.

As an aside, when I was a young Secret Service agent, we went to school to learn all the ins and outs of counterfeiting, including how they put blue jean scraps into the mix when making the paper, giving it a linen quality, a toughness to stand up to the kind of wear and tear money goes through, including bills being washed because people forgot to remove them from their pockets. Interestingly, the fluorides from the detergent create a fluorescence of the jean scraps under a black light, which is why some experts would wash bills and use a black light to detect counterfeit bills.

A while later, I got a call about the bill I had sent for analysis. I was told to go to the encrypted phone in our office so that we could have a confidential conversation. On that call, I was told the bill was quite significant, and that Blackie found imperfections that verified Margie's suspicions. I was then told it was one of the Super Notes that no one was allowed to talk about. This triggered a series of investigations, because the Philippines had information on how they came into possession of that Super Note, which allowed backtracking to what local bank had turned it into a regional bank which then had turned it into a central bank.

I was sleeping in my hotel room when I got a phone call from Toad, a former counterfeit agent with me in the Los Angeles Secret Service office. It was three thirty in the morning and he apologized for the odd hour, but he assured me it was important. He told me he was calling from the headquarters of the counterfeit division, and I needed to get over to the consulate and call him on the encrypted line. At the time, there was no US embassy in Hong Kong, because Hong Kong was not a country. It was a British colony. Even so, the building housing the consulate was much larger than most US embassies I worked in around the world, and it was always being expanded.

I dressed in a hurry and took off walking across a park to the consulate. Hong Kong is basically a safe city, unless of course, you happen to get lost and find yourself in the wrong alley somewhere, but that's true anywhere you go. I arrived at the consulate and got on the phone to Toad, who told me I couldn't say a word to anyone about what he was going to tell me, and that included all US agencies. The big news was they had just received information that a large quantity of Super Notes had been deposited in the Hang Seng bank in Macau. This, indeed, was big, and it was huge for me as I was the one being sent to retrieve the notes.

Toad requested a Royal Hong Kong Police dog team, meaning a surveillance unit to ensure my safety when I went to pick up the Notes.

None of the people on the dog team appeared to be what they were, which was what made them effective. There were young and old, males and females, dressed up and dressed down, folks who blended in without standing out. I knew none of them would approach me, and I wouldn't know who they were, but I felt confident they were always close by, and that no one would bother me. I felt better about having their protection, because on my return trip, I would be carrying 210 $100 Super Notes on me.

I was instructed to jump on the first jet boat later in the morning and get over to Macau. The jet boats were amazing as they cranked up these huge engines, raising the boats out of the water like on skis, allowing incredible speeds. I splurged and for a few extra dollars, I purchased a first-class ticket, earning me a padded seat with a view, as compared with coach class down below on wooden benches. Periodically, I would get up from my seat and walk around, trying to get a feel for how many people were watching me, not only my dog team, but also possibly the CIA. It was a game I was playing, having a little fun along the way and doing some counter surveillance. Every time I moved, I'd stop and catch a reflection in the glass or a mirror, or act like I was looking closely at something, trying to see who might have moved with me.

It was a quick 30-minute trip to Macau, and as I walked down the exit, I spotted Armando, my contact, flanked by armed plainclothes officers. Fortunately, we had met before and established a personal relationship, always a priority with me, and obviously a good thing at times like this. He greeted me, then whisked me toward customs, because technically, I was coming in from a foreign country. There were long lines, of course, but Armando with his credentials escorted me through an emergency exit to a car with a driver waiting for us. We all hopped in and off we went. Other than small talk, there was no real conversation in the car, because this business was so hush-hush.

We arrived at the bank headquarters and went through several layers of security checks, then on to a meeting with some bigwigs who handed over 210 Super Notes. I didn't want any screw-ups and was careful not to touch the bills with my fingertips as I counted each note to make sure I had every single one in my possession, then I signed the chain of custody— essentially an inventory of the stash—documenting that they had handed off the contraband to me. I put the notes in a case that went into a satchel, zipped it up, thanked them, and shook hands. With that, we were off, not even stopping for lunch or a few brews and the exchange of war stories. Strictly business.

They took me straight back to the jet boat, escorting me around all the lines like a VIP, and there I was back in my first-class seat, where I'm sure my dog team was waiting for me in the crowd of over 100 passengers. We took off again, that exhilarating feeling of flying over the water, and in no time, I was back in Hong Kong and off the boat. Agent Barn and his guys were there to meet me, and they zipped me through customs. On the way to their car, I was stopped by a couple of fellows I recognized from the CIA, who asked me if I would like to have a ride back to the Consul General. I thanked them but declined and told them I had a ride. They insisted a bit, but pleasantly, telling me it was no trouble for them as they were going my way. Uppermost in my mind was that I was not to share any information with anyone, including the CIA, and I sure didn't want to be in the car with them holding an obvious conversation piece on my lap, a sealed diplomatic pouch.

I did my job, and someone signed for the pouch that quickly was transported by diplomatic courier back to the United States and straight to Secret Service headquarters. Handing off that pouch felt like I had released a massive weight from my shoulders, which was replaced by a pat on the back for a job well done. That's all I needed, because it was enough for me to know I helped secure the Super Notes, and from them, we got intel that led to significant arrests. That, plus knowing it turned out to be one of the biggest cases in our history is heady stuff.

I later learned that the money had come into Macau through some North Korean diplomats who made the bank deposit, and there was talk that the notes might be headed to Iran. Why? Perhaps to help them improve the quality of their own counterfeiting schemes. Back in the 1950s, when Iran and the United States had a friendly relationship, we gave them printing presses to make their own currency that, like ours, would be hard to counterfeit. But the Shah, Mohammad Reza Pahlavi, was overthrown, and militant Islamic forces took over. Although it took them several years, eventually they were able to use the printing presses to make credible counterfeit US bills. The Super Note could have helped them improve on the quality of their efforts.

Let me add as an aside that Macau is the Las Vegas of China with many casinos, so it might seem that bogus bills could be passed along easily through a casino. Not true. Because casinos deal with cash constantly, they have an eagle eye for counterfeit bills and are sharp at detecting them.

CHAPTER 41

UNDERCOVER DOWN UNDER

After paying my dues in the Honolulu field office and spending my first few years in Bangkok, Manila, and Hong Kong, I finally got my choice assignment, which took me to Australia and New Zealand every couple of months for at least three weeks at a time. Of the more than 70 countries I have visited, Australia is my favorite. This is true, even though I had to go to Canberra, the capital of Australia and the site of the US embassy. Canberra was too quiet, the streets folded up at five o'clock in the afternoon, so I didn't spend any more time there than I had to. In contrast, I sure enjoyed working in Sydney and Melbourne, huge cities that never sleep.

It's funny, I guess you could say, but after each of my three-week stints in Australia, when I would come home, my wife would take one look at me and say, "Greg, you sure look like crap."

She was right, of course, because that's what happens after three weeks of heavy beer drinking into the wee hours of the night, not working out, and allowing my food choices to deteriorate substantially. It would take a few days of detoxing, eating right, sleeping right, and working out again to get me back on the straight and narrow. But it was worth it, because I made some close friendships with several guys, friendships that persist to this day.

When I was in Melbourne, I got a call from the Victoria police, nicknamed the "Vickies." Melbourne is in the state of Victoria. Down there, they do things a bit differently in that they don't have big city police departments. Instead, they have a state police department protecting the entire state, including policing what goes on in the various cities. The call came from a guy I knew on the force, a member of their SWAT team. They call it the Special Operations Group or SOG. I was told they had some guys, some bad actors, tough guys who had fought in the war in Serbia, and they were running counterfeit US money into Melbourne through a contact. They wanted to know if I'd be willing to work as an undercover agent and make a buy from them, with them covering me. I said yes right away because one thing I've done throughout my career that I've always enjoyed is going undercover and acting like a bad guy, carrying out hand-to-hand buys from targets.

When this came my way, I was smart enough to know not to call back to Secret Service headquarters and ask for permission because they never would have given it to me. And the Vickies told me that if their bosses found out what was going down, that an American Secret Service agent was working undercover for them, they never would approve it. Basically, they would be scared to death that something might happen to me that would blow up to be a big international incident.

I felt perfectly comfortable working undercover with these guys because I had spent so much time with the SOG and knew they were highly trained, a top-notch SWAT operation. What's more, I trained shoulder to shoulder with them, and I knew they would cover me as good as any American unit would. So, I agreed to it and met the target down in the city of Melbourne, which is somewhat like our city of San Francisco, located on a large bay, and all artsy and fartsy with boutique coffee shops, which is where we met.

We talked over coffee, and I was wired so that my team could listen in. I tried to give them something to laugh about, the smart-aleck in me taking over periodically, but I also had to keep in mind that this could be evidence admitted in court, so I couldn't make it too outrageous, and certainly not to the extent I would have preferred. I told my target guy that my name was Greg, I was from Kentucky, and we talked about the Derby and such. Then he pulled out some fifty-dollar bills for me to look at. I examined them and found the craftsmanship to be acceptable, and I asked how much he wanted for the bills. The going rate typically is about 10 points, or 10 percent of the face value, five bucks per fifty-dollar bill. As part of my approach, I always tried to bargain, to undercut, and get the best deal possible, which is what a real contact would do. I pointed out imperfections on the bills and told him I'd give him 5 percent, to which he replied, no, no, no, he had to have a minimum of 10 percent. My response was that the highest I could go was 6 percent. So, we negotiated back and forth, which helped my cover, because they would assume that if I was a cop, I'd immediately take the deal, make the buy, and grab him.

We made progress and I bought a couple samples from him, supposedly to take back to my boss and see if he would be comfortable buying a large quantity, which was the goal. I had been told how to dry clean myself after the deal, which meant if I had a tail on me I would know how to lose it. I flagged down a taxi, jumped in, and rode a few blocks and around the corner, got out and walked into a big inner-city mall where I took the escalator downstairs, looked at a store window awhile, then took the elevator up to the third floor, got off, looked again, then came right back down the escalator, and went out a different door than the one I came in. The whole time I was doing this, a surveillance team made up of Victorian police officers followed my every move—a couple of the guys I recognized, the others I didn't. When I came out of the mall, I was picked up by another cab, this one driven by a member of my surveillance team. No doubt, if anyone had been following me, I would have either discovered them or lost them quickly.

We ended up making a big buy from this guy, and since they surveilled him after our first encounter, following him to his distributor, it was easy pickings from there. This, of course, exposed me as working undercover, but they weren't worried because they knew I'd be leaving the next day to go back to the United States. It was a good case in several ways, including the fact that these bad guys had ties to terrorists, helping to fund them so that they could make their mark in that part of the world.

It was fun working in this way, and it gave the Vickies something different to do. It also gave us an excuse to celebrate mightily before I left for home.

CHAPTER 42

MELE KALIKIMAKA

While I was working in Hawaii, I received a call about a guy who was sending altered cell phones to some criminal syndicates in Australia. US Customs intercepted a package that he had someone from LA mail to him in Hawaii; he planned to take a flight down under the next day with the package. This prompted an emergency response call from the LA Secret Service field office, informing me of the interception. The guy who was to receive the phones had been indicted by a federal grand jury in the Southern District of California and they wanted me to arrest him before he had the opportunity to leave the country. Timing was critical because if he got wind that we were on to him and he got away, we'd never see him again. These altered cell phones were a big deal, and I'll tell you why when I wrap up this story.

This was all going on Christmas Eve morning, not good timing because we were working with a skeleton crew. But I knew I had to get on this right away, so I threw together a mini task force by calling some contacts in the Honolulu PD, my Harley-Davidson buddies. I was close to them and felt comfortable asking for a big favor to help me with the arrest. Problem was, the guy I was after lived in this beautiful beach house in a gated community, and as I surveilled it earlier, it was clear he wasn't going to let anyone in he didn't trust and know well. So, we concocted a plan where I contacted an associate who worked for an express delivery service. We borrowed shirts and hats to look official, took one of the delivery vans, and intended to deliver the package of altered cell phones that had been intercepted. The plan was to tell the guy he had to sign for the package, which would get us in.

At the front gate, we looked up at the video camera and rang the doorbell. I let Billy O., a full-blooded Hawaiian, do the talking over the intercom with his local dialect, pidgin English.

"Hey, Brah," he said. "We got this package and need ya to sign for it. Bein's we're going into the Christmas weekend, I figured maybe you'd be wantin' this right away. Otherwise, it'll be a while before you get it, like not till Tuesday."

The guy seemed perturbed, but our act was convincing with the van and the Hawaiian delivery man, and he opened the gate for us. I grabbed the box from the van. It was a large square box, and I left the edge open, allowing me to insert my Sig Sauer .357 semiautomatic handgun. In other words, the butt of my gun was near my chest as I carried the box, and the intact side was facing away and toward the recipient.

I approached the door with my hat pulled down, covering most of my face, and with my dark hair, I looked the part. When I knocked, he opened the door and I said, "Mr. So-and-So?" He says, yeah, and I said, "Here's your special delivery."

I handed him the box, and when he took it, he pulled the box toward him while I held onto my gun, which meant he was looking down the barrel of the .357 in my right hand. In my left hand, I had my Secret Service badge and credentials, which I raised to eye level. I told him, "Mele Kalikimaka," which means Merry Christmas in Hawaiian. Then I told him he was under arrest.

The expression on his face was priceless, the kind of look you get when someone is thinking they are on a reality TV show and that whatever is happening can't be real. It was real, and luckily no one else was in the house that might be in harm's way. The other two guys in the van dashed to the door, grabbed him, assisted him to the floor, and handcuffed him. It was funny watching the guy while we transported him to jail. Stunned is the word, and he kept mumbling to himself in disbelief. Ultimately, he was extradited back to a large Secret Service office on the mainland, where he faced federal charges. Clearly, not your typical Christmas Eve story, but one that ended up good for us.

—

Why were the altered cell phones such a big deal? Every time a number is dialed on them, the phone number changes. This involved a high-tech program that can change the EEPROM (electrically erasable programmable read-only memory) inside the phone. EEPROM is in electronic devices like computers to store small amounts of information, while allowing individual bytes to be reprogrammed or erased. The point is, if criminal syndicates, arms dealers, drug dealers, or terrorists got hold of these phones, the CIA, FBI, or NSA would not be able to get any sort of wiretaps because the number would literally change every time they placed a new call. This was also a problem for phone companies, because they could never send a phone bill to anyone using these phones, which meant they were losing money.

When I was working out of LA, we heard about these phones and were briefed on them, the ins and outs of how they worked, and we identified a guy who was trying to sell them from a motorcycle. We tracked this guy in cool cars and decided we needed to take him because we followed him from a deal and knew he had the phones in the storage compartment on his motorcycle. We pulled him over on the side of the road, and when we did, he thought we were bad guys trying to kill him. We straightened him out, then took him in. Turns out he was on probation and if he went down again, he would be a PFO, a persistent felony offender, facing heavy prison time. The threat flipped him, and he started working for us.

We wired him and sent him to his supplier, an absolute genius who cooked up this scheme to alter the phones. Once they completed their deal, we came in with a search warrant and arrested the supplier who also was sitting on probation time. Although he was a genius, he wasn't smart when it came to cocaine and was hopelessly addicted, which required lots of cash to feed his habit. We flipped him as well, and he cooperated, schooling us on his method for altering cell phones and giving us his contacts. From this, we were able to break up the entire organization.

It was a big case in Secret Service fraud history, and Dan, my partner, and I were invited back to Washington, DC, to teach other federal agents what to look for and how we investigated it, which earned us a few attaboys.

CHAPTER 43

DIAMONDS ARE FOREVER

Late in my career as a Secret Service agent and after being promoted, I was put in charge of the Secret Service Financial Crimes task force, based out of the Louisville metropolitan area. A cool part of this was that I was able to handpick my crew from four or five different agencies. I had an IRS agent, a postal inspector, detectives, police officers, and state troopers, and I deputized them as Special Deputy US Marshalls, which gave them the power to investigate and make arrests outside their individual jurisdictions. Our role was to investigate the financial fraud cases that police or sheriff's departments couldn't follow up, usually meaning that leads might take them beyond their jurisdiction. These might be called intermediate cases, too big for local police, but not big enough for the Secret Service to take over and use all their resources.

Not to brag, but we had an all-star team. We were extremely effective, arresting a lot of people and amassing so much evidence we filled up the US Marshall's storage depot and had to rent more storage space to accommodate. One case stands out. It involved two individuals, the main actor and his getaway driver who were working jewelry stores located in shopping malls across the Midwest.

The main actor, I'll call him Jack, would case a jewelry store, then enter and give the clerk a story that he wanted to buy his wife a nice anniversary diamond. As he looked over the stock, he'd always pick a diamond that was worth around $9,000, and short of $10,000, as anything over that amount might draw unwanted attention. Jack would tell the clerk he was interested in the diamond only, because he wanted to set it in his mother's ring. An important factor for choosing these stores was that the clerks worked for commission and they were always eager to make a big sale.

Jack would tell the clerk, "Look, I have to make sure this is the diamond I want because I'm also looking at some other options. So, will you be working tomorrow?"

Excited about the potential for a big commission, the clerk would affirm that, indeed, he or she would be there when needed. Then, the next day, Jack would call the store and tell the clerk that his meeting ran over and he's running late, but he wants to purchase the diamond he saw yesterday before he leaves town to go home. "Tell you what, I think I can be there in an hour or so, if that's okay with you."

The clerk would, of course, agree and anxiously await.

As promised, Jack would arrive, but it would be later, a bit after five p.m., and he would produce a cashier's check for the full amount of the diamond. The problem was, the banks were now closed, and the clerk could not call and verify the check. This put the clerk in a bind because he couldn't verify the check, but he sure wanted the commission. Here was the hook. Jack made it clear he was leaving town right after the purchase, and that meant it was now or never.

Greed invariably would prevail, and the sale was made. Unfortunately, the next day the bank would determine that the check was counterfeit. Now, this was decades ago and well before computerization streamlined everything. It was a time when it was common to make big purchases with a cashier's check, so there were no red flags, nothing particularly suspicious about the transaction.

This scheme worked beautifully and was successful 18 times throughout the Midwest, and we wanted to get this guy. As a starting point, we made the rounds of all the mall jewelry stores in the region, and I would give my card to the clerks and tell them the story, step by step in detail.

"Just in case you experience this, call me right away, and we'll catch him when he comes back the next day to make the purchase."

It took a while, but eventually I got a call from a store clerk telling me he encountered everything I told him. Immediately, the task force went to the mall and set up surveillance teams. Soon after and according to script, Jack walked in just after five p.m. He bought the diamond and we let the purchase go through. Then, as he was getting into his car in the parking lot, we blocked him in with our cars, and like you see on TV, with guns drawn, we took him down and arrested him. We also arrested Jack's partner who was driving the car.

After the arrest, Jack's partner didn't have anything to say. Jack, on the other hand, was aggressive when I tried to interview him. He was a typical alpha male, a tough guy who got in my face, cussed me out with numerous F-bombs and even threatened me.

He said, "Look, I'm an ex-cop from St. Louis who got jammed up and wound up in a maximum-security penitentiary. Having been a cop in prison and survived, you know what that means. So, what do you think you're gonna do to scare me?"

He talked a strong game, and I had the feeling he looked at me like I was some wet-behind-the-ears yahoo who didn't have a clue what I was up against.

Jack made it clear he knew his rights, and he didn't want or need a lawyer. The good thing for me was, he was talking. I started plotting a strategy to use on Jack to try to open him up. You see, I had a good reputation for getting perps to talk using my own methods, and often this led to a confession, either written or video recorded. A confession done the right way is critically important, because if the suspects decide they want to go to trial, it's hard for them to go against what they have already confessed to.

In my approach, I never screamed or yelled, never slammed my fist on the table or threw things. I had seen this play out countless times to no avail, because when officers act that way, it puts the perp on guard, braced against the interviewer. It also comes across as being desperate and not professional. Instead, I treated Jack like a human being and asked if he'd like something to drink: coffee, water, a soda. He told me his blood sugar had been acting up and he needed something sweet like a candy bar.

I got him a candy bar, and since he refused to answer any of my questions, I quit interrogating him. Instead, I shifted gears and talked to him person to person. If you have patience and know how to listen, it can be effective and with Jack it was. After a while, things went a little deeper, more personal, and he began talking about his daughter, an adult living in another state. The more he talked about her, the more it became apparent that he really cared about her, and that caring and concern might be his Achilles heel, my opening.

I concentrated the conversation on his daughter, and told him, "To be honest with you, you're headed to jail for quite a stretch. You've successfully pulled this scam 18 times across the country, and once not so successfully and you ended up sitting where you are. This adds up to a big case."

Jack shook his head and he gave me a look that told me he knew I was telling him straight, no bull. Then Jack's face softened, and he said, "I've got $280 on me and I'm wondering if there is any way you could get that to my daughter. She's struggling bad and barely making it, and I send her money when I can."

"That's what dads are supposed to do," I said. "It's your pocket money and I can't link it to any crime, so, yeah, I'll send it along and make sure she gets it."

With that, Jack's entire demeanor changed, and he was grateful. Sensing the breakthrough, I let him call his daughter, but she wasn't home, so he left a message. When he hung up, he said, "Man, she's gonna be so disappointed in me because I told her I've been keeping my nose clean."

Then he opened up and told me his story. After hearing it, I was able to confirm that, yes, he had been a St. Louis cop. More than that, he had earned the medal of valor when he risked his life saving some kids from a burning building. But after being hailed as a hero, he made a bad choice and agreed to protect some organized crime mobsters who were transporting stolen electronics. Problem is, it turned out to be a federal sting operation. He was fired as a police officer, arrested, and charged with using his authority as a cop to commit crimes, a "color of law" violation that added time to his sentence. He served time in a federal penitentiary, got out, returned to his home town, and vowed to stay on the straight and narrow.

Unfortunately, that didn't last long, but this time, it wasn't his fault. As he was walking down the street, he ran into someone who knew him as a cop, and they had bad blood between them. But now that he was no longer a cop, this guy wanted a piece of him, and he attacked. During the fight, the guy pulled out a knife, but he ended up getting stabbed and died. Jack was charged in the death, manslaughter or whatever, and served more time in state penitentiary. Given his record, Jack was going to serve a long time and maybe die in jail.

After he talked himself out, Jack said, "I appreciate you letting me contact my daughter and helping me get some money to her." Then he went silent a moment, shrugged, nodded, and opened the spigot and told me everything I needed to know: the who, what, when, where, and how they did what they did.

He told me I'd find a box under the bed in the hotel room they were staying in about an hour from Louisville. I contacted the field office there and they got a search warrant, went in, and found the box. In it was a series of FedEx envelopes, and in each envelope was a counterfeit cashier's check, matching fake work documents, fake driver's license, etc. He'd enter a jewelry store with a kit of materials and convincingly pull off the scam.

Next, we got to work and determined who was printing the fake documents and took him into custody. And after that we caught the guy who was buying all the "hot" diamonds. He was working in a diamond exchange, and was eager to buy diamonds for a much-reduced rate.

All in all, it was a great case leading to many arrests, and the key was simply listening and offering a small act of kindness.

CHAPTER 44

THE CROOKED CHINESE CREDIT CARD CASE

When I was assigned to the Honolulu field office for investigations, I was frequently called to Asia, especially Hong Kong, where I worked closely with the Royal Hong Kong Police Department and a friend I mentioned earlier, Agent Barn, a high-ranking supervisor. We worked a lot of fraud cases together in the early and mid-1990s. In particular, we worked on and blew up the Crooked Chinese Credit Card Case, the largest counterfeit credit card case in Secret Service history up to that date. It involved several Chinese triads. A triad is one of many branches of transnational organized crime syndicates based in countries with significant Chinese populations. In other words, they are sophisticated gangs of Chinese criminals, the Chinese version of the Bloods and Crips, except much more powerful.

The triads operated in Hong Kong much more easily and effectively than they could in mainland China. The police in China don't worry about human rights. If they catch someone doing something wrong, or even suspect someone of doing something, they might beat that person, or shoot or imprison him or her for life. Not a good atmosphere for criminals. In contrast, Hong Kong was under British rule at the time, and because folks living there had more rights, the criminals got away with a lot more and more easily avoided prosecution.

At first, rival Chinese gangs would fight continuously with each other, turf wars for control of criminal activities. Then they wised up and realized that if they worked together, business would be better and without the bloodshed. One example of this is when they joined up to produce counterfeit credit cards: Visa, MasterCard, and American Express. At first, their counterfeiting wasn't great, but gradually, every few months we'd see marked improvement in their craft to make the cards look more and more like the real thing, with the magnetic strips that were encoded and all the technical stuff that is involved in making a good mock-up of a credit card. As agents, we had tons of training on all the ins and outs of credit cards so that we could hold our own when cross-examined, and I did testify on several occasions as an expert witness in Hong Kong courts.

The triads were manufacturing the cards in mainland China, and the cops were being paid off to let the factories crank out the products without interference. Now, although the credit cards looked good, they weren't perfect, and I could certainly tell the difference between the real and the fake. But the average Joe would not be able to make the distinction and would easily accept it and move the transaction forward. Even though the name and credit card number on the front were made up, meaning the bill did not come back to a real person, the magnetic strip was encoded with real information from a credit card that had been compromised or stolen. Thus, when the card was swiped, the card, if it hadn't been reported stolen and cancelled, would work.

While I was in Honolulu, not on assignment outside the country, which was rare, I got a call that somebody was using what they thought was a counterfeit credit card at one of the stylish shopping malls to purchase Rolex watches. Suspicions were raised when a credit card didn't work, and the crooks pulled out another one that did. When this happened, the store clerk confiscated the card. Even so, he let the purchase go through, probably because clerks are paid on commission, and he would certainly want the purchase of several Rolex watches to be completed.

I responded immediately, and since our field office was close by, I got there quickly and missed the crooks by only a few minutes. I pulled up the video on the cameras in this high-end jewelry store and got some pictures printed, then I cast a wide net to all the other jewelry stores in the area to see if these guys had been making the rounds. I also did a name search for anyone who might be leaving the country, but the name on the confiscated credit card was bogus. Dead end. With that, I went to the airport with pictures and showed them around to all the airlines. To my surprise, when I got to Japanese Airlines, I was told the guys in the picture had bought a ticket and their flight was boarding right now.

Unfortunately, getting through a security line and stopping a flight takes nearly an act of Congress. That meant I couldn't get there in time and had to stand by helplessly and watch the plane taxi down the runway, the crooks smug with their stash of Rolex watches. Disappointed, I went back to the office and got on the phone with my contacts from over the years in Hong Kong, China, and Japan, and faxed them pictures of these guys and asked that if they come into their country to please hold them for me. This is where socializing and making friends paid off, because they all knew me and knew that I was good for my word and that the US government was willing to prosecute if we could get our hands on the suspects.

All this effort paid off, because they caught these guys leaving Tokyo for Taipei. How much the extra muscle brought into play by big stakeholders MasterCard, Visa, and American Express helped, I don't know. I do know that in many other countries, getting things done that require cooperation across the board typically takes a lot of bribery, but who knows.

Now, on a much larger scale, when the Hong Kong police finally caught on to what was happening and turned up the heat, the tons of counterfeit credit cards they were manufacturing began to be exported to Canada, Australia, and the United States. They would ship them out in picture albums, the large ones with hard covers that have plastic slots. Typically, these plastic slots have generic pictures in them to show you how to place your own pictures, one facing in each direction, and they would slip the cards into the slots between the pictures and ship them out. This was already a highly successful operation, but things changed, and the export of illegal credit cards escalated tremendously when it became known that Hong Kong would cease to be under British control and be turned over to the Chinese government. This terrified criminals because they knew they had it good under the British, but things would change dramatically with the Chinese in control, so they left the country in hordes, taking with them their counterfeiting business.

All in all, counterfeited credit cards ballooned into a massive international case. Solving it required every resource we could muster, working the case to the max with relentless surveillance and tracking, constant communication from continent to continent, sharing intel of the highest sensitivity, arresting people and flipping them to work as informants and wear wires, and lots of undercover professionals on the job. It was essentially good old-fashioned police work coordinated among the Secret Service in LA, the Royal Hong Kong PD, the Vancouver police intelligence unit and organized gang unit, and the New South Wales police in Sydney, Australia.

One of the interesting aspects of this case is that we charged those we caught with racketeering, using the RICO statute (the Racketeer Influenced and Corrupt Organization Act created to combat Mafia groups). We were told that it was the first time in American history that the US Attorney's Office decided to charge foreigners with the RICO statute, which has severe penalties. This required us, the boots on the ground, to prove the conspiracy, and that's exactly what we did, indicting every last one of the bad guys, including one of the biggest Chinese leaders. I can't remember his Chinese name, but it translated into "Two Thumbs," because he had a birth defect and was born with two thumbs on one hand.

In my opinion, what helped this case was not so much that we were all super sleuths, brilliant beyond compare, although I think we were good, but the key was that we all worked so well and so closely together.

Too often when cases get big and are sensationalized, guys start worrying about who and what agency will get credit for masterminding the bust. This can lead to withholding information, lack of cooperation, and even downright competition, which seems childish and unproductive, and, of course, it is. Instead, we had unusually strong camaraderie, the "all for one and one for all" spirit that clicked and helped us move forward and excel as a group, each of us going out of our way to help the others. It was, indeed, the ideal situation for catching bad guys and putting them away.

With that said, let me wrap up this section by giving a shout out to our incredible team. My friends and colleagues with the Royal Hong Kong PD, Agent Barn, Sheriff, and Slugger and Chook, my good mates from Australia. (Slugger has made the trek to visit me in Louisville on many occasions, and when I go there, I can always count on Slugger standing there with a big grin waiting for me to deplane, no matter what time of day or night it might be.) Esmund, from the private sector, did some amazing work in China with the Hong Kong police. And, of course, indispensable US Secret Service agents who traveled all over the world on this case, and in particular, from Honolulu: the professional's professionals, Pic, Zygo, and Chodo. Thanks, guys, for the thrill of a lifetime.

PART FOUR

SACRED SERVICE: DEACON AND CHAPLAIN

CHAPTER 45

SNEAKIN' DEACON

Up until I was nearly 50 years old, the thought of being any kind of clergy, chaplain, deacon, or whatever never occurred to me. It never occurred to me even though I guess you could say I was a religious person; regardless of where I was serving around the world, going to church on Sundays was a priority for me, and I rarely missed because somewhere in the area there would always be a Catholic church. I've attended Catholic churches in Hanoi, all over Africa, South America, and Asia, and some of the services, especially in poverty-stricken countries, are crazy different, but the purpose and intent are the same. Attending church was my dad's influence. Sunday was church day, no exceptions, and it was a time to be thankful for our many blessings. And every year at Christmas, my dad would give me a missal, a worship aid for Catholic masses that are celebrated daily throughout the world. It contains all the scripture readings for the coming year, so no matter where I was, I felt part of a larger, worldwide congregation.

But that was the extent of my religious endeavors, a face in the crowd, in and out without any sort of true involvement. However, that began to change after my personal encounter with the Pope as a Secret Service agent. Seeds were planted deep inside me that began to take hold, changing me. How, I wasn't sure, but I knew I needed to become more involved in my church, and not merely go through the motions of attending Mass.

This led to me taking what was for me was a giant leap forward and I became an usher. Not much of a leap in retrospect, but it sure seemed like it to me at the time. I liked being of use and helping out as an usher, which inspired me to do more. I got involved as a Eucharistic minister, assisting with Holy Communion, and I also became a minister to the sick. As I became more involved, someone offhandedly mentioned that maybe I was being called to become a deacon. Who, me? Sorry, but you got the wrong guy.

In the Catholic Church, a deacon is what you might call a hybrid, a bridge between the layperson and the priest, and they are very much like priests with two major differences. Deacons cannot celebrate Mass, and are restricted to assisting the priest, as only the priest is endowed with the apostolic authority to call down the Holy Spirit and change bread and wine into the body and blood of Christ. The other difference is that deacons cannot hear confessions. Beyond that, deacons do about everything else, including baptisms, weddings and funerals, visiting the sick and those in jail, and helping with discussions of spiritual matters. Although deacons may have better insights into how families function and dysfunction because we are allowed to marry and have children, and we typically are working full-time jobs, we don't engage in formal marriage and family counseling unless we are certified, but we listen and can offer advice if it is requested.

I couldn't see myself as a deacon for several reasons, including the fact that I knew the training was demanding and intense. I had had a lot of training in my career and I benefited greatly from it, but now that I was retired from my full-time duties, I wasn't eager to take on a five-year program that was much like getting a college degree. To become a deacon requires lots of schoolwork with classes in the evenings and on weekends as most deacons have full time jobs elsewhere. We also had periodic three-day retreats. The schoolwork was challenging and included a heavy reading schedule, writing papers, discussing issues, debating, and participating in training masses. Anyway, I chuckled and dismissed the thought of becoming a deacon.

Then, a while later, the idea reappeared more forcefully and began to percolate. I was part of the men's Bible study group that met at seven o'clock on Saturday mornings for about an hour and a half, and Deacon Jack was part of that group. Jack was a guy I liked, a man with great leadership qualities, someone who folks looked up to, and he offered to head up a men's retreat at a seminary in Bardstown. I accepted the invitation eagerly, and Jack offered to drive me down there. I was glad to ride along, and I figured he simply didn't want to drive by himself. Actually, Jack had an agenda and that was to talk to me about becoming a deacon, but he didn't talk about it on the way down. Instead, he waited for the trip home and told me he'd been watching me in Bible study, how when I spoke up, others listened, and he knew of my involvement with the church as a Eucharistic minister and minister to the sick, and he was aware that I had been running a camp for kids with cancer.

Gee, Deacon Jack sure knew a lot about me, and it was flattering. Then he hit me with the punch line. "Greg, I believe God is calling you to become a deacon."

I was surprised at this because there was no warning, and I began backpedaling immediately. I told him I was nearly 50 years old, I'd been in law enforcement the past 30 years, and I didn't see myself in that clergy role, preaching to groups and all the rest that goes with it.

He listened attentively, nodding to affirm what I was saying, then he said, "No obligations involved, and all you have to do is apply for it, go through a background check and some routine procedures. Let's see what God has in mind for you and how he might play it out. I'm simply asking you to consider it."

It's hard to tell a guy like Deacon Jack no, and I didn't, but that was my thought. So, I figured, okay, I'll throw my hat in the ring and go through the motions, but I honestly didn't think it would go far as I was convinced it wasn't in the cards for me, wearing a collar and doing all the things that deacons do. Even so, because I didn't decline, I moved forward and met other deacons, then I took a series of psychological tests and had a mentor couple assigned to me to essentially tutor me and answer my questions. This part of the process goes on for about a year in which people considering it have the opportunity to discern about it, then if they feel like it's right for them and they are interested in going further, and if they think they are deacon material, the archbishop gives his okay to apply for entrance into the next deacon class.

At the time I was accepted for training, my wife, Tracy, was a Southern Baptist and her response to the whole business was, "What did you get me into?"

This is because the wives were expected to attend classes and go on the three-day weekends with their husbands. Back then, she would attend Mass with me, her choice to do so, and she was familiar with the Catholic faith, but this was an entirely different matter and it required quite a commitment from her.

She had a demanding career as a pharmaceutical rep which required a fair amount of traveling. She was plenty busy keeping up with all the responsibilities and demands associated with raising our three kids, and two of them were babies. She looked at me with what can only be described as incredulity and told me point blank, "There's no way we can do this, and why would you think it's even remotely possible for us?"

In other words, it was okay for "me," but "us" was an entirely different matter. Among other things, originally when the whole deacon thing came up, she saw herself as staying home with the kids while I was off doing deacon things, and that was fine with her. But the Church was strong on the idea that wives needed to be part of the process, and most importantly, they wanted the process to strengthen the husband-and-wife bond, and not do the opposite and pull spouses apart.

Admittedly, the whole thing seemed like an arduous uphill struggle, but one of the reasons I love my wife so very much is that, notwithstanding all the things lined up against the likelihood of success, she was willing to give it a try. And that was a big deal, because she had supported me for many years as a Secret Service agent, with all my traveling and the long separations we experienced at times, and here I was imposing a big load on her again. Says a lot about her, doesn't it? You bet!

Once people started hearing about me applying to be a deacon, a lot of them started asking me why I'd want to do that. This was because the publicity surrounding sexual abuse carried out by priests was soaring and at its peak. In fact, the first day of deacon school, a priest said, "Are you guys crazy for wanting to become deacons and march right into the heart of this whole sordid business?"

I heard from friends, especially law enforcement friends, asking me why I'd want to be part of that. I accepted these as fair questions, and the only way I could answer was that it had to be the pull of the calling. Why else would anyone in their right mind want to commit to all it would take: the classes, endless hours of studying and writing papers, all stacked on top of my other commitments as a husband and a father, plus my nearly full-time duties as a security consultant. And at the end, I would be tied to an organization targeted in daily headlines as harboring and protecting sexually abusive priests.

Clearly, in my view, the church needed new blood, guys who would stand up to this and help with a new beginning. But why me, and what about my career in law enforcement where I had spent years putting bad guys, like these guilty priests, in jail? Would I be conflicted if I encountered a similar thing as a deacon?

I said with some force, "Hey, don't think for one second that I would protect someone who was harming a child. And don't be mistaken; I am completely disgusted with not only these priests who did these horrible deeds, but also the bishops and cardinals who at the least looked the other way, and at worst, actively protected them. They are all guilty and should be punished, and there would be zero sympathy from me. In fact, it would take a great effort on my part not to get the cop in me all worked up and do my best to seek justice."

I gave this a lot of thought in private and tried to be even tempered about it. Like, for example, knowing that only 5 percent of priests were guilty in this way. That is 5 percent too many, and there is no way around it, but it also means that 95 percent of priests were doing God's work and shouldn't be painted with the same broad brush. I had to consider the backlash arising from the incredible hypocrisy of having priests who supposedly stand above all others as devoted examples of the "right" way to live, dictating what is right and wrong to their parishioners, hearing their confessions, passing out penance, and then being exposed. Things were bad to be sure, but were they as bad as publicized? I had to believe they could be fixed with effort, dedication, doing the right things, and setting a good example.

—

I was accepted into the class of 15 men and we started with a three-day weekend retreat at Saint Meinrad Seminary and School of Theology in Indiana, a few hours west of Louisville. It's quite a beautiful spot on a mountain top and a place you'd want to visit in the fall with the leaves changing. We went up Friday afternoon, walked around, familiarized ourselves with the place, then we had dinner; after that, we observed the monks doing their thing. Then it was off to bed, because we were up early the next morning and into classes for the day, then church with the monks on Sunday and more classes. All in all, it was intense, packing a lot into three days, a prelude of what was to come.

Back home again, there were more classes and lots of book time, and a variety of activities, including taking credit hours at Spencerian College, being involved with hospital chaplaincy, learning how to visit patients and interact effectively, knowing what to say and what not to say, and learning the ins and outs of conducting Mass, how best to support the priest, so forth and so on.

The several years of training to become a deacon are quite a haul, that's for sure, but it wasn't a burden, and I got through it and was ordained in August 2010. It was a powerful ceremony. The first thing we all did was lie down on the floor in front of the crucifix, like priests do, demonstrating that we were submissive, swearing our allegiance to Christ, and submitting to the authority of the archbishop. The archbishop laid hands on us and called down the Holy Spirt to anoint us with holy orders, placing us in the apostolic succession of 2,000 years, from Jesus to Peter and on down the line.

Among the many things I cherished about my training was how members of my class bonded, much like cops bond, and for life. When you bond like that, there is always a lot of good-natured ribbing that goes on. For example, I recall the day we were in class and taking a break, sitting around talking about nothing in particular when one of my classmates who knew I had been a Secret Service agent piped up and gave me a nickname, dubbing me the "Sneakin' Deacon." It stuck.

In my other life, when I'm with police buddies or on a bodyguarding assignment, usually people don't know my background. But occasionally, someone will say or do something off color and someone might say, "Hey, watch it, Gitsch is a deacon." I'll see a sheepish face and hear something like, "Oh, sorry about that."

But I don't walk around holier-than-thou or even hint in that direction, because I want everyone to feel comfortable in my presence, regardless of which hat I am wearing. With that said, I try to be careful of what I say and how I say it, what I tweet, and so on. I'm also careful to keep many of my personal and political views to myself, not taking sides and not wanting to be seen as taking advantage of my role and using it to influence others in any way.

I discovered quickly that because I'm a deacon, people tend to treat me differently, according me more respect than they might extend otherwise and quite in contrast to how many folks respond to cops, and this takes some getting used to. The other side of this is that it's natural for them to also expect a higher order of behavior from me. For example, one time I was engaged in a co-ed volleyball game for fun, but it got heated as the game came down to the wire. A ball was hit and bounced close to the line where I was positioned, but it wasn't clear whether it was in or out of bounds. Obviously, when something like that happens in a flash, everyone will have their own opinions and opinions tend to be influenced by what is favorable to your team. Anyway, a guy on the other team who was invested in the game began to yell at me. "Hey, you're a deacon and you have to be truthful and make the right call. Was it in or out?" As if I would cheat if I weren't a deacon. He kept at it until folks on his own team told him to shut up, and at that point, I think it occurred to him that he was making a fool of himself. No problem, I've been there, and in the heat of the moment, people can sometimes get goofy.

CHAPTER 46

Preachin' Deacon

At the time of this writing, I am in my eighth year as a deacon, and I love it more than ever. I've been blessed to be assigned to my home parish, allowing me to stay home and not be forced to travel long distances every weekend, and all three of my kids went to the parish school there.

It's ideal, I'm truly blessed, and I get to preach every few months which I enjoy doing, but there is pressure involved to be sure. We all have sat through bad sermons that seem to go on for days, and I never want to put people through that. I found early on that one characteristic of a bad sermon is trying to do too much, make too many points, so many that no one has a clue what I'm talking about. Instead, I try to focus on one main theme and examine it from different perspectives, provide examples and analogies, and throw in a little humor here and there as I believe God has a good sense of humor. When appropriate, I'll toss in stories from my former life as a cop or Secret Service agent. I can tell you this about giving a sermon: there is instant feedback. I know immediately if I am on or off by the facial expressions and the response or lack of response when I think I have said something clever or humorous.

In everyday life, I look for opportunities to serve. Perhaps I come across a bad scene where someone is injured or died, or it's obvious someone is grieving or in emotional pain—whatever—I offer to help in any way I can. I always look forward to a new day, and I have a simple prayer that bolsters me and it's how I start every morning: "Thank you for my rest and show me how I can serve you today." Boom, that's it, but I must warn you that you'd best be careful what you ask for because the Lord can bring you all kinds of interesting ways that challenge you to serve.

Nowadays, my sense of being a deacon is like everyday life on steroids. I experience lows and highs, but they tend more toward the extreme. I see people at their worst and witness a lot of family tragedy, which exerts heavy pressure. When people get angry at God and leave the church, it hurts, because I believe if they would hang in there, I could help them. At such times, I feel powerless, and that's the worst feeling of all. On the other hand, the highs are magnificent, being part of special moments in the lives of others, the birth and baptism of a child, youngsters making their first communion or confirmation, conducting the wedding of two people deeply in love, and even funerals which, of course, are sad in many ways. I believe that almost everything I do can be an opportunity to witness for Christ and offer comfort, like when I led the opening prayer at the candlelight ceremony downtown at Jefferson Square Park commemorating a Louisville police officer who was killed in the line of duty.

One of my favorite duties as a deacon for the past several years is reading for the 30-minute TV show, *Mass of the Air*, a program that has been on for about 20 years at ten thirty Sunday mornings on WHAS in Louisville. The day's Mass readings for the world are read on the show, and there is a brief homily (sermon). I share this duty with many other deacons, so I do about five or six tapings a year. The reason this is so important to me is that it's personal. When my dad or mom was ill and bedridden, whether at home or later in a nursing facility, and could no longer attend Mass on Sundays, they would watch *Mass of the Air*. My mom became familiar with several of the deacons and after I became a deacon, she delighted in asking me about them, if I knew them, what they were like in person.

The TV program makes a nice companion to our ministry of bringing the Eucharist to those who are ill and cannot make it to church, helping them to commemorate the Last Supper in which bread and wine are consecrated and consumed. This is carried out by our Eucharistic ministers of the sick, and that's something I did for one year. Actually, the way I got involved was a mistake. Years before I became a deacon, I was supposed to be attending a Eucharistic ministry meeting for folks who assist at Mass, but instead I went to the wrong meeting. I guess God wanted me to be there, because I was trapped in the front of the room and the door was a long way away in the back. I stayed and am glad I did because it turned out to be a wonderful experience for me, seeing how important my visits were in making Holy Communion available to anyone, anywhere.

As they say, and I fully believe, let go and let God. And remember, if you ask God how you can serve today, be prepared for an answer that might challenge you in a big way.

CHAPTER 47

Part Clergy/Part Cop

When I was on patrol as a young officer, every once in a while, a police chaplain would show up at our roll call before we went out on the street and we knew that meant he wanted to ride with someone. Usually, the older guys who never wanted to ride with a chaplain would push him off onto younger officers. The sergeant didn't care who the chaplain rode with, as long as somebody took him.

It's not that we didn't like chaplains or respect what they do. On the contrary, we knew they were volunteering their time and for all the right reasons. And sometimes we liked and valued having a chaplain available, like when bad news had to be passed along about an accident, a drug overdose, a murder, and so on. At those times, if a chaplain was available, we cops were spared having to perform that duty. I witnessed this firsthand when I was working as a cop and had to tell a mother her child was hit by a car and wouldn't be coming home. Worse, the mother was preparing a gift for her child at the time. Thank God, I was able to get a chaplain to help me, because the feelings were overwhelming, and I wasn't sure how to even begin to carry this out.

At issue, and it wasn't fair to chaplains, was our lack of trust of outsiders, including chaplains, because we were wary of anything we said and did being reported back to the command officers, or even to the chief's office. So, the general attitude toward chaplains, unless they were picking up broken pieces, was if we did get stuck with one on our ride, we couldn't wait to take him back to the district and get rid of him, allowing us to return to our normal day.

Looking back on it, I feel bad about the way we often reacted to these guys, the feeling we had that we weren't comfortable sharing personal problems with outsiders like the chaplains, even though I'm sure most of them were good people who were eager to help. The problem was, when it comes to cops, people have to earn our trust first before we'd open up. As I mentioned previously, in our department we had a chaplain, Preacher Pete, who got personal with a couple of the police officers' wives that he was counseling and that certainly didn't help the situation as far as trust was concerned.

Nowadays, the shoe is on the other foot. When it became known that I was in training to become a deacon, I was invited to come on board as a chaplain. The process was a simple one, basically signing on to help, and it seemed like such a natural fit with all my police experience, enabling me to bridge the gap and more easily earn the trust of the officers. In fact, one of the first things I did as a chaplain was to push for us to do more for the officers. My suggestion was to have a chaplain come into the police academy when new officers are in a classroom, a captive audience that can be educated about what chaplains do and in what ways we can be helpful and how to reach out to us. It also would be helpful to warn about how police work takes a toll on a marriage, the signs to look for, and what kinds of strategies might help before things go downhill too far.

Although I was one of them, it's still not easy for most cops to reach out for help. Cops are loath to admit they need help because they see it as a sign of weakness. It's the biggest no-no for a cop, and this mindset means I rarely get calls. Instead, it's more often a spontaneous reaction, like when I'm at a scene that takes a toll on everyone, and someone will approach me, usually by first telling me they heard I was a cop, as if to verify that approaching me is okay. Then we talk, and I mostly listen, hoping they want to go further with more counseling.

When I counsel cops, the issues vary widely, from coping with senseless violence, to wondering how God can let things happen the way they do, to problems in marriages or with sons and daughters, financial crises, the list goes on. Sometimes, believe it or not, I get requests from people who want to be baptized. I have baptized many police officers on the side of the road, in living rooms, and at my church after mass. Sometimes it's important to them to keep it low-key and they don't want a big to-do about it. They want it personal and private, and I honor that and would never turn anyone down for that opportunity, no matter where I was or what was going on, because as my faith teaches me, it's important to that person, to their soul, especially regarding the afterlife. I'm so thankful that I am empowered to baptize officers who witness horrible things and have strong spiritual needs, and that I'm able to do so right there on the spot.

As a chaplain, one of the first things I learned is, if I got called out, something bad had happened and it usually caught everyone by surprise. Normally, someone got up that morning expecting to have a typical day, then catastrophe struck, and they were suddenly gone. When I'm called, I go to the scene and assist in any way I can to provide spiritual help to the family. I never ask what their religion is, what denomination or whatever. Some people have no religious or denominational orientation, no church, or they'll tell me they haven't been to church in a long time. Or, they tell me they don't believe in God. At times, people react with anger toward God for allowing whatever went down to happen. My response is to encourage them to react as they choose, to scream and yell. God can take it and he'll never turn his back on people, no matter what, and at some point, when the time is right, He will be there waiting to help them in any way that they may need.

I never know when I might get a call; it could be morning, noon, or night. No matter what, I have to get there, but it could take me a half hour, an hour, or more, especially if I'm not home and have to go home to change clothes to look the part of someone representing the police department and the church. Regardless, I always try to get there as fast as I can. If there is a death and the victim has been tended to by paramedics, the next steps are up to the coroner to declare the victim deceased, then notify the family. Then it's my turn as the chaplain. In my experience, the toughest challenge is when a police officer is injured, perhaps in a car accident or maybe a shooting. If he or she is killed in the line of duty, it makes everything much more difficult and intense because all available police officers are going to respond, and it will be a very active situation, brimming with chaos as one of their own has been harmed or killed.

Before I step into any scene, I like to talk with an officer to fill me in and give me a better idea of what happened: Was it an accident, was it deliberate, or perhaps a suicide? Knowing helps me prepare how best to approach family members and talk to them, get a feel for them, and console them in any way I can. By far, the worst scenario is a suicide; it's devastating when people are so down and in such despair that taking their own lives is their only answer. Not only that, it's hard on family members, particularly if the suicide was completely unexpected. I wonder at times, if someone who is considering suicide would stop and consider what it does to loved ones, the devastation it causes, the guilt, the confusion, the anguish of not doing something to stop it, not doing enough. I have attended many suicide scenes, especially around the holiday season, and imagine the impact of a child finding a parent, or vice versa, and the overwhelming feelings that arise. It's perhaps my greatest challenge coming up with something meaningful to say at a time like that.

Some folks are eager to talk at the scene; others don't want to bothered right then. I continue to find it amazing how differently people react to the same circumstances, the different ways people engage in the grieving process. At a recent scene I attended where an infant had died, upon hearing the news, half the people present were stone silent, while the rest were screaming and wailing, falling down, rolling around on the floor.

In certain situations, if I respond and reveal that I'm a police chaplain, it's possible that members of the victim's family do not like the police for some reason, or the police are the ones who took actions resulting in the victim's death. Obviously, it's a delicate situation, because I'm viewed as part of the police department, and at times, I've been asked not to come in, and I've been thrown out of houses because of hatred for the police. Regardless, I understand. I realize each case is different and each must be dealt with individually.

Beyond the needs of the victim and the family at the scene, I am also keenly sensitive to what is too often overlooked, and that is the needs of involved police officers. I know what it's like, and even though cops stand around looking strong and tough, inside they could be in anguish and in need of help. For example, the scene could involve a child that is deceased. This is challenging and difficult even for the most hardened police officers because most of them have children.

At the scene, I don't push forward too aggressively with the officers. Having been on the other side as a cop, I know this is exactly the wrong thing to do. Instead, I make it known that I'm there by perhaps doing something as simple as going to get coffee. I am especially on the lookout for signs a cop may be in trouble emotionally, maybe depressed or worse, considering suicide. At such times, I stay close and do my best to intervene, and this is where my past life as a cop comes in handy. I get it, I understand.

It's also helpful that I'm highly sensitive to not contaminating the scene by touching or moving anything. Legally, when we as clergy go into a crime scene, we can be subpoenaed for a trial as one of the people who were there. That means given all that's involved, it's best that chaplains do not enter a crime scene unless it's necessary. I always ask permission from the officer in charge and make it clear that I understand my role and the obligations I assume when I am there.

I have sometimes found myself at a scene seriously doubting whatever story was being told of how the crime happened. My cop mind speeds there, but as a chaplain, it's not my place to make such judgments, or to say or do anything with what I am feeling. Even so, I can't turn it off when I see someone acting out, or not acting in a way I would interpret as appropriate and consistent with the story that is being told. This, admittedly, makes me suspicious, but I keep it to myself.

On the gentler side, as a chaplain, at times I am asked to lead prayers at a police officer promotion ceremony, or when a new recruit class graduates. Fortunately, I have not been asked to lead prayers at a police officer funeral, and hopefully, I'll never be asked to do that. All in all, it has been a wonderful opportunity to come back to my community where it all started and again be of service to my brothers and sisters in law enforcement. Hopefully, and God willing, I'll be able to serve in this capacity for a good long while.

CHAPTER 48

TRIAL BY FIRE

My first experience as a chaplain could best be described as a trial by fire. I would have liked to believe that all my training, my experiences in so many different venues, including years as a cop, and the wisdom I have accumulated simply from being on this earth for so many years, would have prepared me for whatever it is I might face. Such assumptions were immediately put to rest when I responded to my first chaplain call.

En route, I was nervous, unsure if I would do the right things, say the right things, be a comforting presence. I was informed there was a work accident, which could mean many things, ranging from someone falling and breaking an ankle to the unthinkable, someone being killed on the job. This case was the latter, and I was called to a major construction site where someone had died in a horrible accident. The deceased, a man, had been run over by one of the massive trucks moving in and out of the site.

When I arrived, I walked toward the site of the accident. EMS personnel were there, along with a couple of police officers standing with the body, which had been covered up. I was told the coroner had been notified. The coroner must process the scene and formally declare the individual dead. All work had stopped, of course, and there were massive construction vehicles everywhere. As I approached, I felt the emotions emanating from workers upset at what had happened right there in the middle of the worksite late in the afternoon as they were finishing up their day.

One of the police officers introduced me to the deceased man's supervisor who was visibly shaken. He told me they had already called the family of the deceased and they should be arriving shortly. I asked him if there was a place where I could gather friends and family, and he took me to his office. Soon, the first family member arrived, a sister who was overwhelmed with emotion. I cannot imagine what that must be like, to see your brother in the prime of life the day before, then be informed that the body under the cover was him.

Here, face to face, was my first test as a chaplain. The sister was screaming and crying, and my first instinct was to try to hold her and offer some comfort, not stopping to think that she didn't know me from Adam, nor did she know why I was there. I guess you could say she was so emotionally distraught that she didn't question my actions, which allowed me to hold her and inform her that I was police chaplain and was trying to help in any way I could. As she began to calm down slightly and was able to speak, she told me her other sisters were on their way.

As each sister arrived, the crying and wailing escalated, getting louder and louder. It was obvious I was helpless, and there was nothing I could do to control what was happening as the emotions of each sister fueled the others. Thankfully, another police chaplain stopped by. He knew I was brand new and he had an idea of what I might be facing. I don't think I was ever more elated to see anyone in my life. It was like he was throwing me a lifeline, but instead of it pulling me to safety, it was as if he had failed to secure it, and we both were thrust headlong into the mix. He recognized immediately that he was helpless, as well. He put a hand on my shoulder and gave me a look that told me the best we could do was simply be there for them, and let them mourn without restraint.

Now, stop for a moment if you will and imagine yourself in an office that's not terribly large with several sisters of a man who had died suddenly and tragically, and the sisters had brought their children—all daughters ages, eight to sixteen—for a total of 10 or so females letting out their emotions. It was heartbreaking, and I so much wanted to be able to do something, anything to help. Through the office window, I could see that someone had thought to move a truck into position to block the view. Otherwise, as bad as things were, we would have been looking directly at the body on the ground.

The sisters decided they wanted to see the deceased, and they insisted as I tried to explain that it was best they remember him as he was the last time they saw him. I was very concerned about them charging out the door, throwing the cover off the body, and seeing the damage the truck had done to their brother. It would have been a sight they would never be able to put out of their minds, a sight that would haunt them forever. I stood in the doorway, imploring them to heed my words to remember their brother as he was, praying the whole time that God would send some energy my way to help me make my point.

There were some tense moments, but I was able to breathe a sigh of relief when it was decided that what I was saying was best. It allowed me to ask them if they had a religious leader, someone they could depend on at this time of need. They responded that they were Catholic, which helped me feel slightly better because I knew I could move forward in a known direction with some Catholic prayers. I told them I was a Catholic deacon, and for the first time, I felt that I was some use.

As I coped as best I could with the strong emotions in the office, I was informed that the driver of the truck that ran over the dead man was also on-site nearby. This stung me, because I knew he needed attention, obviously devastated that his actions had unintentionally caused the death of his colleague. In his defense, these trucks are so big, and the drivers sit so high, it's virtually impossible to see clearly what is in front, especially if someone steps out from nowhere. This, combined with the fact that the deceased was unaware that the truck was going to move as he stepped in front of it, made for a perfect storm, setting up the accident. All I can say is what a blessing it was to have a second chaplain there, because I knew I couldn't leave this group. He gave me a nod and took off to be of service elsewhere.

I was there about three hours, but if you had asked me at the time how long it was, I wouldn't have had a clue; the emotions were so intense among the sisters, daughters, and coworkers. Eventually, other family members showed up and some of the men were a blessing and helped me restore a little order. A fellow police officer also lent a hand and showed great compassion, for which I was most grateful. I led the group in the prayer Our Father, and I prayed for the deceased man's soul. As things began to wind down, they thanked me and told me they would continue with the priest from their parish.

In my career as a police officer and Secret Service agent, I certainly have experienced my share of emotionally grueling circumstances, but I have to admit that by the time I left that day, I was wrung out completely, as if my insides had been ripped open and devoured by some large beast, leaving nothing behind. It was something that would stay with me forever.

I also knew for certain that I had made the right choice to serve God in the role of police chaplain. And I accept all that goes with that, including being on call for God, a familiar role for me. As a police officer on the SCUBA team, if somebody needed to be rescued or a body found, I'd get a call. As a Secret Service agent in the investigations unit, I had to take my turn as the duty response agent, which meant if something happened after office hours at night or on weekends, it was my responsibility to respond immediately and represent the Secret Service, whether it be an investigative case or a threat against the president.

And now, once again I'm on a roster for call outs, but this time it's the Sneakin' Deacon in the role of chaplain for the Louisville Metro Police Department. I can be called to go at any time, knowing that I am needed, but not knowing how or why or what to expect. I may be dealing with an injury, death, or suicide, strong emotions, deep depression, anger at the police, anger at God, a feeling of hopelessness, or whatever. Regardless, I believe it's important that I get there as quickly as possible, because it's likely that whatever happened is going to strongly affect a family for the rest of their lives. I must do what I can to ease the burden.

—

In closing, when I was a young child I wanted to be a guardian angel, and I mean that literally. I had an ongoing fantasy, a daydream about how I would go about rescuing Jesus from the cross. Don't laugh, it's true. I conjured up this scenario in which my friends and I would come in there, armed with swords, bows, and arrows covered up by the capes we wore, doing our best to blend in with the crowd. At the right moment, we'd take out the Roman soldiers and then help Jesus down from the cross, ease him into a wagon we had waiting, and take off. Sounds bizarre, I know, but that's how my mind worked at the time.

Ironically, in an earthly sense, the role of guardian, protector, and helper seems to fit the route I've taken in life. As to the angel part, well, I'm sure there are some who might see me as otherwise, but that comes with the territory. I began my role by earning my safety patrol badge in the sixth grade, then moved on at 18 to be a store detective, where I guarded and protected the people working in the store, the customers, and the merchandise. As a police officer, I protected the people living on my beat. As a Secret Service agent, I protected the people allotted protection by the US government and protected the US financial system. As a private security consultant and bodyguard, I protect people who need my services, and as a Catholic deacon, I protect my parishioners and the church. And, finally, wearing my most recent hat as a police chaplain, I am honored to receive the call and do what I can to help. I am well aware that the Angel of Death can come at any time.

As I think back and reflect, my daily life can best be summed up by one of my dad's favorite expressions, words that captured his approach to life as a dedicated FBI agent. When he'd get a call, and it could be any time, day or night, he'd move quickly and be ready in a flash. Then, after slipping his gun into its holster, adjusting his fedora just right, and giving my mother a kiss goodbye, he'd open the door, hold it a moment, then say with a smile, "We doze, but never close."

I can still hear his words echoing in my mind and I must admit, that's exactly how I like it, and I wouldn't have it any other way. This, even knowing that when anyone takes on the role of guardian and protector in all its variations as I have, they find that it's a relentless task with long hours and few breaks, efforts more often than not go unrecognized, and at times it can be life threatening. But, through it all, I have believed in the power of Jesus Christ to sustain me and never let me down, and I am most thankful for my opportunities to serve. Yes, it has been challenging, but it also has been more rewarding and fulfilling than anything I can imagine. What's more, I firmly believe it's what I was supposed to do.

God has a plan for all of us and the sooner we learn what it is, the happier we will be. Amen.

Cancer from Both Sides

On a summer morning 20 years ago, I was reading the newspaper before heading off to my job as a Secret Service agent. When I turned the page, an article caught my eye. It was about people who give up a week of their vacation to work at a camp dedicated to children with cancer. The gist of the story was that kids come to this camp and everything is structured to help them forget about their cancer and have fun, to just be kids again. I was impressed by the idea of the camp, especially since it was free for the kids and their parents, and it was able to survive and operate due to the sacrifice these people were making as volunteers. Good for them, and I'm sure God was smiling about that. Then my mind went on to other things.

Later that day, and this is the honest-to-goodness truth, I got a call from a guy asking me if I would like to go with him and a bunch of University of Louisville football players who were going to this same camp to visit with the kids. I was a mentor at the time to football players who wanted to go into law enforcement. I guess they figured that as a former U of L football player, I'd fit in well with the group, and because I was a Secret Service agent, the kids might get a kick out of my being there.

Interesting, I thought, that I had two messages about this camp full of kids with cancer in less than 12 hours. Hmm, what should I make of that? Well, over the years, I have come to learn that this kind of thing is not mere coincidence. I was supposed to pay attention, and no doubt God was nudging me in that direction for some reason. So, I signed on and went for a visit. Sure enough, I was blown away by the experience of meeting 55 kids with cancer in different stages, ranging from a recent diagnosis to very advanced, kids getting chemo and valiantly battling the disease.

It was quite a day, and when it ended, I went to the camp director and asked if there was anything I could do to help. He smiled, the kind of smile that said, you bet, I've got a long list from which to choose. Then he told me the camp was more than 50 years old and before the kids arrived, the camp needed to be scrubbed top to bottom the day before. He emphasized top to bottom, because some of these kids have compromised immune systems, and everything must be spic and span. The day before the kids arrive is also a training day for the counselors; there is too much to cover and it wasn't possible to handle the training and do the kind of cleaning they needed on the same day. This necessitated soliciting a group of helpers to come up for the day and tackle the unpleasant task. He put a hand on my shoulder and told me it would be great if I could help next year before the camp started. He added, "And maybe bring along some friends." I agreed on the spot and left knowing I would be contacted the next year.

The year went by quickly and it was time to make good on my promise. I sent out a bunch of emails to people I knew from church (this was before I became a deacon) and elsewhere like the Knights of Columbus, asking for help. I made it clear that this was not a glamorous task. It was pure grunt work, cleaning a rustic 50-year-old camp top to bottom, but it had to be done and I told them why. I received some vague commitments, but nothing firm. I know folks are busy and I was asking a lot, but I hoped for the best.

I had told folks I'd meet them at the rest stop on Interstate 64 near Simpsonville on Saturday morning if they could make it. We'd work, have some lunch, and then head for home at around three that afternoon. I vividly remember driving up the highway and saying, "God, please let me have at least a couple of guys there to help me with this, or I'm going to look pretty foolish showing up by myself to clean 10 cabins." I turned off into the rest stop and didn't see anyone. I frowned at the thought of working alone, then I took a breath and said to myself, "Well, Lord, if that's the way it is, I'll just do my best and work till it's done."

A moment later, I saw a guy I knew coming out of the restroom. He waved to me and I thought, oh, good, at least there's two of us, but that meant it was still going to be a long and ugly day.

I pulled my car over toward him and I'm sure I was still frowning when I lowered my window. He placed his hands on my car door, bent forward, and said, "Hey, Greg, looks like you really shook the tree on this one." Then he pointed to the far end of the parking lot and what a relief. There were 20 or more guys with mops and pails.

I about swallowed my tongue as the words poured from my mouth. "Thank you, God, this is awesome, so much more than I expected!"

We got the cleaning done in record time, and since then, our group has continued to clean the camp every year. Talk about dedication; showing up annually for that onerous job demonstrates it in spades. But we don't want too much to be made of it, and, in fact, we have an unwritten pledge to secrecy: Nobody can know that we men can actually clean toilets!

When the cleaning was done that first year, I decided to hang around the rest of the week and see what the camp was all about. It was a powerful experience, deeply moving, and at the end of the week, I was asked if I would like to be a member of the Kids Cancer Alliance Board of Directors. I was told they had only three or four members and they really wanted new blood. I wasn't looking for more things to add to my plate, but I couldn't think of a reason not to do it, so I signed on and started attending board meetings.

The key issue, as always, was the challenge of raising money to pay for the camp. As I had learned from the newspaper article, the camp is entirely free, no fees for the campers or their parents. One thing led to another and we started doing a better job bringing in money. I put on a few golf scrambles and conjured up some other fund-raising activities. But to take the next step up the ladder, we decided we needed to be a more credible organization, and it would help to join a camping association. This necessitated our having an executive director, and guess who was elected? Yep, me, and I'll tell you it was more than a little intimidating, because it was a whole new world for me, quite different from law enforcement. But I'd give it my best shot.

My office was impressive: my wife's minivan and a cell phone. I'd drive around to different clubs and organizations trying to raise money. With God's helping hand, we grew and had more and more kids participating, and our board greatly expanded to quite an impressive group. At that point, it was clear we needed a real, bona fide executive director who could put the kind of time and effort into the job that it required—someone with experience and a vision for what we could become. We made the hire and she has really paid off for us.

That's the background of my involvement, but the real story is the kids. Some of them are like three, four or five years old, fighting cancer and all that that entails. Some of them have very little, if any, chance of survival.

Over my 19 years of involvement, there have been times when kids attached themselves to me in a big way. The first was a young man who took me under his wing and taught me what the camp was all about. We became very close, and when he passed away, it broke my heart. Later, I met his mom at a fund-raiser and she said, "You must be Mr. Greg. My son talked about you all the time, and you really added so much to his life, so much so that he told me he wanted to be buried in the hat you gave him." That really choked me up and touched my heart. Unfortunately, he was only the first of many children I would bond with and then lose to this dreaded disease.

To be honest, after losing my first couple of kids in this way, I felt that I couldn't allow myself to get as close as I was because it was too painful. I tried to limit my emotions, to be friendly and supportive, but to protect the deep, vulnerable part of myself. That, of course, didn't work at all, and soon new kids won me over, and I gave my heart completely, only to have it broken time after time. But that's what God was directing me to do: connect with these kids and form a meaningful bond, comfort and love them during whatever little time they had on this earth, and I was honored to do so.

Seven-year-old Patrick was one of my kids, and I remember him walking in that first day wearing a red University of Louisville jersey. That stood out because most of the folks there supported Big Blue, the University of Kentucky, U of L's bitter rival. That red shirt instantly brought Patrick and me together. Then I saw his mom bringing in a Ziploc bag filled with medicines. I could tell by the look in her eyes that she was weary of the struggle, but I could also see that she was more than up to the task and there was no doubt she would keep fighting with all she had for her son. Images like that burned deeply into my memory and they inspired me constantly to want to do as much as I could to help in any way I could. Patrick and I became close and our relationship continues.

Patrick's is an amazing story in so many ways. Imagine beating cancer six times, only to have it return a seventh time, as it has now. You would think that fighting cancer and believing you won only to have it attack you again and again, seven times, would beat you down to the point of giving up. Not Patrick. He's remarkable, a true inspiration and one of my heroes. As you may recall from my chapter on Jennifer Lawrence, before she became too famous, she came up to the camp and spent the day and a picture was taken of her and Patrick. It meant a lot to him, so much so that seven years later, he still had the picture on his phone.

—

My involvement with Kids Cancer Alliance has exposed me to cancer in a very real and personal way. I am not sure how many times I have visited hospitals to see a sick or dying child, or how many funerals I have attended. I still have pictures of these kids on my computer because I never want to forget them, even though it breaks my heart thinking about them.

My dad had prostate cancer, which inspired me to be more aware of my situation and the potential for a hereditary connection. But other than that, I had not been involved with cancer until my work with the camp and the alliance. It's interesting that over the years so many people have asked me about the source of my intense involvement with the kids. Do I have a child with cancer? Thankfully, I could always say no.

As an ordained deacon, I have counseled people with cancer and we have discussed God's will, and what that might mean. Is it a test, possibly serving some higher purpose that we are not aware of? Hard to say. Regardless, I emphasized the need to be strong and fight hard and to have faith that it will turn out as God intended. With that said, if I'm going to talk the talk, I must walk the walk.

I was recently diagnosed with a sizeable tumor on one of my kidneys. They couldn't determine how serious it was until it was biopsied and analyzed, and the only thing I knew for certain was that the tumor would be removed. Beyond that, I was warned that, because of the size and location, there was a chance I could lose the kidney. Boy, coming from out of the blue the way such news often arrives really took me back and made me realize the devastating impact such news must have on children and their parents.

My tumor was biopsied, and I had to wait for results. At such moments, time stands still and confusion reigns. On the one hand, I was desperate to know the results, but on the other hand, I would rather not know if the results were going to be bad. Either way, I had to stay positive and accept what I had told so many others, and that is to embrace the will of God and know that it was not my place to question. In other words, Greg, practice what you preach.

Because of my involvement with kids suffering from cancer and having seen firsthand what it's like, many times I have prayed that if there was a way I could take their suffering upon myself and away from them, I would do so. I really mean that. And when my own children were ill, and we didn't know exactly what was wrong with them, I feared the worst, and in the midst of their illness, I would pray to God that if anyone in my family was going get cancer, please let it be me. I'm begging you, God, let it be me.

While finishing this book, I had my operation. A buddy of mine told me that, with four incisions across my abdomen, I looked like I had been in a knife fight. The tumor was the size of an orange and the biopsy was positive, meaning the tumor was cancerous. What's more, there was no way the doctor could remove the tumor without taking the kidney, so I'm down to one kidney. The good news is the cancer was confined with no margins. Even so, I must go back every few months for additional tests to ensure that the cancer has not returned.

How am I feeling about the whole thing? Because I have prayed so often that if anyone in my family was going to get cancer, please let it be me, it is my hope that my children and my wife have been spared, and if so, I accept my fate as a true blessing. After my operation, the doctor informed me of something quite extraordinary. On top of the tumor there was a scar that resembled a cross. He had a picture of it and showed it to me. A coincidence? I don't think so. I see it as a *God-incidence*, a symbol that God is with me, and whatever is to come, He and I will work through it together.

I am blessed abundantly, and my morning prayer remains the same as always. "God, thank you for my rest, and show me how I can serve you today."

ACKNOWLEDGMENTS

This book is about my life and the many roles I have played and continue to play. I could not have accomplished what I did or enjoyed the benefits associated with the many hats I wore without the incredible love and support of my family, and the glow of love emanating from God. He watches over us all, removing seemingly immovable obstacles and making each step we take possible and rich with blessings.

I want to thank my extended families:

- The kids from the Kids Cancer Alliance who taught me how to hope, cry, rejoice, and fight the good fight
- The police officers, federal agents, and all the first responders I worked with closely—professionals who inspired me with their dedication to duty, daily risking their lives and rushing in where angels fear to tread
- My fellow clergy who selflessly dedicate their lives to saving souls

And, of course, a big thank-you to those who helped bring this book to life: my coauthor, Bryant Stamford; my friend, Jennifer Lawrence, author of my book's foreword; my publisher, Carol Butler; my editor, Susan E. Lindsey; and my book designer, Scott Stortz, who worked tirelessly on my behalf to make it happen.

ABOUT THE AUTHORS

Greg Gitschier, a Louisville native, has been a police officer, US Secret Service agent, and senior special agent, and is now a bodyguard and security consultant (Greg Gitschier Consulting LLC). Gitschier was a police officer in Louisville for 11 years and a Secret Service agent for more than 21 years. In the Secret Service, he worked as a bodyguard, criminal investigator, firearms instructor, fitness coordinator, and police task force supervisor. He was assigned full-time to protect President Ronald Reagan's family and has protected other heads of state and dignitaries, including the Queen of England, the Emperor of Japan, and Pope John Paul II.

Gitschier is now a security consultant for numerous Kentucky and Indiana businesses, schools, and churches, and he was the senior member of the Louisville HIRT (Haz-mat/SWAT team). He has worked with the largest grocery store chain in America and similar organizations to prepare for active shooter situations, was security chairman for six major PGA events at Valhalla Golf Club, was security advisor for the Ryder Cup, and helped prepare and lead security for the 2015 Breeders Cup. He attended three Olympic Games as a security planner and escort to GE and NBC senior executives, and also provided security to the 2016 National Republican Convention in Cleveland.

For five years, Gitschier was a bodyguard for Louisville Mayor Greg Fischer and, when needed, he acts as a bodyguard for celebrities. Gitschier lives in

Louisville, Kentucky, with his wife, daughter, and two sons.

Bryant A. Stamford, PhD, is a professor at Hanover College and for 42 years authored a newspaper column on health, nutrition, and fitness issues for the Louisville *Courier-Journal*. He has served as editorial advisor for several magazines and has authored or coauthored six books.